GURKHA

25 years of The Royal Gurkha Rifles

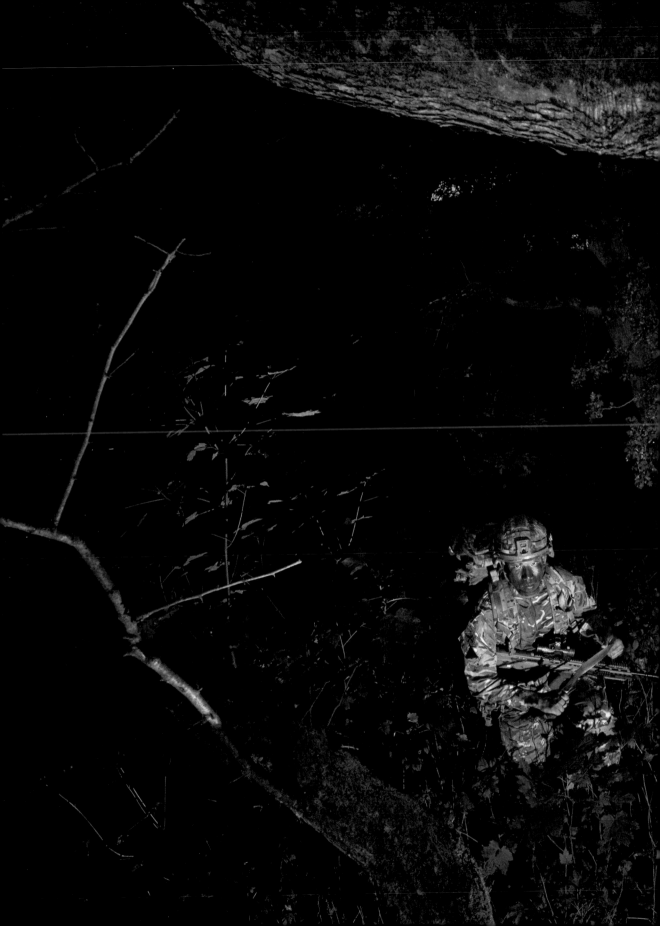

GURKHA

25 years of The Royal Gurkha Rifles

Major General (Retd)
J C Lawrence CBE FRGS

First published by Uniform
an imprint of Unicorn Publishing Group LLP, 2019
5 Newburgh Street
London W1F 7RG
www.unicornpublishing.org

10 9 8 7 6 5 4 3 2 1

ISBN 978-1-912690-23-7

Design by Matthew Wilson
Printed by Jellyfish

Front cover: Photograph by Corporal Amrit Thapa
RLC of Rifleman Ekbahadur Gurung RGR. Corporal
Amrit served with the RGR from 2004 to 2018 and
then transferred to the Royal Logistic Corps to
pursue a career as an army photographer. A black and
white version of this image won the on-line category
in the 2018 Army Photographic Competition.

Following page: A painting of His Royal Highness
The Prince of Wales, Colonel-in-Chief of The Royal
Gurkha Rifles, by Mark Shields RUA. Commissioned
in 2001, the painting, which hangs in the Officers' Mess
in Sir John Moore Barracks, the home of the UK based
Gurkha infantry battalion, shows His Royal Highness
wearing the Mess Kit of the Regiment. The painting
was made possible through the generosity of Ellice
and Rosa McDonald (photograph by Marcus Leith).

Contents

Appendices

CLARENCE HOUSE

On 10th September 1994, I reviewed the Formation Parade of The Royal Gurkha Rifles as the new Regiment's first Colonel-in-Chief. It was a remarkable day – even though it marked the end of nearly 200 years of Gurkha service to the Crown by some of the most distinguished Regiments in the history of the British Army, it also celebrated the beginning of a new era.

In my Address to the Regiment, I said that The Royal Gurkha Rifles must look to the future, and that the Regiment must rise to whatever challenges present themselves. I hoped that it would do this not only by maintaining the traditions and standards of its forebears, but also by building a reputation of its own.

I am delighted that it has succeeded in doing both these things; from the first operational deployment to the Balkans in December 1995, to its most recent tour in Afghanistan earlier this year, the Regiment's performance on operations has been exemplary. During the last twenty-five years, I have felt incredibly proud to see so many members of the Regiment receiving honours and awards for their gallantry and leadership.

I also recognize that the Regiment's reputation for military excellence has been hard won. Since its formation, fourteen members of the Regiment have lost their lives, and many others have sustained life-changing injuries on operations. Although this has brought unbearable hardship and sorrow, I draw some small comfort from knowing that the Regiment will never forget them, nor the sacrifices they made.

As I reflect upon the Regiment's first quarter century, it is sometimes difficult to remember exactly just how much has been achieved. This is why this book is invaluable – carefully researched, and with hundreds of fascinating images, it will perhaps help the reader to understand my deep personal pride in being Colonel-in-Chief.

We have so much to celebrate this year – not only past achievements, but also a bright future as we look forward to the creation of a new, third Battalion.

Introduction

Major General G M Strickland DSO MBE
Colonel of The Royal Gurkha Rifles

I n the semi-twilight of the Borneo jungle, shadows moved silently as soldiers prepared their positions for the night. I sat, cleaning my rifle, as a figure slid up to me and slipped a small wrap of brown paper into my hands. Curiously, I peeled back the layer to reveal a glint of silver – the crown of the cap badge of The Royal Gurkha Rifles. And so my life in our new Regiment began.

Since that day in 1994, I have had the privilege of serving with the most remarkable people in journeys and

Above: Major General G M Strickland DSO MBE.

Left: The last Commander British Forces Hong Kong inspects an honour guard from the newly formed Royal Gurkha Rifles (RGR). The last RGR unit left Hong Kong in 1996 prior to the Colony being handed back to the Chinese Government in 1997.

conflicts around the world. Our Gurkhas have proved themselves second to none as soldiers, and as friends.

It has been a rich 25 years. We came together as a Regiment that had become accustomed to its role in Hong Kong and Brunei, slightly apart from the rest of the British Army but with its own proud institutions and ways. The approach of the return of Hong Kong to China, and the end of the Cold War in Europe had triggered a reappraisal, with profound implications. As a new Regiment, we began to embrace the United Kingdom and shift closer to the heart of the British Army.

We knew we stood on the shoulders of giants. The exploits of the 7th Duke of Edinburgh's Own Gurkha Rifles in the Falklands War were recent history, and the reputation for excellence in jungle warfare forged through Burma, Malaya and Borneo

rang loud in our new collective conscience. Each of our forebear Regiments had incredibly proud history, for which we now assumed responsibility.

We did not have to wait long. It was almost with relief that in 1999 both battalions were fully tested, first in Kosovo, and then in East Timor. It marked a coming of age, and the confidence that emerged was palpable. Both operations showed in different ways some of the strengths of light, fast-moving Gurkha infantry. Kosovo was the final deployment of 5 Airborne Brigade before it reformed as 16 Air Assault Brigade. It was ironic that this preceded a gap in our close association with airborne forces, but one that would be reinstated fifteen years later. East Timor provided an equal challenge. Deploying as part of the Australian led force to oversee the withdrawal of the Indonesian military from the ravaged remains of

Below: Soldiers from A Company Group 2RGR completing their final checks in Australia before boarding RAAF C130s for a tactical air land operation (TALO) onto Komoro Airfield on the outskirts of Dili, the capital city of East Timor. The Company Group deployed on Operation Langar as part of the UN International Force East Timor (INTEFET) on 20 September 1999 and remained in-theatre until early December 1999.

Right: Gurkhas from 1RGR boarding an aircraft to Macedonia at the start of Operation Agricola. On 12 June 1999, 1RGR crossed the border from Macedonia into Kosovo as part of the NATO-led Kosovo Force (KFOR). The deployment lasted until late August 1999.

A soldier from the RGR, completely at ease in the jungle. The RGR has continued the tradition for excellence in jungle operations established by its antecedent regiments in Burma, Malaya and Borneo.

a conflict torn territory, the second battalion played midwife to the birth of the world's newest nation. In both these operations, Gurkhas were in their element, menacing when needed, ready to apply lethal force, but reassuring and warm with people who had suffered so much.

The Balkans drew the Regiment in. Over the course of the 1990s and early 2000s we completed several tours in Bosnia overseeing the Dayton Peace Agreement. As ever, our Gurkhas won friends, and came away with impressive Serbo-Croat linguistic skills. Their ability to root out hidden weapons without alienating the population, bitterly divided by the war, was impressive. It also allowed skills such as covert observation and surveillance to be honed.

The jungle holds a special place for Gurkhas. With a battalion permanently stationed in Brunei, we have built on the knowledge so hard-won by those before us. Ambush positions held for days, silent troop movements, navigation through thick forest, and the ability to launch violent attacks instantaneously, all in an unforgiving environment with movement snagged by thorns and roots, constant wet, and sapping heat. These are the features of jungle training. In my own induction, I watched amazed as Gurkhas laid animal traps, whittled baskets out of rattan, kept their kukris sharp, and were so completely at home in this alien environment.

As we have grown as a Regiment, so has Nepal changed. The civil war of 1996–2006 raged in some of our recruiting heartlands. The subsequent rejection of the monarchy, and the institution of a federal republic fundamentally changed the political landscape. But at the same time, the country was modernising. Education standards rose, roads opened up into remote hill regions, mobile phones became ubiquitous, and awareness of the outside world grew. As we accepted that modern warfare requires modern skills, we began to adjust the criteria for entry for our soldiers. Whilst there has been no reduction in fitness standards required, a premium has been placed on education. The long debate about the relative merits of 'hill boys' versus educated soldiers has continued, but the evidence speaks for itself. Gurkhas today exhibit a range of skills and talents, and courage and fortitude remain evident. There have been many tales of daring. When I spoke to Sergeant Dipprasad Pun one dusty morning in Afghanistan just after he had single-handedly fought off an attack by 12 Taliban fighters with his machine gun, grenades, rifle, and eventually a heavy tripod, he told me that the last time he had experienced anything like the fear of that attack was when he believed he was drowning in a river in Nepal. But Afghanistan also brought out countless examples of quieter courage and determination. Stepping out through a dusty gap between two walls, knowing that your friend from recruit training lost his leg in the same spot the previous week to an improvised bomb, takes a deep strength. I never saw a Gurkha waver in these incredibly testing circumstances. Always professional, our soldiers rarely cut corners, and they reaped the benefits from it. A willingness and desire to practise over and over again is a feature of our Regiment from which we have derived much strength.

The mix of British and Gurkha officers gives the RGR a real strength that few other regiments can match. It has stood the test of time and remains as important today as it has always been.

Opposite (above): Soldiers from 1RGR on patrol in Afghanistan during Operation Herrick 7 (September 2007 to April 2008). Defeating the Taliban requires a high standard of basic infantry skills, something the RGR works hard to excel at (image copyright Peter Nicholls 2007).

Opposite (below): A soldier from 1RGR in Afghanistan on Operation Herrick 7 pauses in front of a house – it takes courage and quiet resolve to enter a doorway when you have no idea what lies beyond.

We are fortunate to have retained a structure unique to the Gurkhas, in which our officers are drawn both from Britain and Nepal. Whilst the rank of Queen's Gurkha Officer has disappeared to be replaced with the somewhat more pedestrian 'Late Entry' title, most Gurkha officers still rise through the ranks and are commissioned after many years of service and experience. They are joined in the Officers' Mess by their British and occasionally Nepali counterparts who have come straight from The Royal Military Academy Sandhurst. The blend of culture and experience is invaluable. The British platoon commander brings youth, enthusiasm and innovation, whilst his Gurkha counterpart brings a deep understanding of the soldiers, the wisdom of experience, but an openness to new ideas. In the last 25 years, we have slightly shifted the numerical balance towards British officers, but have retained the essential ingredient, which has stood the test of hard conflict.

A feature of our first 25 years has been the widespread reinforcement of other Regiments of the British Army with formed Companies of Gurkhas. This has taken a delicate balancing act, retaining The Royal Gurkha Rifles' identity, ethos and tradition, whilst also assimilating into a series of fine Infantry Regiments, each with their own legacy and way of doing business. Tight bonds have been forged with The Parachute Regiment, The Royal Scots, The Highlanders, The Princess of Wales's Royal Regiment, The Royal Irish, The Mercians and The Yorkshire Regiment through this mechanism. Whilst Iraq has not featured so directly in the Regiment's tally, the initial operation to remove Saddam Hussein in 2003 included one of these reinforcement companies with The Royal Irish, charged with securing key sites in Iraq as the invasion began.

Above: Lieutenant General Sir Hew Pike greets members of the parachute trained Gurkha Reinforcement Company. The company was attached to the 2nd Battalion The Parachute Regiment (2PARA) from 1996 to 2002. Known as C (Cassino) Company, it saw operational service in Afghanistan, Bosnia and Herzegovina, Macedonia and Sierra Leone.

It is unlikely there is another Infantry Regiment in the British Army that has been as committed to Afghanistan as The Royal Gurkha Rifles. From the first deployment to Kabul in 2002, to a return there in 2019, we have charted the course of events in this shattered nation from within. We witnessed the initial optimism in Kabul, and took part in the expansion of the NATO footprint up to the North West in Mazar e Sharif and Meymaneh. We watched the Taliban regain confidence in the south and were part of the very first UK deployment to Helmand, occupying and defending isolated positions in Now Zad and Sangin, at times close to being overrun. We saw the British approach shift to counter-insurgency and were given the role of launching surprise attacks on the Taliban in their areas of perceived strength, often by night-time helicopter assault, across the whole of Southern Afghanistan in support not only of the UK but also the Netherlands, Canada, Romania and the US. We held ground in areas contested by the Taliban in a battle for the support of the people, in Musa Qaleh,

Members of 1RGR training on an urban range in Kabul during Operation Toral 7 (November 2018 to May 2019). Note the board in the background which refers to 2RGR's tour on Operation Toral 3 in 2016.

A young British officer from 2RGR anoints the head of one of his soldiers during the Hindu festival of Dashain in Afghanistan during Operation Herrick 14 (April to October 2011) (image Crown copyright 2011).

On 16 February 2011, a small parade was held in Queen Elizabeth Hospital, Birmingham to award Rifleman Sachin Limbu with his operational service medal for Afghanistan. The parade was attended by contemporaries from Rifleman Sachin's intake into the RGR, as well as the Colonel of the Regiment and his Commanding Officer. Rifleman Sachin was initially wounded in an IED strike on 24 June 2010 and subsequently died of his injuries on 2 January 2012.

Garmsir and Gereshk, and we returned to Kabul to train the officers of the Afghan National Army, and to protect the international force. Even at this point, we know we may yet return.

Whilst it is tempting to focus solely on operational deployments, life in The Royal Gurkha Rifles is about much more than that. The time-honoured traditions of Gurkha life persist. A passion for sport, a tightly knit family community, a thirst for new experiences, and a constant commitment to excellence endure. For the young British officer sitting around a fire eating Nepalese food, sharing a drink and stories of life around the world, and breaking into song and dance as a soldier beats out a rhythm on the traditional madal drum, there can be fewer more rewarding experiences. Similarly, the welcome received by every new soldier who passes recruit training and finally joins the Regiment is heartfelt and honest. Our soldiers and their families belong.

These first 25 years have not been without pain. Fourteen of our officers and soldiers have

lost their lives on operations, and many more have been wounded. The fortitude of those who deal with life-changing injuries is humbling. Rifleman Sachin Limbu suffered the most grievous wounds in an explosion in Helmand, Afghanistan. For over a year he endured unimaginable pain and suffering in hospital before he finally succumbed. His courage and dignity inspired us all. The Regiment's legacy is his.

As we enter our 25th year, we find ourselves in a position of tremendous strength. The Army's request that we now re-form our third battalion in the specialised infantry role, configured to train, advise, assist and accompany other nations' forces, indicates a hard-won confidence in our approach to the profession of arms. As a Regiment we could not have asked for a more timely and resounding vote of trust.

This history is an important milestone which marks our place in the British Army as a new and vibrant Regiment. Major General Craig Lawrence, a former Colonel of the Regiment, has brought this to life with superb clarity and humour, and we owe him an

Men of the 4th Gurkhas pose for a photograph on a balcony in the Bala Hissar, the old citadel that dominates the Kabul skyline in Afghanistan. This image was taken during the Second Anglo-Afghan War (1878–80).

enormous debt of gratitude for doing so. Recalling his time serving with Gurkhas in Palestine in the First World War, Sir Ralph Turner MC immortalised the bonds of trust and friendship in words. The first 25 years of The Royal Gurkha Rifles have again proved those bonds. Like him, I have watched our Gurkhas in their bivouacs or about their fires, on forced march or in the trenches, shivering with wet and cold or scorched by a pitiless and burning sun. They have readied for attack in the pre-dawn hush, fought off waves of attack, suffered terrible injury and loss, and yet remained compassionate in victory. Like Sir Ralph Turner, I can vouch for their unparalleled courage and generosity. We are fortunate indeed to share such a bond.

Over a hundred and thirty years later, soldiers from 1RGR on patrol in the ruins of the Bala Hissar during Operation Toral 7 in March 2019.

Author's Preface

Major General (Retired) J C Lawrence CBE FRGS

When I did the research for the book *The Gurkhas: 200 Years of Service to the Crown*, I was struck by just how much The Royal Gurkha Rifles (RGR) had managed to achieve since its formation in July 1994. My regret at the time was that I was not able to do these achievements justice, as space was limited and the book had to be about the 200 years of the wider Brigade of Gurkhas, not just my own Regiment. I was therefore delighted when the 25th Anniversary of the RGR presented an opportunity to produce another book, but this time one focused exclusively on the RGR.

At the launch of the *The Gurkhas: 200 Years of Service to the Crown* at the Royal United Services Institute (RUSI) on 30 April 2015. All royalties from the sales of the book over the last four years went to the Gurkha Welfare Trust, raising several thousand pounds to help retired Gurkhas and their families live out their lives with the dignity they deserve.

The original intention had been to produce a coffee table book with lots of pictures and very little text. However, it soon became apparent that images alone would not suffice in trying to tell the story of the RGR's first quarter century of life. I have therefore included a fair amount of narrative. In doing this, the aim is not to provide a detailed Regimental history – others have this in their sights – but to provide sufficient background that the images, and the achievements they represent, can be seen in context. The other thing that became apparent is how much harder it is to write recent history than that of the distant past. When I did the Gurkha 200 book, I was able to draw on a number of other well-researched histories to help me get the facts right. But for this book I had to piece the story together from Regimental newsletters, newspaper cuttings, articles in the Kukri, official letters, e-mails, the results of online searches, conversations with those who were there, hand-written notes in the archives of the Gurkha Museum and comments from my expert proofreaders. For any historian, working from such primary sources is exciting but it brings with it the possibility that some mistakes will be made. To some extent, this book should therefore be seen as a stalking-horse, flushing out errors and omissions in order that when the more comprehensive Regimental history is produced, it can avoid making the same mistakes. To that end, I should be extremely grateful if, when you spot what you think is a mistake, a misrepresentation of the truth or a significant gap in the Regiment's history, you would let me know.

The RGR's many achievements are down to the people who have served, and continue to serve, in its battalions and sub-units. I have therefore tried to include photographs of as many of them as possible in telling the story of the Regiment. Inevitably, the later years benefit from the ubiquity of digital cameras and I have therefore been able to draw on a rich seam of imagery. This is not the case with the earlier years and I have struggled to collate sufficient imagery to adequately illustrate some of the key events in the Regiment's first ten years or so of life. Despite putting out several trawls, I have also struggled to find photographs of some of the RGR's later operational tours, particularly those undertaken by the Gurkha Reinforcement Companies and independent sub-units. I would like to reassure those whose images do not appear in the book that their absence is a consequence of the imagery available to me, not a lack of respect for their contribution. However, this paucity of material does raise a serious point about the importance of chronicling the life of the Regiment, with both imagery and documentation, as it unfolds. Some serving officers, such as Captain Michael Barney, whose help has been invaluable in putting together much of the detail in the Appendices, have a passion for our history which we must encourage. The creation of Heritage Officers in each battalion should also make a difference but we need to take this seriously otherwise we run the risk of many of our accomplishments and, more importantly, the people who worked so hard to achieve them, being forgotten as the years pass. I would therefore urge those who have any material relating to the RGR, whether photographs or documents, to get in touch with the Gurkha Museum and share what they have.

Right: Laying a wreath with another RGR officer at the headstone of Captain John Cook VC's grave in Kabul's British Cemetery in September 2014. Captain Cook, an officer in the 5th Gurkhas, was awarded his Victoria Cross during the Second Anglo-Afghan War for his bravery at the Battle of Peiwar Kotal in November 1878. Whilst it might surprise many, our distant past is far better documented than our recent past.

Below: Although the Gurkha Museum has a remarkable archive of material covering more than 200 years of Gurkha service to the British Crown, it has very little relating to the RGR. The material they have fits into only five of the green box files on the far wall.

In the acknowledgements section of the book, I have tried to identify, and thank, those many people who helped me with the book, particularly those who very generously gave me access to their personal photo archives. Some of these deserve mention here because they also contributed so much of their time. Lieutenant General Sir Peter Duffell spent many hours patiently explaining the background to the Regiment's formation, an event he was intimately involved in as Major General Brigade of Gurkhas, Commander British Forces Hong Kong and the Regiment's first Colonel. Lieutenant General Peter Pearson acted as chief proofreader and made numerous sensible suggestions for improving the quality of the book. As well as writing the book's Introduction, which I think does a great job of highlighting what makes the Regiment so unique, Major General Gez Strickland worked hard to ensure that the chapter describing Afghanistan was not only as accurate as possible but also captured the essence of the Regiment's many tours there. As well as my two predecessors and one successor as Colonel of the Regiment, I owe particular thanks to Major (Retired) Bruce McKay, the Regimental Secretary, for his unstinting support despite my constant, and often unreasonable, requests for information and to Gavin Edgerley-Harris, the Director of the Gurkha Museum, whose patience and resources have been very much appreciated.

I am particularly grateful to the Regiment's Colonel-in-Chief, His Royal Highness The Prince of Wales, for writing the book's Foreword. Not only does it explain why His Royal Highness is so proud of the Regiment but, importantly, it reminds us all that whilst the last 25 years have given us much to celebrate, so does the RGR's future, which looks brighter now than it has done for many years. I am

Left and below: Having commanded an RGR company and an RGR battalion, both in barracks and on operations, it was a great privilege to be invited to be Colonel of the Regiment from 1 July 2009 until 1 February 2016. Throughout my service, I have never failed to be impressed by the officers and soldiers of the RGR, whose hard work and personal sacrifice make the Regiment what it is.

also very grateful to my family and to Laura, my wife, in particular. This book has taken me more than two years to research and write. Throughout, Laura has been hugely supportive despite the many evenings, weekends and holidays that I have spent working on it, rather than spending time with her and the rest of the family. She has been a tower of strength and I am in no doubt that without her good-humoured encouragement, this book would not have been possible.

Lastly, I would like to thank those members of the Regiment, past and present, who have made writing this book, like my 22 years of service with the RGR, such a fascinating and enjoyable endeavour, as well as an honour and a privilege. Their many achievements over the last 25 years, which have come at a very real human cost, have made our Regiment what it is. My only hope is that I have done them justice.

My year in Afghanistan working on the Presidential Elections of 2014 gave me an insight into the incredibly tough nature of the fighting that the RGR has been involved in since it first deployed to Afghanistan in January 2002.

CHAPTER 1

The Need for Change: the Formation of The Royal Gurkha Rifles

O n 3 May 1994, the UK Ministry of Defence issued a general staff order authorising:[1]

- The amalgamation of the 1st Battalion 2nd King Edward VII's Own Gurkha Rifles (2GR) and the 6th Queen Elizabeth's Own Gurkha Rifles (6GR) to form the 1st Battalion The Royal Gurkha Rifles (1RGR);
- The retitling of the 1st Battalion 7th Duke of Edinburgh's Own Gurkha Rifles (7GR) to become the 2nd Battalion The Royal Gurkha Rifles (2RGR);
- The retitling of 10th Princess Mary's Own Gurkha Rifles (10GR) to become the 3rd Battalion The Royal Gurkha Rifles (3RGR).

The order directed that these changes were to be implemented on 1 July 1994. It further directed that 1RGR was to be operationally effective from 1 August 1994[2] and that 2RGR and 3RGR were to be so from 1 September 1994. In December 1996, the 2nd and 3rd Battalions were then to merge to become a new 2nd Battalion, leaving the British Army with just two Gurkha infantry battalions, one in the UK and one in Brunei.

The changes scheduled for the 1 July 1994 took place as directed, with the merger of 2RGR and 3RGR taking place a few weeks early on 18 November 1996.[3] Fortunately, this latter event had less impact than

Opposite: A watercolour painting of The Royal Gurkha Rifles' Formation Parade by Alix Baker showing the uniform of the new regiment.

Below: The front page of the Ministry of Defence's official order authorising the amalgamation and retitling of the existing Gurkha infantry regiments to form The Royal Gurkha Rifles.

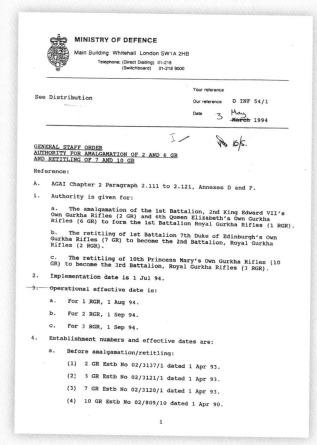

MINISTRY OF DEFENCE

Main Building Whitehall London SW1A 2HB

Telephone: (Direct Dialling) 01-218
(Switchboard)   01-218 9000

See Distribution

Your reference

Our reference   D INF 54/1

Date   3 May 1994

GENERAL STAFF ORDER
AUTHORITY FOR AMALGAMATION OF 2 AND 6 GR
AND RETITLING OF 7 AND 10 GR

Reference:

A.   AGAI Chapter 2 Paragraph 2.111 to 2.121, Annexes D and F.

1.   Authority is given for:

a.   The amalgamation of the 1st Battalion, 2nd King Edward VII's Own Gurkha Rifles (2 GR) and 6th Queen Elizabeth's Own Gurkha Rifles (6 GR) to form the 1st Battalion Royal Gurkha Rifles (1 RGR).

b.   The retitling of 1st Battalion 7th Duke of Edinburgh's Own Gurkha Rifles (7 GR) to become the 2nd Battalion, Royal Gurkha Rifles (2 RGR).

c.   The retitling of 10th Princess Mary's Own Gurkha Rifles (10 GR) to become the 3rd Battalion, Royal Gurkha Rifles (3 RGR).

2.   Implementation date is 1 Jul 94.

3.   Operational effective date is:

a.   For 1 RGR, 1 Aug 94.

b.   For 2 RGR, 1 Sep 94.

c.   For 3 RGR, 1 Sep 94.

4.   Establishment numbers and effective dates are:

a.   Before amalgamation/retitling:

(1)   2 GR Estb No 02/3137/1 dated 1 Apr 93.

(2)   5 GR Estb No 02/3121/1 dated 1 Apr 93.

(3)   7 GR Estb No 02/3120/1 dated 1 Apr 93.

(4)   10 GR Estb No 02/809/10 dated 1 Apr 90.

1

expected because the Regiment was also directed to provide three Gurkha Reinforcement Companies (GRCs) at the same time. These companies, each about a hundred strong, were formed to support British infantry units struggling to recruit and retain sufficient manpower to meet their operational establishments. The three GRCs formed up in November 1996 and were attached to the 1st Battalion The Royal Scots, the 1st Battalion The Princess of Wales's Royal Regiment and 2nd Battalion The Parachute Regiment.[4]

The order to amalgamate the four existing Gurkha infantry regiments to form a single new regiment was the culmination of years of detailed planning by Headquarters Brigade of Gurkhas and the Ministry of Defence. To understand why this decision was taken, it is necessary to go back to July 1990 and 'Options for Change', the UK Government's attempt to reap a peace dividend from the collapse of the Warsaw Pact and the end of the Cold War. Introducing the proposed reductions in the size and capabilities of the armed forces, Tom King, then Secretary of State for Defence, told the House of Commons that the Government had "...sought to devise a structure for our regular forces appropriate to the new security situation and meeting our essential peacetime operational needs".[5] When combined with his assertion that the "...overall reduction in service manpower would be about 18%",[6] his proposals arguably made sense given the diminished threat facing the UK. However, they hid the fact that the Brigade of Gurkhas was being hit disproportionately hard. In retrospect, this might seem unfair but it was

a real victory at the time given the widely held view, particularly across the infantry, that "...all Gurkha Battalions should go before a single British Battalion went to the wall".[7] Fortunately, the Army Board, and not the infantry, was responsible for determining the future size and shape and size of the Army.

In the summer of 1990, Lieutenant General Sir Peter Duffell, then Commander British Forces Hong Kong and Major General Brigade of Gurkhas, submitted a paper to the Army Board setting out the case for the retention of a viable Brigade. In some ways, the timing of 'Options for Change' benefitted the Brigade of Gurkhas because it coincided with the Government's preparation for the handover of Hong Kong to the Chinese in 1997. Although the Royal Hong Kong Police had primacy for dealing with civil disorder in the colony, the paper explained that the retention of a capable British garrison able to assist with maintaining security in the run-up to the handover was essential. It argued that if the Gurkhas were disbanded under 'Options for Change', they would need to be replaced with British troops, a much more expensive option that would have been extremely unattractive to the Hong Kong Government because it paid a large proportion of the garrison's costs. In addition, the Gurkhas knew the Territory well and 'fitted in' with the local population. The paper went on to argue that the Gurkhas would need to have an assured future of some sort beyond 1997 if they were to be effective right up until the handover. As General Duffell explains:

"The central tenet of my paper rested ultimately on the simple proposition that if it was deemed necessary

Lieutenant General Sir Peter Duffell, the first Colonel of the Regiment, inspecting soldiers from The Royal Gurkha Rifles in February 1995, eight months after the Regiment's formation. General Duffell was Major General Brigade of Gurkhas, as well as Commander British Forces Hong Kong, during the 'Options for Change' process and played a key role in ensuring that the British Army did not cut Gurkhas from its order of battle as it down-sized and that it retained two Gurkha infantry battalions.

to retain the effective services of a Gurkha garrison until the Hong Kong commitment ended, then it would be necessary to offer some proper future for some Gurkhas for some time thereafter".[8]

It helped that the Sultan of Brunei had committed to maintaining a Gurkha battalion in his country, largely at his own expense, and that many British infantry regiments were struggling to recruit. The paper alluded to these considerations but majored on the need to ensure a smooth transition of power in Hong Kong, something the Government was particularly concerned about. The case was compelling and, despite the protestations of the wider infantry, the Army Board eventually agreed that a force of some 2,500 Gurkhas should endure. This provided sufficient headroom for two infantry battalions, as well as a small infrastructure component and individual squadrons of Gurkha engineers, signals and transport.[9]

Having secured a viable future for the Brigade of Gurkhas, the next problem was how to reduce

the Gurkha infantry component down to just two battalions, one in the UK and one in Brunei. Brigadier Christopher Bullock, then Brigadier Brigade of Gurkhas and very much involved in the process, describes how this was resolved:[10]

"Headquarters Brigade of Gurkhas' original plan had anticipated the two Western regiments 2nd and 6th amalgamating to form 2nd/6th Gurkhas (the two battalions of 2nd Gurkhas having amalgamated in 1992) and the two Eastern regiments forming 7th/10th Gurkhas, thereby retaining the historic titles. However the Colonels of the Regiments concerned thought otherwise and decided to go for an entirely new regiment 'The Gurkha Rifles' which being duly honoured became 'The Royal Gurkha Rifles'. Vexatious but secondary issues such as order of amalgamation, dress and accoutrements, etc, were settled by animated discussions in the smoke-filled conference rooms of various London military clubs".

Above: His Royal Highness The Prince of Wales, Colonel-in-Chief of the RGR, talking to Lieutenant General Sir Peter Duffell (on the left) and Field Marshal Sir John Chapple (on the right) on 14 March 2017 at a parade in Buckingham Palace to celebrate His Royal Highness' 40 years as the Colonel-in-Chief of Gurkha infantry. Field Marshal Chapple was the Chief of the General Staff (CGS) during the 'Options for Change' process and oversaw the reductions in the size of the Army. A Gurkha officer, he had to remain impartial as the decisions regarding which regiments to cut were taken but he insisted that these decisions were based on objective analysis and not emotion. This helped ensure that the Gurkha infantry survived 'Options for Change' despite the view of the wider infantry that "...all Gurkha Battalions should go before a single British Battalion went to the wall" (image Crown copyright 2017).[13]

Right: The design for the cap badge of The Royal Gurkha Rifles as approved by the College of Arms on 13 January 1994.

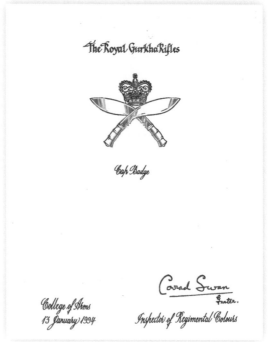

The Royal Gurkha Rifles

Cap Badge

College of Arms
13 January 1994

Conrad Swan
Exeter.
Inspector of Regimental Colours

The Queen's Truncheon in its case in the Indian Army Memorial Room at the Royal Military Academy Sandhurst. It was placed in the case on 24 June 1994 and remained there until 28 April 1997 when it entered service with The Royal Gurkha Rifles.

At the time, there was a great deal of emotive discussion within the battalions about whether the move to a single large regiment was the right thing to do but, as General Duffell notes, there were several strong arguments for adopting this course of action:[11]

- A single large regiment would match the structure that many British infantry regiments were also adopting post 'Options for Change'.
- The name 'The Royal Gurkha Rifles' was "... clean, easily memorable and evocative" and avoided the need for complex numerical titles that might have favoured one antecedent regiment over another.
- It provided an opportunity to take the best of every unit and incorporate it into the new Regiment.
- It would ease cross-posting between the battalions and enable the mixing of eastern and western Gurkhas.[12]
- It would present no complications should the Regiment need to contract or expand, a remarkably prescient consideration given the need to produce GRCs over the years and the formation of 3RGR in 2019.

Once the decision had been made, the battalions got on with the difficult business of shedding the surplus manpower not required in the new regiment. It helped that the Government had eventually agreed to improved conditions of service and a generous redundancy package but discharging so many capable and experienced officers and soldiers was still a painful process; as one commanding officer rather poignantly noted, "one was always saying goodbye".[14] Writing in December 1993 for the 1994 edition of the 6GR Newsletter, Major Gordon Corrigan, then the Formation Officer for the 2GR and 6GR amalgamation, gives a sense of what it was like to be involved in the formation of the new regiment:

"All of us regret the disproportionate reduction of the Brigade under the misnamed 'Options for Change', and believe that our Gurkha soldiers have deserved better of the nation. However we have no choice but to bite the bullet and allow surgery to take place, however painful it undoubtedly is. We will merge with 2GR, 7GR and 10GR and that being the case attempts to score points off each other or to refuse to recognise reality can only be damaging to the cause that really matters – that of Gurkhas as a part of the British Army. I am glad to say that the atmosphere amongst officers of all four Battalions at regimental duty is friendly and co-operative".[15]

Although many officers and men serving in the four infantry battalions wanted the new regiment to have the honour of carrying forward the Queen's Truncheon of the 2nd Goorkhas (as 2GR were

Opposite: The Queen's Truncheon being presented to The Royal Gurkha Rifles on 28 April 1997 by His Royal Highness The Prince of Wales, the Colonel-in-Chief of the Regiment (image Crown copyright 1997).

Right: One of the invitations to the 'Queen's Truncheon Parade' sent out by the Colonel and All Ranks of The Royal Gurkha Rifles. The recipient of this invitation, Colonel D R Wood, was one of the trustees of the Sirmoor Rifles Association (UK) Trust, the organisation that manages the affairs of the disbanded 2GR, the regiment to which Queen Victoria presented the Queen's Truncheon in recognition of its loyalty during the Indian Mutiny of 1857.

accepted 27/3/97

The Colonel and All Ranks of
The Royal Gurkha Rifles
request the pleasure of the company of
Colonel D R Wood
at the Queen's Truncheon Parade *on* 28th April 1997
at RMAS *at* 3 pm

R.S.V.P
P.H.Q R.G.R
Queen Elizabeth Barracks
Church Crookham
Hants. GU 13 ORJ

Dress: See attached letter.

called),[16] this was not initially agreed in case it was interpreted as favouring one antecedent regiment over the others. Awarded to the 2nd Goorkhas after the Indian Mutiny of 1857 by Queen Victoria in recognition of their loyalty, the Queen's Truncheon was therefore taken out of service and, on 24 June 1994,[17] laid up in the Indian Army Memorial Room at the Royal Military Academy Sandhurst.

Once the new regiment had established its own identity it was agreed that the Queen's Truncheon should be returned to service and, on 28 April 1997, the Queen's Truncheon was removed from its display case and handed to The Royal Gurkha Rifles by His Royal Highness The Prince of Wales, Colonel-in-Chief of the new Regiment.

As explained in Special Interest Section 1: The Queen's Truncheon, an iconic symbol of "the emergence of *all* Gurkhas from the ruck of sepoys into the elite of riflemen",[18] remains in service to this day and will play a key role in the celebrations taking place in 2019 to commemorate the 25th Anniversary of The Royal Gurkha Rifles, just as it did in 2015 during the celebrations to commemorate 200 years of Gurkha service to the British Crown.

The Queen's Truncheon on parade during the celebrations to commemorate 200 years of Gurkha service to the British Crown in 2015. This photograph was taken at a parade in the presence of Her Majesty The Queen on 9 June 2015. Captain Rambahadur Limbu VC MVO, the only living Gurkha recipient of the Victoria Cross, stands behind the Queen's Truncheon with recipients of the Conspicuous Gallantry Cross and the Military Cross (image Crown copyright 2015).

Royal Gurkha Rifles formed

A SMALL but poignant ceremony at Church Crookham near Aldershot marked an historic turning point for the British Army's Gurkhas, as the 7th Duke of Edinburgh's Own Gurkha Rifles welcomed their new commandant, Lt Col David Hayes, and were officially renamed the 2nd Battalion, The Royal Gurkha Rifles.

The Vesting Day parade on July 1 was marked with a Guard of Honour and the rebadging of company commanders who then distributed badges to the Gurkha soldiers. As the Royal Gurkha Rifles flag was raised outside Battalion Headquarters for the first time, Gurkhas shouted a traditional "Jai (Victory) Royal Gurkha Rifles" salute to symbolise the birth of the new regiment.

On the same day, the 2nd King Edward VII's Own Gurkha Rifles (The Sirmoor Rifles) and 6th Queen Elizabeth's Own Gurkha Rifles amalgamated to become 1st Battalion, The Royal Gurkha Rifles, while 10th Princess Mary's Own Gurkha Rifles retitled as 3rd Battalion, The Royal Gurkha Rifles.

The new 2 RGR has now taken up duties in Brunei, and will be replaced in the UK later this month by 3 RGR. The Gurkhas will move from their Church Crookham base later this year to take up residence at Elizabeth Barracks, Pirbright. The barracks with its original 1942 wooden accommodation blocks will be demolished to make way for a housing estate.

Initially the 1st Battalion will be stationed in Hong Kong, the 2nd Battalion in Brunei and 3 RGR in the UK. After the withdrawal of Gurkha troops from Hong Kong in 1996, 2 RGR and 3 RGR will merge to form the 2nd Battalion in Brunei, while 1 RGR will move to the UK.

The commandant of 2 RGR, Lt Col David Hayes, presents new badges to Queen's Gurkha Officers at Church Crookham

Picture: Terry Champion

Truncheon in safe keeping – Page 7

3

Left: An article in *Soldier Magazine* describing the 'Vesting Day' parades that took place on 1 July 1994 to mark the formation of The Royal Gurkha Rifles. During the symbolic parades, which took place in UK, Hong Kong and Brunei, soldiers were invited to replace their existing cap badges with that of their new regiment.

Below: Officers of The Royal Gurkha Rifles take post during the Regiment's Formation Parade, 10 September 1994.

The formal parade to celebrate the formation of the RGR did not take place until September 1994 but there was still a need to mark the birth of the new regiment. To that end, symbolic 'Formation Day', or 'Vesting Day', parades were held on 1 July in UK, Hong Kong and Brunei during which soldiers were invited to replace their existing cap badges with that of their new regiment. For many, it was an emotional experience as regiments that had served the British

The programme produced for the formal parade to mark the formation of The Royal Gurkha Rifles. The parade took place on 10 September 1994 in Queen Elizabeth Barracks, Church Crookham. His Royal Highness The Prince of Wales took the salute.

Crown for well over 150 years ceased to exist as living organisations. But there was also a spirit of optimism as this short extract from the speech given by the CO of 10GR/3RGR on 1 July 1994 suggests:[19]

"So, my message to you today is simple. Do not be sad about the passing of 10th Princess Mary's Own Gurkha Rifles. The Regiment and those who served in her will not be forgotten. Take forward with pride the good things and particularly the 10GR way of life. And be prepared to build a new and equally distinguished Regiment – The Royal Gurkha Rifles. Our motto should perhaps therefore be, 'never forget but look forward'. DAS KI JAI"

Six weeks later on 10 September 1994, the official Formation Parade took place in Queen Elizabeth Barracks, Church Crookham. His Royal Highness The Prince of Wales, as Colonel-in-Chief of the new Regiment, took the salute accompanied by General Duffell, the Regiment's first Colonel. In his speech, His Royal Highness recognised the importance of the past but also acknowledged the bright future that lay ahead:[20]

"As your Colonel-in-Chief, it is with great pride that I have reviewed your Formation Parade today. The Regiment is new, but the Gurkha soldier's reputation, his superlative standards and traditions reach back through 180 years of loyal and courageous service to the British Crown.

The reputation for excellence and gallantry achieved over the last 200 years by the Gurkhas is second to none. Sadly, over the past few years some of the most famous and distinguished Regiments and Corps of the British Army have been amalgamated, and the Brigade of Gurkhas has been no exception. By the time the amalgamations are complete 5000 Gurkha officers and soldiers of our Battalions will have gone. I am all too well aware of the hardship that those made redundant may face as they seek new employment, but also I am heartened by how much is being done to help and assist them.

31

The Formation Parade of The Royal Gurkha Rifles which took place on 10 September 1994 at Queen Elizabeth Barracks, Church Crookham in the presence of His Royal Highness The Prince of Wales. As this painting by Alix Baker shows, the backdrop to the parade consisted of the cap badges of the four regiments that amalgamated on 1 July 1994 to form The Royal Gurkha Rifles. Note that the cap badge of the new regiment is in the centre of the display.

For all of you gathered here today, this Parade marks the beginning of a new era. From now on The Royal Gurkha Rifles must look to the future. The world is still a dangerous and uncertain place, and the British Army is frequently called upon to help contain the less stable areas of the globe.

Gurkhas have recently served with great distinction in the Falklands, in the Gulf and with the United Nations in Cyprus and Cambodia. Gurkha signallers are even now in Bosnia and I hope more of you will have the opportunity to serve there.

The Regiment must be ready to rise to whatever challenges present themselves and these may lie just round the corner. You are lucky not only to be a Rifle regiment, with its traditional speed of reaction and indirectness of approach, but you also have all the flexibility that a large Regiment offers.

And, above all, you are a Gurkha Regiment; one that I know will continue to strike fear and a healthy respect in the minds of any enemy, and pride

into the hearts of your many friends. Wherever your service may take you, I wish the Regiment a long and distinguished future.

I do congratulate you all on the splendid way in which you are carrying on the traditions and standards of your forbears and the way in which you have conducted yourself on parade. I need hardly say how enormously proud I am to be your Colonel-in-Chief and to be associated with such a splendid Regiment. I would have been very sad indeed if I had been unable to maintain my association with the Gurkhas.

Good luck and best wishes to you all. Jai Royal Gurkha Rifles.'

Left: A close up image of the Colonel-in-Chief inspecting the front rank of the Formation Parade. Lieutenant General Sir Peter Duffell, the Regiment's first Colonel, smiles as he listens to His Royal Highness talking to a Rifleman.

Below: His Royal Highness The Prince of Wales at the reception following The Royal Gurkha Rifles' Formation Parade. His Royal Highness has been the Regiment's Colonel-in-Chief since its formation.

Prince Charles' words proved to be prophetic as, only 15 months after the Regiment's formation, A Company 3RGR departed for Bosnia on Operation Resolute,[21] the first operational deployment of Gurkha infantry since the Falklands War of 1982. Since then, the Regiment has continued to maintain a high tempo of operational deployments to the Balkans, Afghanistan, Africa, Iraq and many other theatres, earning a reputation as a highly professional and capable infantry force and consolidating its position as a worthy successor to its distinguished antecedents. The chapters that follow aim to provide an insight into the Regiment's many achievements over its first 25 years of service to the British Crown.

THE QUEEN'S TRUNCHEON

In 1857, The Royal Gurkha Rifles' (RGR's) antecedent regiments were called upon to demonstrate not only their fighting skills but also their loyalty as the native troops of British India started to turn against their imperial masters. The violence started on 11 May in the town of Meerut. Although it came as a surprise to the British, it had been brewing for years. Arguably, the main catalyst was the cartridge that accompanied the new Enfield rifle which the firer had to rip open with his teeth. This was usual practice with weapons of the time but rumours soon began to circulate that the cartridge for the new weapon was greased with cow or pig fat. As a sacred animal, the use of cow fat was offensive to Hindus and, to Muslims, the pig was considered unclean. Native soldiers were therefore reluctant to put the cartridges to their mouths.

The Queen's Truncheon being marched on parade by the Truncheon Party. On this occasion the parade took place in front of Her Majesty The Queen at the Royal Hospital Chelsea on 9 June 2015 to commemorate 200 years of Gurkha service to the British Crown (image Crown copyright, 2015)

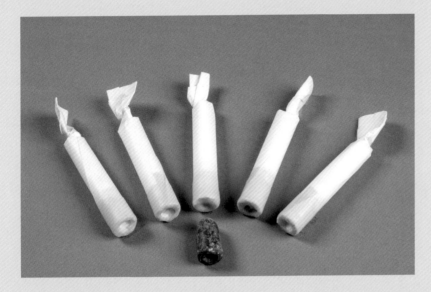

Left: The cartridges that went with the new Enfield rifle. The firer had to rip open the end of the cartridge with his teeth.

Below: A painting by Jason Askew showing the guns aimed at Delhi.

The Gurkhas, ever practical, had few such reservations, even demonstrating to other native troops on a musketry course that the new cartridges were fine.[22] However, discontent turned into open rebellion when native troops were forced to use the cartridges against their will. On 14 May 1857, the Sirmoor Battalion, later to become the 2nd Gurkhas, one of the RGR's antecedent regiments, was ordered to proceed to Meerut to help suppress the rebellion.[23] But events were moving fast and the battalion was soon redirected to Delhi to reinforce a British column under Lieutenant General Sir Henry Barnard.[24]

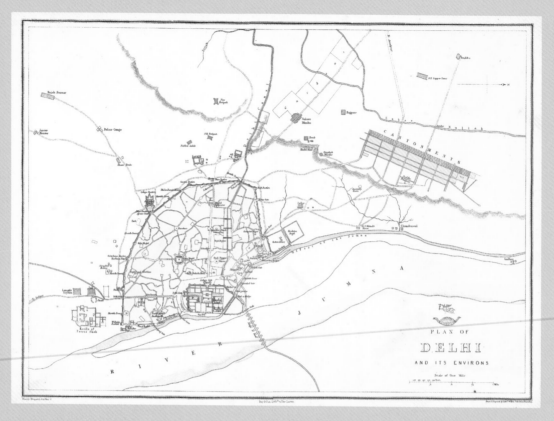

Above: A contemporaneous map of Delhi showing the ridgeline to the north east where the Sirmoor Battalion occupied a defensive position in the house of the merchant Hindu Rao.

The battalion's arrival was greeted with some suspicion. Worried that the Gurkhas might also mutiny, their tents had been pitched close to the artillery which, unbeknownst to the Gurkhas, had been given orders to turn their guns on the battalion at the first sign of rebellion.[25] However, it was not long before the Gurkhas, fighting alongside the 60th Rifles, quickly dispelled any doubts about their loyalty.

The rebels consolidated their position by withdrawing into the heavily fortified city of Delhi. This allowed the British to occupy a ridge to the north east which overlooked the approaches to the city.

The mutineers realised the tactical importance of the ridgeline and, in particular, a sprawling villa which dominated the ridge belonging to a local merchant

called Hindu Rao. But the men of the 60th Rifles, the Sirmoor Battalion and the Corps of Guides held firm, repulsing 26 separate attacks between the first week of June and the 14 September 1857.[26] Conditions were dire. As well as the constant artillery bombardments and rebel attacks, the defenders had to contend with cholera. The casualties continued to mount but the defenders fought on. Eventually, in mid-August a relief column arrived, headed by Brigadier General John Nicholson. Known as the Lion of the Punjab, he commanded a force of some 4200 men, including 90 reinforcements for the Sirmoor Battalion which, by this stage, had lost well over half of its men.[27]

On 14 September 1857, reinforced and determined to put an end to nearly four months of constant combat, the British and loyal East India Company forces went on the offensive. Organised into four fighting columns, their aim was to break into the city in order to take the fight to the mutineers.[28] Brigadier General Nicholson, with the Kumaon Battalion (later the 3rd Gurkhas) in the vanguard of his force, led his column towards the mighty Kashmir Gate. The mutineers resisted, mortally wounding Nicholson,[29] but eventually the gate was blown and the city's formidable defences breached.

Left: A view of the walled city of Delhi taken from the ridgeline to the north east which overlooks it. The Kashmir Gate is at the bottom right of the image.

Above: A painting by Jason Askew showing Gurkhas of the Sirmoor Battalion repulsing an attack on Hindu Rao's House, the defensive position they occupied along with the 60th Rifles and the Corps of Guides on a ridge overlooking Delhi.

37

A painting by Jason Askew showing the assault troops breaking through the Kashmir Gate on 14 September 1857. The assault was led by Brigadier General John Nicholson. Known as 'The Lion of the Punjab', he was mortally wounded in the attack and died of his injuries on 23 September 1857.

A photograph of the Kashmir Gate taken in 1857 after the storming of the city. Note the damage to the walls sustained during the 'break in'.

A photograph of the Kashmir Gate taken on 13 May 2019. Although the moat in front of the gate has now been filled in, much of the damage from the assault of 1857 can still be seen.

Bahadur Shah Zafar, the elderly King of Delhi, who became the reluctant figurehead of the Indian Mutiny.

The attacking troops surged into the city, driving the mutineers from street to street. The fighting lasted for six days; the attackers showed little mercy. The elderly King of Delhi, who had become the mutineers' *de facto* figurehead, was captured. Although three of his sons were killed, his life was spared, a remarkably lenient act given he had offered a 10 rupee reward for the head of every Gurkha.[30][31]

The storming of Delhi was arguably the turning point of the mutiny but it took well over a year for the last embers of rebellion to be extinguished.[32] One of the most significant skirmishes of this period, at least from the Gurkha perspective, occurred on 10 February 1858. Lieutenant John Adam Tytler, a 33-year-old officer of the 66th (later to become the 1st Gurkhas), was part of a force which encountered two rebel groups of about 5,000 infantry and 1,000 cavalry near the town of Haldwani.[33] Although heavily outnumbered, the British had little option

Soldiers of the Sirmoor Battalion (later the 2nd Gurkhas) in front of Hindu Rao's House on Delhi Ridge. The ridge dominated the city of Delhi which, in 1857, became the focus of the Indian Mutiny. Despite suffering tremendous losses, the Sirmoor Battalion, along with the 60th Rifles and the Corps of Guides, succeeded in holding the ridge until reinforcements arrived.

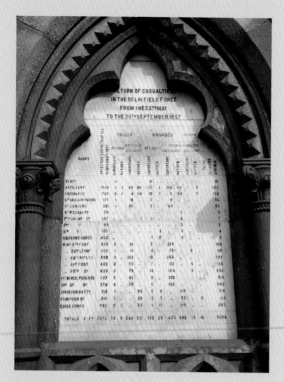

In 1863, a memorial was erected on the ridgeline overlooking Delhi in memory of the officers and soldiers of the Delhi Field Force killed fighting the mutineers between 30 May and 20 September 1857. This panel on the memorial gives the casualty figures for the units involved. Note that those for the Sirmoor Battalion, the Corps of Guides and the 60th Rifles are disproportionately high as they bore the brunt of 26 attacks by the mutineers between the first week of June and 14 September 1987.

For its remarkable service at Delhi, the Sirmoor Battalion was granted the following Honours and Distinctions:[35]

a. A third, honorary Colour inscribed 'Delhi' in English, Hindi and Persian. An additional jemadar (Gurkha lieutenant) was added to the establishment to carry this Colour.

b. Other Ranks became known as riflemen because of the opprobrium attached to the title 'sepoy'.

c. The Battalion was granted the privilege of wearing the facings and uniform of the 60th Rifles.

d. Although a Rifle Regiment, the Battalion was further authorised to continue to carry Colours (not something Rifle Regiments traditionally did).

e. The title of the Battalion was changed from the Sirmoor Battalion to the Sirmoor Rifle Regiment.

but to fight. The enemy's artillery was proving to be devastatingly effective until Tytler, alone, rode forward to the guns and started to engage the enemy in hand-to-hand combat. Shot in the arm and with a spear in his chest, he continued to fight until the guns had been taken.[34] Perhaps not surprisingly, he was awarded the Victoria Cross, the first Gurkha officer to receive the award.

A painting of the storming of Delhi in 1857 showing 'the incident at Subjee Mundi'. A soldier from the Sirmoor Battalion (later the 2nd Gurkhas, one the RGR's antecedent regiments) is about to draw his kukri and decapitate a mutineer taking refuge in a house.

Soldiers from the 66th or Goorkha Regiment (previously known as the Nusseree Battalion and later the 1st Gurkhas) circa 1857. During the Indian Mutiny, the regiment was involved in heavy fighting with mutineers in the north of India. Lieutenant John Tytler, one of the regiment's British Officers, was awarded the Victoria Cross for his actions, becoming the first recipient of this award in a Gurkha battalion. Tytler is seated at the head of the table with his head resting on his hand.

The two Colours of the Sirmoor Battalion (later 2nd Gurkhas) at the time of the Indian Mutiny. A third 'honorary' Colour was awarded in recognition of the Battalion's performance during the Indian Mutiny. This was eventually replaced by the Queen's Truncheon.

The Honours and Distinctions granted to the Sirmoor Battalion were a significant privilege, but one of them presented something of a problem. Infantry regiments carried their Colours into battle and because they were seen as embodying the spirit of the regiment, they had to be protected from the enemy at all costs. The award of a third Colour therefore meant that additional soldiers would need to be taken out of the line of battle and assigned to its protection. The impact of this was not lost on Lieutenant Colonel Charles Reid, the Sirmoor Battalion's Commandant (as the commanding officers of the Sirmoor Battalion were known). In December 1858, Reid wrote to the Adjutant General of the Indian Army expressing his concern and asking that an "ornamental bronze truncheon be presented to the Battalion" instead of the third Colour.[36] Reid's request,

which included a design for the truncheon, was forwarded to the Secretary of State for India, a new appointment that had been created following the Mutiny and the Government's decision to liquidate the British East India Company and assume direct control of India.[37]

However, carrying a truncheon in lieu of a Colour was so "contrary to all the established rules of the service"[38] that there was considerable nervousness about submitting such a proposal to Queen Victoria. Buckingham Palace therefore suggested that a truncheon be carried by the Bugle Major in addition to, rather than instead of, the third Colour. The advantage of this was that it would not need to be agreed by the Queen. In October 1859, Reid duly received authorisation for "a bronze Truncheon, in the shape of a Drum Major's stick, to be made up and presented to the Regiment".[39]

When he left the Regiment having handed over command, Reid was made an Aide de Camp (ADC) to the Queen, an appointment that brought him into routine contact with Her Majesty. In the course of his duties, the subject of the Truncheon must have come up as the Queen began to take an interest in it. After seeing the finished item at the 1862 International Exhibition,[40] she gave permission for the Truncheon to replace the Regiment's third Colour. The following article, which was published in the Illustrated London News a few weeks before the International Exhibition officially opened to the public, provides a first-hand account of the newly made truncheon:

"We give above an Engraving of an 'Honorary Truncheon' which is about to be sent out to India for presentation to her Majesty's 2nd Goorkha or Sirmoor Rifles, for their service to the State during the siege of Delhi in 1857. The Truncheon, designed by Colonel Charles Reid CB and ADC to the Queen, and manufactured by Messrs. Hunt and Roskell, is composed of Indian ornaments and the staff is so arranged as to divide into four pieces. On the summit of the staff is an Indian minaret, surrounding which stands three figures representing privates of the Sirmoor Rifles supporting the Imperial crown of Great Britain. Surrounding the rim on which these figures stand is the inscription – 'Main Picquet, Hindoo Rao's House Delhi 1857', and in the minaret hang two crossed 'kookeries', the national Goorkha weapon. The Goorkha figures, we are informed, are admirably modelled, and no better idea could be given to the men of the Sirmoor Rifles. The truncheon will always serve as a rallying point, and will be carried in the centre of the regiment by a Goorkha officer especially appointed by Government; in fact, the truncheon will take the place of an 'honorary colour' which was at first given by the Government, but at the suggestion of Colonel Reid, a truncheon was substituted as being more appropriate to a rifle regiment".[41]

The Regiment finally received the Truncheon from the Commander-in-Chief of India, Lieutenant General (Acting General) Sir Hugh Rose (later to become Lord Strathnairn) at a parade held on 30 November 1863 in Lahore (then in India, now in Pakistan). By this time, it had been decided that it would replace all three of the Regiment's Colours. Interestingly, ever since it entered service with the 2nd Gurkhas, the Queen's Truncheon has usually been referred to as 'the Nishani Mai' (meaning 'Symbol of the Great Mother') by Gurkhas.

A close up of a replica head of the Queen's Truncheon showing three soldiers of the Sirmoor Rifles supporting the Imperial Crown of Great Britain. The soldiers are in turn supported by two crossed kukris contained within three pillars.

The Queen's Truncheon being carried by the Truncheon Jemadar during a parade to mark the Changing of the Guard at Buckingham Palace. An officer carrying the Colours of the Welsh Guards, the regiment handing over the guard, marches alongside the Jemadar. This picture was taken on 6 May 2015 when the RGR was carrying out Public Duties as part of the celebrations to mark two hundred years of Gurkha service to the British Crown (image copyright Richard Pohle).

Right: The Truncheon Jemadar, the officer who carries the Truncheon when it is on parade, is often the most junior Gurkha officer. He is flanked by two sergeants and two corporals as in this photograph taken on 28 January 2011 during a parade to award operational service medals to members of 1RGR and G (Tobruk) Company 1MERCIAN, a Gurkha Reinforcement Company, both of which had recently returned Operation Herrick 12 in Afghanistan (image Crown copyright 2010).

Since it was presented to the Sirmoor Rifles in 1863, the Truncheon's continued service with Gurkha infantry has only been called into doubt on two occasions. The first of these was after India achieved independence and the regiment to which it belonged, the 2nd Gurkhas, transferred from the Indian Army to the British Army. After the history of the Queen's Truncheon had been explained to King George VI, he authorised it to continue in service with the British Army and for it to continue being accorded the respect of a Colour. The second time was when The Royal Gurkha Rifles was formed on 1 July 1994. As explained in Chapter 1, the Queen's Truncheon was taken out of service on 24 June 1994, a week before the new regiment was formed, and laid up in the Indian Army Memorial Room in the Royal Military Academy Sandhurst. This was done in case its retention in the new regiment was seen to favour the 2nd Gurkhas over the other antecedent

The Queen's Truncheon is only ever lowered (as in this photograph) during a Royal Salute to a member of the Royal Family. On this occasion, the Royal Salute was for His Royal Highness The Prince of Wales who was about to review the parade as the Colonel-in-Chief of the RGR (image Crown copyright 2010).

Right: Her Majesty The Queen inspecting the Queen's Truncheon on 10 June 2015 at Buckingham Palace. The Truncheon was presented to Her Majesty as part of the celebrations to commemorate 200 years of Gurkha service to the British Crown (1815 to 2015). Whenever the Queen's Truncheon is presented to the Monarch, a silver band engraved with the date is added to the staff just below the head of the Truncheon.

Below: During the Hindu festival of Dashain, the Queen's Truncheon is presented with garlands made of flowers as a mark of deep respect. In this photograph the Truncheon Jemadar holds the Truncheon whilst the Gurkha Major places the garlands over the crown.

regiments. By 1997, the new regiment was judged to have established its own identity and the decision was therefore taken to bring the Queen's Truncheon back into service. It was presented to the Regiment on 28 April 1997 by His Royal Highness The Prince of Wales, the Regiment's Colonel-in-Chief.

When on parade, the Queen's Truncheon is carried by a Gurkha officer – the Truncheon Jemadar – and escorted by four armed guards, two sergeants and two corporals, whose drill and turnout are expected to be immaculate.

On very special occasions, the Queen's Truncheon is presented to the reigning sovereign for formal inspection. The last time this happened was in June 2015 as part of the formal commemorations to mark 200 years of Gurkha service to the Crown.

Many of the Honours and Distinctions awarded to the Gurkhas as a consequence of their exemplary conduct during the Indian Mutiny, such as the privilege of carrying the Queen's Truncheon, have been carried forward from the antecedent regiments into the RGR. In addition, the RGR continues to celebrate the close relationship that was formed on Delhi Ridge between the Sirmoor Battalion and the 60th Rifles by having The Rifles as an Affiliated Regiment.

Right: Having finished their basic training at the Infantry Training Centre in Catterick, new recruits join the RGR and complete a short induction package. At the end of this, they swear their allegiance to the Crown and the Regiment on the Queen's Truncheon. This photograph was taken in Bosnia in January 2006 when 1RGR was deployed on Operation Palatine (taking part in Operation Althea, the European Union name for the Balkans deployment). It shows the Gurkha Major holding the Queen's Truncheon whilst soldiers who have recently joined the battalion swear their allegiance.

CHAPTER 2

The Balkans

From December 1995 until September 2007, battalions and sub-units from the RGR did multiple tours in the Balkans, both in Bosnia and Herzegovina and in Kosovo. The Gurkha soldier's natural ability to relate to the rural populations of these relatively poor countries was a force multiplier in terms of gathering low-level intelligence.

Following the end of the Cold War, ethnic tensions started to surface in countries that had been under the iron control of the Soviet Union for decades. Nowhere was this more apparent than in Yugoslavia, then comprised of Bosnia and Herzegovina, Croatia, Macedonia,[42] Montenegro, Serbia and Slovenia. In June 1991, Croatia and Slovenia declared independence from Yugoslavia, prompting Serb militias, supported and armed by the Serb dominated Yugoslav People's Army, the JNA, to occupy those areas of Croatia that had large Serb populations.[43] They did this forcibly, driving people from their homes and killing thousands of non-Serbs.

Within a few months, Serbia controlled nearly one third of Croatia's territory. In Bosnia and Herzegovina the situation was also deteriorating. On the pretext of needing to protect Serbs from the inter-ethnic violence that was erupting across the country, the JNA began occupying areas populated by Bosnian Serbs. When, in March 1992, Bosnian Muslims (known as Bosniacs) and Bosnian Croats voted for Bosnia and Herzegovina to become independent, the Bosnian Serb population refused to recognise the outcome of the plebiscite and declared their own independent state within Bosnia, the Republika Srpska. Inter-ethnic tensions then escalated into civil war. Led by Radovan Karadžić, and backed by the

Serbian government of Slobodan Milošević,[44] the Bosnian Serbs, again supported by the JNA, carried out a violent campaign of 'ethnic cleansing' across Bosnia and Herzegovina, forcing some 170,000 people from their homes and laying siege to Sarajevo, the capital of the country. Although they were fighting against the Serbs, the situation became more complex when Bosnian Croats also began targeting Bosniacs, evicting them from Croat dominated areas of Bosnia and Herzegovina. Atrocities were committed on all sides as the civil war raged but it risked becoming an all-out Balkans war when Croatia entered the conflict "with an eye toward taking Bosnian territory that nationalists considered Croatian".[45] The situation could be succinctly summarised as Serbia, which arguably formed the heart of the old Yugoslavia, and the newly independent Croatia fighting "...for territory and influence in the land that separated them, Bosnia-Herzegovina, initiating a brutal war that lasted for much of the first half of the 1990s".[46]

The international community's response to the deteriorating situation in Bosnia-Herzegovina was initially rather muted. On 25 September 1991, the United Nations (UN) Security Council passed its first resolution to try to deal with the situation. Although Resolution 713 (1991) expressed deep concern at the fighting and called on those involved to try to agree a peace deal,[47] it had little effect. On 7 April 1992, the Security Council took a more robust position and passed Resolution 743 (1992), which authorised the deployment of a UN Protection Force (UNPROFOR) to "...create conditions of peace and security required for the negotiation of an overall settlement of the Yugoslav crisis".[48] The UN's position continued to harden and, in June 1992, the North Atlantic Treaty Organisation (NATO) became involved, agreeing to "...support peacekeeping activities under the responsibility of the Conference on Security and Co-operation in Europe (subsequently renamed the Organisation for Security and Co-operation in Europe (OSCE))".[49] NATO's operations were initially limited to imposing a no-fly zone over Bosnia and Herzegovina and to enforcing sanctions, which included an embargo on the supply of arms to the former Yugoslavia. On 18 March 1994, Bosnian Muslim and Croatian leaders agreed to a ceasefire and to the formation of the Federation of Bosnia and Herzegovina within Bosnia. The agreement – known as the Washington Agreement after the city in which it was negotiated – was a significant step forward as it brought two of the sides together but the Bosnian Serbs refused to recognise either the ceasefire or the newly-formed Federation. Instead, they continued their military offensive.

The situation took a dramatic turn for the worse when, in July 1995, units from the Army of the Republika Srpska (VRS) massacred around 8,000 Muslim men and boys near the town of Srebrenica in one of the supposedly 'safe-zones' established by the UN. Although the safe-zone was patrolled by Dutch soldiers from UNPROFOR, they were unable to prevent the massacre, which has been described as the worst atrocity in Europe since the Second World War.[50] NATO responded by carrying out air strikes throughout August and September, protecting UN 'safe-havens'[51] and targeting VRS installations. This markedly reduced Bosnian Serb military effectiveness and helped shift the balance of power on the ground. NATO's overwhelming military superiority, and its willingness to use lethal force, helped convince the Bosnian Serb leadership that "the benefits of negotiating a peace agreement outweighed those of continuing to wage war" and, on 14 December 1995, after negotiations held near Dayton, Ohio in the US, the General Framework Agreement for Peace in Bosnia and Herzegovina was signed in Paris.[52] This agreement – known as the Dayton Peace Agreement (DPA) – established Bosnia and Herzegovina as a single multi-ethnic democratic state with two entities: the Federation of Bosnia and Herzegovina (largely populated by Bosniacs and Croats); and the Republika Srpska (largely populated by Serbs).

The DPA brought the three-and-a-half year war to an end. Once signed, NATO took over from UNPROFOR on the ground in Bosnia and Herzegovina, deploying an Implementation Force (IFOR) with a one year mandate not just to maintain peace but, where necessary, to enforce it. IFOR's main task was "to guarantee the end of hostilities and separate the armed forces of the Federation of Bosnia and Herzegovina, on the one hand, and Republika Srpska, on the other".[53] On the ground, this task translated into overseeing "the transfer of territory between the Federation of Bosnia and Herzegovina and Republika Srpska, the demarcation of the inter-entity boundary and the removal of heavy weapons into approved cantonment sites".[54]

On 6 December 1995, several days before the DPA had been formally signed, the officiating

Commanding Officer of 3RGR, Major Gerard Hughes, received a phone call from Headquarters 5 Airborne Brigade telling him that the battalion was to deploy a rifle company group on Operation Resolute, the name given to the UK's contribution to IFOR. It was an exciting moment as it marked the first operational deployment of Gurkha infantry since 7GR deployed to the Falkland Islands in 1982 as part of the UK Task Force.[55] On 18 December 1995, the last elements of 3RGR's A Company Group were piped out of Queen Elizabeth Barracks, Church Crookham on their way to Bosnia.

Once in theatre, the company group was split into four platoons and given responsibility for guarding key installations across the country. These

Soldiers from 1/7th Gurkhas with a captured Argentinian anti-aircraft gun in the Falkland Islands in 1982. The battalion deployed as part of 5 Infantry Brigade and took part in the final battle for Port Stanley. The next time that Gurkha infantry would deploy on operations in a formed unit or sub-unit would be 14 years later when A Company 3RGR deployed to Bosnia in December 1995 on Operation Resolute.

Soldiers from A Company
3RGR on Operation Resolute
in Bosnia and Herzegovina
in 1996 as part of the NATO
Intervention Force (IFOR).

included: the British Brigade Headquarters in Sipovo;
Headquarters of the Allied Rapid Reaction Corps
(ARRC) in Sarajevo; the ARRC's Rear Headquarters
in Kiseljak; 237 Electronic Warfare Squadron in
Vitez; and Headquarters National Support Element/
Rear Headquarters Multi-National Division (South
West) (Rear HQ MND(SW)) in Split, Croatia.
The company was also responsible for guarding
the main headquarters of MND(SW), initially in
Gornji Vakuf and then, when the headquarters
moved, in Banja Luka. The company's own
headquarters was collocated with HQ MND(SW),
an ideal arrangement as it enabled the company
commander[56] to convince the HQ MND(SW) staff
that his men could do more than just guard static
installations. As a result, the company was soon
deploying three-man teams to support Psyop Patrols
in Sipovo and Banja Luka, as well as conducting
weapons inspections at three VRS barracks. The
deployment lasted seven months. As 3RGR noted at

the time, "whilst our primary task was unexciting it
required great motivation and professionalism which
the men were more than equal to".[57]

By September 1996, IFOR had achieved the
majority of its objectives but the situation in Bosnia
and Herzegovina remained potentially unstable.
NATO therefore agreed to deploy a Stabilisation
Force (SFOR) from December 1996. SFOR's
primary task "was to contribute to a safe and
secure environment conducive to civil and political
reconstruction. Specifically, SFOR was tasked to
deter or prevent a resumption of hostilities; to
promote a climate in which the peace process could

On completion of their deployment
on Operation Resolute (from
December 1995 to July 1996),
members of A Company 3RGR
were awarded the NATO medal
with the clasp 'Former Yugoslavia'.

Soldiers from B Company 1RGR delivering electoral material to a polling station in September 1997 prior to the provincial elections in Bosnia and Herzegovina. The company deployed on Operation Lodestar for six weeks in September and October to support the elections. Once the elections were over, the company was given its own area of operations near the town of Jajce.

continue to move forward; and, to provide selective support within its means and capabilities to civilian organisations involved in this process".[58] On the ground, this meant SFOR troops carrying out a wide range of different activities such as: patrolling and providing area security; supervising de-mining operations; arresting individuals indicted for war crimes; and assisting the return of refugees and displaced people to their homes.[59] When IFOR was replaced by SFOR in December 1996, the UK name for deployments to Bosnia and Herzegovina changed from Operation Resolute[60] to Operation Lodestar.[61]

The RGR's next deployment to the Balkans, and first contribution to the SFOR mission, took place in September 1997 when B Company 1RGR deployed on Operation Lodestar for six weeks as part of a surge to provide additional support to provincial elections

taking place that month. The company group, which was initially based in Gornji Vakuf, was under the command of the Second Battalion The Royal Regiment of Fusiliers (2RRF). Interestingly, one of the company's platoons was detached to provide Warrior dismounts for A Company 2RRF which, at the time, formed part of a battlegroup commanded by the RGR's affiliated regiment, The King's Royal Hussars.

At the start of the tour, B Company was responsible for delivering sensitive electoral material to eight different 'opstinas', roughly equivalent to municipal districts. However, once the elections were over, the company group was given its own area of operations centred on the village of Divicani, near the historical town of Jajce.[62] Over 400 Bosnian Muslim families had been encouraged to return to their homes in the area having been driven out during the civil war. Based in a dilapidated school – which they renovated whilst there – the company's task was to provide security in order to "...buy time for the returnees, free from intimidation, to rebuild

The Second in Command of B Company 1RGR stands proudly in front of one of the Saxon armoured vehicles used by the company on Operation Lodestar to deliver sensitive electoral material during provincial elections in Bosnia and Herzegovina in September 1997.

One of the armoured Saxon vehicles used by B Company 1RGR during Operation Lodestar in September and October 1997 showing the crossed kukris of the RGR on the front right of the vehicle.

The utility of NBC protective clothing! Two soldiers from B Company 1RGR on Operation Lodestar wearing respirators as they get down to the serious business of chopping onions for the evening bhat.

4 Platoon of B Company 1RGR outside the dilapidated school in the village of Divicani that became their home in September and October 1997 during Operation Lodestar. The company's task after the elections was to secure the Divicani area and provide protection to over 400 Bosnian Muslim families returning to their homes after the war in order to rebuild them prior to the onset of winter. The mix in the colour of berets is because, at the time, only those who had completed 'P Company' and qualified as military parachutists were authorised to wear the maroon beret of the airborne forces. This policy has since changed and all members of the RGR serving in airborne or assault formations, such as 16 Air Assault Brigade, now wear the maroon beret.

Respirators again! Two soldiers from B Company 1RGR during Operation Lodestar in October 1997 preparing the walls of the school gym for re-painting in the village of Divicani.

their homes prior to the onset of winter".[63] The company assumed responsibility for the area on 16 September 1997 and remained there for four weeks, providing a secure environment for the Muslim returnees but also helping them and their Bosnian Croat neighbours prepare for winter. The company returned to UK in mid October 1997.

B (Gallipoli) Company, a Gurkha Reinforcement Company (GRC) serving with the 1st Battalion The Royal Scots (1RS), was the next RGR organisation to deploy to Bosnia and Herzegovina, this time on Operation Palatine in July 1998. Although the name of the UK's deployments to the Balkans changed from Operation Lodestar to Operation Palatine in June 1998, the task was still to support SFOR in achieving its objectives. B (Gallipoli) Company 1RS was based in the 'Metal Factory' in Banja Luka, the capital of the Republika Srpska. Its role was to be the Divisional Defence Company for HQ MND(SW), an important task that would remain the preserve of GRCs for the next year and a half. As well as patrolling the surrounding area, the company was responsible for monitoring local VRS activity, which included observing training as well as inspecting barracks and other military sites, and distributing leaflets in support of the SFOR information campaign (Operation Kane). The company also played an important role during the general elections on 12 and 13 September 1998 by providing a visible, but low-key, deterrent presence on the streets of Banja Luka in support of the civilian police and the OSCE.

In January 1999, B Company 1RS was replaced as the HQ MND(SW) Divisional Defence Company by

C (Cassino) Company 2PARA. The tour was initially relatively straightforward but it became more challenging in late March 1999 when Bosnian Serbs started to protest against NATO bombing raids in Kosovo. Things reached a head when, on 26 March 1999, the UK and US embassy outstations in Banja Luka were sacked by violent protestors.[64] C (Cassino) Company had a key role to play in ensuring the security of the 'Metal Factory' over this period and dealing with civil unrest in Banja Luka itself. The situation eventually calmed down but, as the company newsletter notes, "for the remainder of the tour the Company battled hard to regain the fragile relationship between SFOR and the local community in very trying times".[65] The company's newsletter went on the note that "things were not made any easier by the excitement and coverage that we were missing out on in Kosovo".[66] The "excitement" they were "missing out on" was the deployment of their parent brigade, 5 Airborne Brigade, to Kosovo as part of the NATO-led Kosovo Force (KFOR).

The situation in Kosovo, a region in the south of Serbia that had enjoyed autonomy until 1989, had deteriorated throughout the early 90s because of growing tensions between its ethnic Serb and Albanian communities. In 1991, the Kosovar Albanians held a referendum and voted for independence. Although this was largely ignored, it did not stop the Democratic League of Kosova (LDK) establishing its own parliament and installing a President, Ibrahim Rugova. When the DPA was negotiated in December 1995, the status of Kosovo was deliberately excluded from the discussions, partly because the western negotiators failed to recognise its potential for future conflict but also because it would have further complicated relationships with Slobodan Milošević.[67] In 1997, support for the Kosovo Liberation Army (KLA), a well-armed militia committed to the country's independence, began to increase. Violent clashes broke out between the KLA and Serb paramilitary forces, prompting the Serbs to deploy large numbers of additional troops (both Serb militia and regular Serb units) to the region. Unlike Bosnia and Herzegovina, the Serbs saw Kosovo as their own territory and they were therefore determined to eradicate the KLA and bring the region back under control. To consolidate their territorial gains, the Serbs again resorted to ethnic cleansing. In 1998, for example, they reportedly killed 1,500 Kosovar Albanians and caused a further 400,000 to flee their homes,[68] although the total number of Kosovar Albanians displaced during the conflict has been estimated at 860,000.[69]

The international community knew that it needed to respond to the mass atrocities being committed in Kosovo but it struggled to achieve consensus on the way ahead. Talks in late 1998 and early 1999 between the so-called International Contact Group (comprised of Germany, France, UK, Italy, Russia and the USA) and representatives of Kosovo, Serbia and the Federal Republic of Yugoslavia (FRY), which by then consisted of the Republics of Serbia and Montenegro, initially appeared to be making progress but failed when the Serbs refused to accept that Kosovo should be granted considerable autonomy.

Russian and Chinese opposition to a military solution meant that there was little point in trying to secure support for a military intervention through a UN Security Council Resolution so, given the failure of the talks and the rising humanitarian cost of the conflict, NATO decided to intervene. On 24 March 1999,[70] NATO began an air campaign against Serbian and FRY forces in order to "halt and reverse the humanitarian catastrophe that was then unfolding"[71] and making it clear that in order to halt the air campaign President Milošević would need to:[72]

- ensure a verifiable stop to all military action and the immediate ending of violence and repression;
- ensure the withdrawal from Kosovo of the military, police and paramilitary forces;
- agree to the stationing in Kosovo of an international military presence;
- agree to the unconditional and safe return of all refugees and displaced persons and unhindered access to them by humanitarian aid organisations;
- provide credible assurance of his willingness to work towards…the establishment of a political framework agreement for Kosovo in conformity with international law and the Charter of the United Nations.

Eventually, on 9 June 1999 and after 78 days of the air campaign, President Milošević acquiesced. On 10 June 1999, the UN Security Council passed Resolution 1244 (1999) authorising the deployment of an international civilian and military presence to provide a transitional administration and security presence to oversee the return of refugees and the withdrawal of military forces from Kosovo. The resolution went on to state that the international civilian presence would facilitate a "political process to determine the future status of Kosovo".[73]

The UK's contribution to Kosovo Force (KFOR), as the NATO-led military deployment was called, went under the name of Operation Agricola and included 5 Airborne Brigade. This explains why, on 10 June 1999, 1RGR was in Macedonia in a forward assembly area near the border with Kosovo waiting to enter the country the following morning. However, the plan was changed at the last minute and the battalion, along with the 1st Battalion The Parachute Regiment, was ordered to prepare for a helicopter assault onto Pristina Airfield to try to seize it ahead of the Russians, who were thought to be intent on stealing a march on NATO having despatched a company-strong force by road from their SFOR deployment in Bosnia and Herzegovina. Fortunately, sense prevailed, and possible conflict with Russia was avoided, and the battalion was stood down and told to revert to the original plan of entering Kosovo by road and helicopter following the line of a pass known as the Kacanik Defile, but this time on 12 June 1999. It was a tense time. The situation across the border was far from certain as the Intelligence Officer of 1RGR noted:

Above: A Gurkha soldier from 1RGR stares wistfully at the camera in a sea of maroon berets as 5 Airborne Brigade prepares to fly to Macedonia at the start of Operation Agricola, the UK name for support to the NATO-led ground deployment into Kosovo in June 1999.

Left: Gurkhas from 1RGR waiting to board an aircraft en route to Macedonia before then deploying across the border into Kosovo.

"Sitting in cornfields in Macedonia looking north towards the range of mountains that form Kosovo's southern border we occasionally received news of what was happening in the Kacanik Defile in the form of photographs taken by Phoenix.[74] These aircraft were regularly shot down by the Serbs who seemed to enjoy a spot of clay pigeon shooting between engagements with the Kosovo Liberation Army (KLA)".[75]

At 0500 hours on the morning of 12 June 1999, C Company 1RGR deployed across the border in helicopters, landing some four miles up the Kacanik Defile. B Company crossed the border on foot with orders to "seize, secure and clear the route" to C Company.[76] C Company was particularly isolated as it would take time for B Company to reach it and the route to the company's north was blocked by a mined tunnel that needed to be cleared before it could be used. Already tense, the situation became more dangerous when the 1RGR Reconnaissance Platoon arrived with a convoy of heavily armed Serbs

Above: Helicopters landing in Macedonia to pick up members of 1RGR and deploy them across the border into Kosovo to begin securing the Kacanik Defile, the route chosen by NATO for its ground forces to enter the country (photo courtesy of Sean Statham).

Below: Members of 1RGR securing the entrance to a tunnel in the Kacanik Defile. At 0500 hours on 12 June 1999, C Company 1RGR was inserted by helicopter four miles inside Kosovo to seize a key bridge. B Company 1RGR then crossed the border from Macedonia on foot and cleared the road to C Company, creating a secure entry route for NATO's ground forces to deploy into Kosovo (photo courtesy of Sean Statham).

Soldiers from 1RGR carry out a vehicle patrol in Kosovo during the summer of 1999 on Operation Agricola.

A 1RGR foot patrol in Kosovo during Operation Agricola. The rail tracks to their rear were most probably damaged during the 78-day air campaign conducted by NATO before ground troops crossed the border from Macedonia into Kosovo.

from the Ministry of Interior Police (MUP) that they had been ordered to escort north to safety. Deciding that the Serbs needed to be disarmed, C Company managed to remove their weapons without a shot being fired, a remarkable achievement given how tense the situation was. Once the tunnel had been cleared by military engineers, the Reconnaissance Platoon continued north, escorting their now disarmed MUP charges as far as the town of Urosevac where, on the personal orders of Commander of 5 Airborne Brigade, Brigadier Adrian Freer, the platoon was re-tasked. Instead of being allowed to return to 1RGR, it was ordered to set up a road-block and to stop any armed Serbs from going further south.[77] Although isolated and outnumbered, the platoon distinguished itself with the platoon commander, Captain Fraser Rea, being Mentioned in Despatches (MiD) for his bravery and level headedness in dealing with the many irate Serbs who tried to force their way through the road block.[78]

By midday on 12 June 1999, B and C Companies had linked up, opening the defile for 4 Armoured Brigade and the rest of KFOR to deploy deep into Kosovo to begin ensuring that all parties involved in the conflict started to comply with the agreement that had been reached. After 24 hours, 1RGR was relieved of securing the road by a US Task Force[79] and flown forward to become the KFOR reserve, a task it carried out for a week before being given its own area of operations in the southern part of the British sector. There, the 1RGR battlegroup had three main tasks: first, the protection of Serbs who, having given the Kosovar Albanians a hard time, were now receiving similar treatment; second, to monitor the demilitarisation of the KLA, which involved

On completion of their deployment on Operation Agricola (from June 1999 to August 1999), members of 1RGR were awarded the NATO medal with the clasp 'Kosovo'.

constant liaison and considerable patience; and third, to maintain law and order.[80] The battalion's tour was a significant success and, having handed over to a Finnish Battalion on 29 August 1999, 1RGR returned to the UK.[81]

Whilst 1RGR was making a name for itself in Kosovo, July 1999 saw B (Gallipoli) Company 1RS deploying back to Bosnia and Herzegovina on Operation Palatine to take over from C (Cassino) Company 2PARA in Banja Luka. When they had handed over to C Company in January 1999, B Company had been the Divisional Defence Company but, in the interim, the role had changed name to become the Banja Luka Operations Company (BLOC).[82] The primary tasks remained guarding HQ MND(SW) in the 'Metal Factory' and patrolling the Banja Luka area of operations. As part of the Household Cavalry Regiment (HCR) battlegroup they also conducted a number of surge operations. For example, the company provided an inner cordon and a small rescue team during Operation Cage 2, a spot inspection of Tunici Prison by members of the International Police Task Force (IPTF). The company also took part in Operation Coriolanus, an operation to secure Banja Luka airfield so that various heads of state and other VVIPs could attend a peace stabilisation summit in Sarajevo. During the operation, the HCR provided an outer cordon mounted in their Scimitar armoured vehicles, B Company provided an inner cordon and an infantry platoon from Luxembourg provided the quick reaction force (QRF). The company's tour ended in October 1999 having been a complete success.

Although the RGR's main Balkans focus was on Bosnia and Herzegovina and Kosovo, C (Cassino)[83] Company 2PARA also briefly deployed to Macedonia on Operation Bessemer from August until October 2001.[84] The company deployed with 2PARA as part of a 16 Air Assault Brigade operation to "...collect and dispose of NLA weapons and ammunition in order to restore stability in the Former Yugoslav Republic of Macedonia (FYROM)".[85] The NLA – the National Liberation Army of Macedonia – had formed in late 1999 with the goal of achieving equal rights for ethnic Albanians within Macedonia. It had close links to the KLA and, from January 2001, it launched a series of attacks against Macedonian security forces, meeting with considerable success and taking effective control of significant areas of the country. The NLA signed a peace treaty with the Macedonian Government in August 2001. When it deployed, 16 Air Assault Brigade's task was to act as Headquarters Task Force Harvest, coordinating the recovery of weapons from the NLA with a multinational force of some 15 nations under command. The Officer Commanding C (Cassino) Company described this as "...a very delicate game to be played keeping the peace between rebels and other factions".[86] The company had a particularly interesting role as it was selected to provide close protection (known as Category 2 Support) to special forces operating in Macedonia as Harvest Liaison Teams. This meant that the company operated "far and wide across Macedonia". As the company commander notes: "we were essentially weapon collecting from the NLA rebels, but very few of them wanted to give up their weapons

A soldier from 2RGR on Manjaca Ranges in Bosnia and Herzegovina training with Portuguese troops during Operation Palatine. The battalion deployed to Bosnia from September 2001 until March 2002 (image is Crown copyright).

The Commanding Officer of 2RGR serves Christmas Dinner to members of his battalion on Christmas Day 2001 in Bosnia and Herzegovina.

Members of 2RGR surrounded by a large cache of illegal weapons and munitions discovered during a search operation. Much of the battalion's time on Operation Palatine was spent conducting intelligence-led operations to try to identify the location of such caches.

Some of the weapons recovered by 2RGR during its tour on Operation Palatine.

(understandably), and so it became a delicate operation of what I called 'deployed diplomacy' – diplomacy in the hands of junior front line soldiers deployed a very long way away from base locations".[87] The company returned to UK in October 2001 and, after a very brief period of post-operational tour leave (POTL), deployed to Afghanistan on Operation Fingal (See Chapter 5).

2RGR's first tour in the Balkans did not take place until September 2001 when the battalion deployed to Bosnia and Herzegovina on Operation Palatine as the United Kingdom Battle Group (UKBG). It was an interesting tour, particularly as 2RGR was the first light role battalion to deploy to Bosnia during the winter.[88] As well as 550 men from 2RGR, the battalion took under command a squadron from the HCR, a battery from The Royal Artillery, equipment

support personnel from 3rd Battalion The Royal Electrical and Mechanical Engineers (REME) and 56 individual reservists, bringing the total strength to over 1,000 personnel. The battlegroup was based in Mrkonjic Grad Bus Depot (MGBD) in the Republika Srpska, about an hour's drive from Banja Luka. The main task was the conduct of so-called 'normal framework operations' at company level. These included: the collection of illegally held weapons and ammunition; the checking of VRS military sites and installations; and a range of community related projects falling under the general heading of Civil Military Cooperation (CIMIC). Throughout the tour, B Company 2RGR was the Divisional Reserve, providing a crowd and riot control (CRC) capability that was in demand, both within MND(SW) but also in neighbouring divisional areas.

Left: Soldiers from 2RGR share a joke about one of the weapons recovered from illegal caches.

Below: A vehicle from B Company 2RGR in action during Operation Palatine.

During its tour, the 2RGR battlegroup carried out a number of large-scale deliberate operations, such as Operation Twister, a cordon and aggressive search of 12 suspected illegal weapon storage sites. The yield from the operation was particularly impressive and included, amongst other things, 230,000 rounds of 7.62mm and 9mm ammunition, 22 rocket launch grenades and 45 anti-personnel mines.[89] The companies spent much of their time carrying out searches for illegal weapons and ammunition in their own areas of responsibility. Known as Operation Harvest, these searches usually achieved their most impressive finds as a consequence of low-level intelligence, essentially 'tip offs', gathered during routine interaction with the local population, something Gurkhas excel at. The battalion returned to UK in March 2002.

Soldiers from 2RGR practice their crowd and riot control (CRC) techniques using Saxon armoured personnel carriers in October 2001 during Operation Palatine.

In March 2003, the 1st Battalion The Highlanders (Seaforth, Gordons and Camerons), known as 1HLDRS, deployed to Bosnia and Herzegovina on Operation Palatine for a six month deployment as UKBG. The battalion included A (Gallipoli) Company, which, until 28 March 2000, had been B (Gallipoli) Company 1RS and therefore had a huge amount of Balkans experience having completed two tours as the Divisional Defence Company/Banja Luka Operations Company.[90]

Throughout its tour with 1RS, the company had its own area of responsibility centred on MGBD, with platoons located in the outlying areas of Knesevo and Kotor Varos. The company's mission was to: "conduct operations to maintain and extend the safe and secure environment (SSE) and, selectively, to support civil implementation within boundaries and consolidate stability in Bosnia Herzegovina".[91] In addition to routine patrolling and intelligence gathering, the company took part in a number of

Above: Used correctly, the shields carried by 2RGR personnel during CRC operations provide considerable protection against objects hurled by protestors.

Training in theatre had to as realistic as possible in order to maintain the high level of
crowd control competency required to deal with riots on the streets of Banja Luka. This
image shows soldiers from 2RGR using their shields to control the flames from a petrol
bomb. The soldier stood behind the shield men has a fire extinguisher to control the flames.

Training for crowd and riot control during Exercise Joint Resolve 25, a Multinational Division exercise that took place in February 2002 during 2RGR's tour on Operation Palatine.

Gurkhas may not be particularly tall but they have lots of initiative! Two soldiers from A (Gallipoli) Company work together to check whether there are any weapons hidden in a shed.

large-scale battlegroup operations, such as Operation Bagration and Operation Timberwolf. Operation Bagration was an A Company intelligence-led cordon and search of Knesevo. It identified evidence of systemic non-compliance in the local police force and acted as a catalyst for significant changes in the area. Operation Timberwolf ran from August 2003 until late September 2003 and was aimed at putting pressure on illegal parallel power structures by finding, and recovering, weapons caches in the north west of the battlegroup's area of operations.

A Company achieved some remarkable successes during this operation, finding 3 towed artillery guns on the first day and recovering 41 tonnes of weapons and munitions, including a working anti-aircraft system, in the first two weeks alone.[92] The company also supported the first visit of Pope John Paul II to Banja Luka on 22 June 2003 under Operation Eleison, providing support to his movements into the city. The company returned to the UK with 1HLDRS in October 2003 at the end of a highly successful tour.

An officer from A (Gallipoli) Company 1HLDRS engages locals in conversation during Operation Palatine in
September 2003. Low level interaction such as this was a critical source of information about possible weapons caches.

A soldier from A (Gallipoli) Company 1HLDRS trying to see whether there are weapons or
munitions hidden inside an old farm building during the company's tour on Operation Palatine.

Right: An SFOR helicopter recovering one of the field guns found by A (Gallipoli) Company 1HLDRS during search operations carried out in September 2003.

Below: Success! A massive find of ammunition and weapons during Operation Timberwolf, a surge operation to find and clear illegal caches that took place in August and September 2003.

A (Gallipoli) Company 1HLDRS find a field gun, one of three, hidden in woods during a search operation.

In October 2003, 1RGR deployed to Bosnia and Herzegovina on Operation Oculus, the operational name for UK deployments to the Balkans that replaced Operation Palatine (for deployments to Bosnia and Herzegovina) and Operation Agricola (for deployments to Kosovo). As had been the case for 2RGR, the headquarters of the 1RGR battlegroup was initially located in MGBD, a bonus for the battalion as it meant there was an opportunity to compare notes with A (Gallipoli) Company 1HLDRS before it left theatre. Interestingly, an infantry platoon from the Chilean Army and several Australian officers had joined the battalion prior to its deployment. The Chileans were a particularly useful group. Although they spoke very little English, and no Nepali, they were physically very large and highly disciplined, making them ideal for CRC. Within a few weeks of its arrival, the battalion conducted its inaugural operation as part of Multi-National Brigade (North West) (MNB(NW)). This consisted of providing support, in the form of a series of cordons, to the International Criminal

Above: The Officer Commanding A (Gallipoli) Company 1HLDRS (in the centre) discusses whether a weapons permit is legitimate with a member of the Royal Military Police (left) and a member of the International Police Task Force (IPTF). The IPTF member, Doug Haywood, had done several tours in Bosnia and Herzegovina and remained with the UKBG in MGBD when 1RGR took over from 1HLDRS in October 2003. He proved to be an invaluable source of information.

Below: The company second-in-command directing operations from the back of a Land Rover during A (Gallipoli) Company's tour in Bosnia and Herzegovina.

Officers and soldiers from 1RGR with a haul of mortar barrels recovered from a shipping container on a farm. The photograph was taken in December 2003 during the battalion's tour on Operation Oculus.

From left to right: the Regimental Sergeant Major, Gurkha Major and Commanding Officer of 1RGR with some of the weapons recovered by the battalion during Operation Oculus in Bosnia and Herzegovina. The battalion deployed from October 2003 to April 2004.

Tribunal for the Former Yugoslavia (ICTY) as it raided the offices of the Bosnia and Herzegovina state security service. In November 2003, the battalion then conducted a three-week operation to find and recover illegal weapons and ammunition. Known as Operation Krajina Kote, the operation was a significant success despite the heavy snow falls that made many roads difficult to navigate and threatened to obscure much of the ground-sign that would indicate where a weapons cache might be hidden.

In December 2003, the battalion began to transition from being the UKBG to being a Multi-National Battle Group (MNBG), taking a Dutch infantry company and a Canadian armoured squadron under command. In January 2004, 1RGR battlegroup headquarters moved from MGBD to a purpose built facility inside the 'Metal Factory' in Banja Luka. As part of the transition, the battlegroup's role changed from one of ground holding with its rifle companies to the provision of a MOST (monitor, observation, surveillance and targeting) capability, backed up by a manoeuvre

strike capability. Midway through the transformation (on 22 and 23 December 2003), the battlegroup conducted a highly successful detention operation (Operation Concession) to lift a suspected extremist in the town of Travnik. Just as the battalion was settling into the routine of its new role, it received an urgent call to deploy a force to Kosovo as violent skirmishes had erupted between ethnic Albanians and ethnic Serbs and the UK standby battalion,[93] which had already deployed, needed help. C Company 1RGR hastily deployed on 19 March 2004,[94] complete with Saxon armoured personnel carriers flown out from the UK and a small tactical headquarters headed up by the battalion's second-in-command. 1RGR recovered back to the UK in April 2004 having had a remarkably interesting and highly varied tour. The Reconnaissance Platoon remained behind for several weeks having been detached from the battalion to provide a covert surveillance capability in Sarajevo.

18 months after its return from Bosnia and Herzegovina, 1RGR was back in the Balkans.

The battalion had originally been due to deploy to Afghanistan in 2005 but Land Command had changed the Operational Commitments Plot to enable a British infantry battalion to complete an Afghan tour prior to being disbanded. Although the news came as a disappointment to 1RGR, the battalion quickly accepted it and started to prepare for its second tour in the Balkans in as many years. The situation in Bosnia and Herzegovina had changed considerably since the battalion's previous deployment, not least because NATO's SFOR mission had come to an end in December 2004 and had been replaced by a European Union Force (EUFOR). Although the UK name for deployments to the Balkans remained Operation Oculus, the EU name for the mission in Bosnia and Herzegovina was Operation Althea. In addition, although the majority of the battalion deployed to Bosnia and Herzegovina, the new pan-Balkans nature of the commitment meant that the battalion also had to deploy an

Members of 1RGR with Republika Srpska police in October 2005 during an operation in a rural hamlet. Note the insignia of the European Union on the left shoulder of the RGR personnel. The EU Force (EUFOR) replaced SFOR in Bosnia and Herzegovina in December 2004 (image Crown copyright).

Above: A patrol from 1RGR uses skis to enable it to reach high altitude villages during the battalion's winter deployment to Bosnia and Herzegovina on Operation Althea.

Right: Even years after the civil war in Bosnia and Herzegovina ended, the threat from anti-personnel mines remained real and constrained patrolling activities.

intelligence, surveillance and reconnaissance company (ISR Company) to Kosovo.[95] Support Company was selected to undertake this task, which lasted from November 2005 to April 2006. Although an exciting and challenging deployment, it brought with it the requirement to complete a particularly demanding pre-course run by the Operational Training Advisory Group (OPTAG) in Folkestone. 1RGR's reconnaissance platoon had completed a similar course in 2003 before deploying to conduct covert surveillance in Sarajevo during 1RGR's last Balkans tour so Support Company knew what to expect but, even so, it was a tough course!

Once in theatre, the battalion conducted a number of highly successful operations to help bring greater security to the region. These ranged from large-scale search operations aimed at finding illegal caches of weapons and munitions and a cordon and search of Banja Luka prison, through to anti-illegal logging activities and targeted operations against covert networks suspected of supporting Persons Indicted For War Crimes (PIFWICs).[96] Given their experience

Soldiers from 1RGR during Operation Orient in November 2005, an EUFOR led operation to disrupt smuggling operations using the transport network. The photograph was taken during 1RGR's tour on Operation Althea (image Crown copyright).

from previous tours, the rifle companies excelled at finding well-hidden caches, with A Company uncovering the largest cache since EUFOR began and B Company seizing a large quantity of counterfeiting equipment, as well as liberating an underage girl who was being held captive in a brothel. The excitement mounted in the run up to Christmas 2005 when the battalion was tasked with releasing personnel to deploy to Afghanistan. There were two main reasons for this: first, the RGR had been directed to form a new composite company (D (Tamandu) Company) to deploy to Afghanistan with 16 Air Assault Brigade on Operation Herrick 4 (see Chapter 5); and second, because manpower was required to help man an Afghan National Army Officer Training Team. Personnel for both tasks left Bosnia and Herzegovina for the UK over the Christmas period, eventually deploying to Afghanistan in April 2006.

Soldiers from 1RGR practise close quarter combat with kukris on Manjaca Ranges in November 2005 during the battalion's tour on Operation Althea (image Crown copyright).

In April 2007, C Company 2RGR returned to the Balkans, this time deploying to Kosovo as the ISR Company. As Support Company 1RGR had done in preparation for their deployment in the same role in November 2005, C Company 2RGR had to complete the physically and mentally demanding Static Covert Surveillance Course run by the Close Observation Training and Advisory Team (COTAT). Once in theatre, the deployment proved particularly interesting as it involved conducting both rural and urban operations, ranging from a few hours to many months, throughout the country.[97] Of note, the company included 15 attached personnel, both

regulars and reservists, from a wide range of cap badges who were employed as drivers because they were able to blend in with the local population when the company operated from covert vehicles, something Gurkhas would have struggled to do given the ethnicity of the local population. In reflecting on on the company's tour, the company commander noted "a huge amount of responsibility is placed in the JNCOs, often without reward".[98] It is therefore fitting that three Gurkha members of the company received commendations from Commander KFOR. The company returned to 2RGR in September 2007.

An RGR soldier talking to a local inhabitant of one of the more rural villages in Bosnia and Herzegovina. The commitment shown by the members of the RGR throughout their many tours in the Balkans helped people, such as the lady shown in this image, to return their lives to normal.

The RGR's many deployments to the Balkans from December 1995 until September 2007 made a significant contribution to improving the situation in Bosnia and Herzegovina, Kosovo and Macedonia. Although not as 'kinetic' as the Regiment's subsequent deployments to Afghanistan, the Balkans tours were not without considerable risk. The 'break in' to Kosovo in June 1999, for example, required 1RGR, which was in the vanguard the KFOR deployment, to step into the unknown. In the years that followed, the ISR Company task in Kosovo placed a premium on soldiers' ability to live undetected as they carried out their covert surveillance, often in very close proximity to dangerous elements from the Albanian and Serb ethnic factions. And in Bosnia, painstaking intelligence gathering, often conducted by very junior riflemen out on the ground in rural villages, led to some of the most spectacular finds of illegal weapons and munitions. Their removal and disposal markedly degraded the military capability of the parallel power structures that seemed intent on returning to violence.

It seems appropriate to conclude this chapter with remarks made by the Commanding Officer of 1RGR shortly after the battalion's operations in Kosovo in the summer of 1999. Although he had Kosovo in mind when he made them, they apply to the Regiment's efforts in all its Balkans deployments:

"We have brought peace to people desperate for the chance to get on with their lives, rebuild their houses and send their children to school; we have shown everybody that RGR is ready and waiting for operations anywhere in the world, and we have reminded ourselves that professionalism, mixed when necessary with guile and imagination will always win through."[99]

THE ROYALS

Although all of the antecedent regiments had royal titles, the only one that had a member of the Royal Family as a serving Colonel-in-Chief when the regiments amalgamated to form the RGR was 2GR. His Royal Highness The Prince of Wales had become Colonel-in-Chief of the 2nd Goorkhas in 1977, continuing a tradition that began in 1876 when his great great grandfather, King Edward VII, became the first Prince of Wales to assume the appointment of Colonel-in-Chief of this famous regiment.[100]

Prior to the amalgamation, Prince Charles was asked whether he would be prepared to continue his association with the Gurkha infantry and become the first Colonel-in-Chief of the RGR. Fortunately, he accepted the invitation and, on 10 September 1994, His Royal Highness addressed his new regiment for the first time at the formal Formation Parade. Since then, he has remained closely engaged in the Regiment's activities, welcoming battalions back from operations, presenting medals, taking part in Regimental birthday celebrations, visiting families when the battalions have been in Afghanistan and hosting members of the Regiment and their families at his home and in many of the Royal Palaces. As the photographs in this chapter show, Prince Charles has played, and continues to play, a very active role in the life of his Regiment.

Soldiers from The Royal Gurkha Rifles mounting guard at Buckingham Palace during the celebrations to mark 200 years of Gurkha service to the British Crown in June 2015. The public duties carried out by the RGR during this celebratory period illustrated the close relationship that exists between the Regiment and the Royal Family (image copyright Richard Pohle 2015).

Above: The Colonel-in-Chief inspecting members of 1RGR in Brunei in October 2008 during a Far East Tour with the Duchess of Cornwall. The visit to the battalion provided Prince Charles with an opportunity to meet some of the wounded from Operation Herrick 7 (September 2007 to April 2008).

Below left and right: On 28 January 2009, the Colonel-in-Chief visited Sir John Moore Barracks in Folkestone to meet the families of 2RGR personnel deployed on Operation Herrick 9. He is shown here signing the Visitor's Book under the watchful eye of the Officer Commanding the Rear Party (who is now the Regimental Secretary) and the Commanding Officer's wife. During his visit, Prince Charles had the opportunity to meet Rifleman Kushal Kumar Limbu who was wounded in action in November 2008 on Operation Herrick 9, losing both legs (images Crown copyright 2009).

In November 2008, two members of the battalion were killed in action on Operation Herrick 9. A number of other soldiers also sustained life-changing injuries in the first few months of the tour, which ran from September 2008 to April 2009. The Colonel-in-Chief's decision to visit the Rear Party and meet the families in January 2009 therefore provided a much-appreciated boost to morale at this difficult time (image Crown copyright 2009).

In February 2010, His Royal Highness The Prince of Wales visited 1RGR on Salisbury Plain as the battalion was completing its mission rehearsal exercise before deploying to Afghanistan on Operation Herrick 12. Rifleman Poshraj Rai was told that he had to brief the Colonel-in-Chief on his duties as a sangar sentry. Once Rifleman Poshraj had completed his briefing, he was expecting his Royal visitor to ask him some penetrating questions. Instead, the Colonel-in-Chief presented him with the Parish Trophy, an annual award for the most outstanding rifleman in the battalion. Rifleman Poshraj was extremely surprised by this unexpected, but very pleasant, turn of events!

Above: The Colonel-in-Chief with members of 1RGR and some of the families during his visit to Salisbury Plain in February 2010.

Left: On 28 January 2011, the Colonel-in-Chief returned to 1RGR after the battalion's tour in Afghanistan on Operation Herrick 12 to award operational service medals for the deployment (image Crown copyright 2011).

The Colonel-in-Chief shares a joke with 1RGR's Buddhist religious teacher who spent time in Afghanistan with the battalion whilst it was deployed on Operation Herrick 12 (image Crown copyright 2011).

After the medal parade on 28 January 2011, the Colonel-in-Chief was able to meet some of the families over lunch.

The Colonel-in-Chief during a visit to 2RGR on 1 July 2015, the Regiment's 21st Birthday. As well as joining in the celebrations, Prince Charles congratulated the battalion on joining 16 Air Assault Brigade and noted that "...your considerable airborne heritage and your fine infantry skills will stand you in good stead".[101] The re-subordination to 16 Air Assault Brigade took place on 1 June 2015 and led to members of the battalion replacing their rifle green berets (albeit temporarily) with the maroon berets of the airborne forces (image Crown copyright 2015).

The Colonel-in-Chief presenting operational service medals for Afghanistan to members of 2RGR following their deployment on Operation Toral 3 (April to December 2016).[102] The parade took place in Buckingham Palace on 14 March 2017 and formed the central part of an event to commemorate Prince Charles' 40 years as Colonel-in-Chief of Gurkha infantry.

The Colonel-in-Chief inspects the honour guard during his visit to 2RGR in November 2017. Prince Charles and the Duchess of Cornwall were completing an official visit of Asia and were able to spend time with the battalion whilst in Brunei (copyright Dharamprakash Limbu 2017).

Her Royal Highness The Duchess of Cornwall talking to the families during a visit to 2RGR in November 2017 (image copyright Dharamprakash Limbu 2017).

Left: The Colonel-in-Chief unveils a painting by the artist Jolanda Aucott to commemorate the Gurkhas' 200 years of service to the British Crown during a parade at Buckingham Palace on 14 March 2017.

Below left: Captain Chandrabahadur Pun and Prince Harry share a joke during His Highness' second tour of Afghanistan on Operation Herrick 17 in late 2012/early 2013.

Above: Reunited again! His Royal Highness Prince Harry and Major Chandrabahadur Pun enjoying another joke at a parade held in Buckingham Palace on 14 March 2017 to celebrate Prince Charles' 40 years as the Colonel-in-Chief of Gurkha infantry and to enable Their Royal Highnesses to award operational service medals to members of 2RGR following their deployment to Afghanistan on Operation Toral 3 (from April to December 2016). The book that Prince Harry is holding was compiled by Headquarters Brigade of Gurkhas and chronicles Their Royal Highnesses many engagements with the RGR (image Crown copyright 2017).

His Royal Highness The Duke of Edinburgh talking to the President of the Gurkha Brigade Association and the Queen's Gurkha Orderly Officers (QGOO) during the 2013 'Field of Remembrance' at Westminster Abbey. Prince Philip has always taken a keen interest in the Gurkhas. Before the RGR was formed, he was a frequent visitor to 7GR, possibly because its full regimental title was 'The 7th Duke of Edinburgh's Own Gurkha Rifles'! (image Crown copyright 2017).

During an official two-day visit to Brunei in November 2004, His Royal Highness The Duke of York found time to visit 2RGR.[103] As well as joining members of the battalion and their families for lunch, Prince Andrew also reviewed a parade, commissioned several new officers, took part in a 'turf-cutting' ceremony to mark the start of the building phase of the Brunei Estate Development Plan and attended a dinner in the Officers' Mess. A short but very full programme!

In August 2014, His Royal Highness The Prince of Wales, accompanied by The Duke and Duchess of Cambridge and Prince Harry, visited members of 2RGR deployed on Operation Comet, the official name for the Ministry of Defence's support to the 2014 Commonwealth Games in Glasgow.

Left: The Earl and Countess of Wessex were able to visit 2RGR in October 2017 whilst they were in Brunei representing Her Majesty The Queen at the Golden Jubilee Celebrations of His Majesty The Sultan of Brunei. The Regimental umbrellas did a marvellous job of keeping Prince Edward and the Countess dry despite the heavy rain!

As well as His Royal Highness The Prince of Wales, other members of the Royal Family have taken the opportunity to engage with the Regiment whenever possible, both in the UK and in Brunei. All of these visits have contributed to the richness of regimental life, for members of the Regiment as well as for their families. The Regiment has also formed a particular bond with His Royal Highness Prince Harry having served alongside him in Afghanistan on Operations Herrick 7 (in late 2007/early 2008) and Herrick 17 (late 2012/early 2013).

His Majesty The Sultan of Brunei

The Regiment is also fortunate to enjoy a close relationship with His Majesty The Sultan of Brunei. Not only has The Sultan kindly included members of the Brunei based RGR battalion in many of the formal events held to celebrate special occasions over the last 25 years, such as His Majesty's Birthdays, but he has also been a frequent, and very welcome, visitor to the Battalion's home in Tuker Lines, Seria.

Above: His Majesty The Sultan of Brunei took the salute at a parade held in Brunei in October 2015 to commemorate the Gurkhas' 200 years of service to the British Crown. He is shown here with the Commanding Officer of 1RGR and General Sir Peter Wall, Colonel Commandant of the Brigade of Gurkhas and Chief of the General Staff.

Her Majesty The Queen and His Majesty The Sultan during the formal celebrations held on 9 June 2015 at the Royal Hospital Chelsea to commemorate 200 years of Gurkha service to the British Crown.

The Sultan of Brunei with the Commanding Officer during a visit to 1RGR in March 2017, shortly before the battalion returned to the UK and was replaced in Brunei by 2RGR.

During his visit to 1RGR in March 2017, His Majesty took the opportunity to meet the families.

His Majesty also took the opportunity to (very convincingly) beat the Commanding Officer of 1RGR in a quad bike race down the beach!

His Majesty The Sultan meets officers of the RGR during celebrations to mark his 71st Birthday in July 2017.

The final inspection of the guard of honour waiting to greet His Royal Highness Prince General Haji Al-Muhtadee Billah, The Crown Prince of Brunei, and Her Royal Highness Princess Sarroya during their visit to 2RGR in March 2005. The battalion deployed to Afghanistan on Operation Herrick 2 (March to October 2005) shortly after Their Royal Highness' visit.

His Royal Highness The Crown Prince talking to officers and men of the battalion during his visit to 2RGR in March 2005.

Her Royal Highness Princess Sarah meets some of the families in Hornbill School during her visit to 2RGR in March 2005.

The first Commanding Officer of 1RGR briefing His Royal Highness Prince Dipendra Bir Bikram Shah Dev, The Crown Prince of Nepal, on the 'new' SA80 assault rifle and its common weapon sight (CWS) during a visit to the battalion in Hong Kong in late 94/early 95. Crown Prince Dipendra died on 4 June 2001 having ascended to the throne of Nepal following the death of his father, King Birendra Bir Bikram Shah Dev, on 1 June 2001.[105]

The Nepalese Royal Family

The Gurkha infantry always had a close relationship with the Royal Family of Nepal. For example, during both World Wars, when Britain was facing an existential threat, His Majesty The King of Nepal allowed the United Kingdom to recruit many thousands of additional young men to fight on behalf of the British Crown. In October 1971, His Majesty Field Marshal King Mahendra Bir Bikram Shah Dev also became the Colonel-in-Chief of the Brigade of Gurkhas. However, the bond that existed between the Royal Family and the Brigade of Gurkhas ended on 28 May 2008 when the Nepalese monarchy was officially abolished[104] and its Royal Family ceased to have a role in the nation's affairs. Notwithstanding this, it is worth remembering that the RGR had a strong bond with members of the Nepalese Royal Family during its first decade of life.

CHAPTER 3

East Timor

For nearly three hundred years, East Timor, the eastern half of a small island about 450 miles off the north-western coast of Australia, was Portuguese territory. Keen to de-colonise, in 1974 the Portuguese tried to establish a national government able to determine the country's final status. However, civil war broke out between those supporting independence and those who favoured integration with Indonesia.[106] Unable to contain the situation, the Portuguese withdrew from East Timor and the Indonesians invaded, occupying the country and, in 1976, integrating it into the Republic of Indonesia as its 27th province. The United Nations (UN) did not recognise East Timor's annexation and, prompted by the frequent civil unrest in the country, the Security Council and the General Assembly repeatedly called for Indonesia to withdraw.

From 1982, the UN began holding high-level talks with Indonesia and Portugal to try to resolve the situation. In June 1998, Indonesia eventually agreed that the country could have limited autonomy provided it remained within the Indonesian Republic. The UN undertook to conduct a "popular consultation" in order to "ascertain whether the East Timorese people accepted or rejected"[107] the proposal and, on 11 June 1999, the UN Security Council authorised the establishment of a UN Mission in East Timor (UNAMET) to facilitate the referendum and then help the country implement its outcome.

On 30 August 1999, the East Timorese voted. A remarkable 98% of registered voters went to the polls. Although 21.5% voted to accept the proposal, 78.5% voted to reject the proposed autonomy and, instead, to begin a process of transition towards full independence. The country then descended into chaos as the pro-integration militia, supported by the Indonesian Army (the TNI), "launched a campaign of violence, looting and arson throughout the entire country".[108] As one RGR observer later noted, "almost all of East Timor was in ruins…my only question was how did the militia and TNI manage to so mercilessly destroy so much in such a short space of time and why was their hatred extended towards defenceless women, innocent children and old folks".[109]

UNAMET

Do you ACCEPT the proposed special autonomy for East Timor within the Unitary State of the Republic of Indonesia?

Apakah anda MENERIMA usul otonomi khusus untuk Timor Timur di dalam Negara Kesatuan Republik Indonesia?

Ita Boot SIMU proposta autonomia espesiál ba Timor Lorosae iha Estadu Unitáriu República Indonézia nia laran?

Aceita a autonomia especial proposta para Timor Leste integrada no Estado Unitário da República da Indonésia?

ACCEPT MENERIMA HA'U SIMU ACEITO

OR   ATAU   KA   OU

Do you REJECT the proposed special autonomy for East Timor, leading to East Timor's separation from Indonesia?

Apakah anda MENOLAK usul otonomi khusus Timor Timur, yang akan mengakibatkan berpisahnya Timor Timur dari Indonesia?

Ita Boot LA SIMU proposta autonomia espesiál ba Timor Lorosae, nebé sei lori Timor Lorosae atu haketak an hosi Indonesia?

Rejeita a autonomia especial proposta para Timor Leste, levando á separação de Timor Leste da Indonésia?

REJECT MENOLAK HA'U LA SIMU REJEITO

Left: The ballot form on which the East Timorese cast their votes during the referendum on 30 August 1999. 78.5% voted not to accept the greater autonomy proposed by the Republic of Indonesia, opting, instead, for complete independence. This is a genuine form used during the election hence its soiled nature.

Below: A ruined house typical of so many after the TNI and pro-Indonesian militia had ransacked the country once the population had voted overwhelmingly for independence.

Under pressure from the UN, Indonesia agreed to accept assistance from the international community and, on 15 September 1999, the UN Security Council passed Resolution 1264 authorising an international force (INTERFET), under Australian leadership, to "…restore peace and security in East Timor, to protect and support UNAMET in carrying out its tasks and, within force capabilities, to facilitate humanitarian assistance operations".[110] Critically, the resolution also authorised "…all necessary measures to fulfil this mandate",[111] which gave the force the authority to use lethal force if required.

Just over 1,000 miles away in Brunei, 2RGR was about to deploy on a three week jungle exercise when it received instructions from the UK that it was to deploy a force to East Timor on Operation Langar, the UK name for support to INTERFET. As the battalion noted, "a planned exercise deployment by sea to Sittang quickly became an operational air deployment to Darwin in the Northern Territories of Australia".[112] At the time, A Company, with attachments from Support and Headquarters Companies, was 'on

duty' as the lead company group. The decision was therefore taken that a force of some 200 based on A Company Group should deploy along with a small battalion headquarters element, headed up by the Commanding Officer, to look 'up and out'. Whilst the command element deployed to Townsville in Australia to begin planning the deployment

The tactical recognition badge worn by members of the UN endorsed INTERFET (the International Force East Timor) when it deployed in September 1999.

Members of A Company 2RGR on exercise in Brunei are delighted that the warning order for Operation Langar, a deployment to East Timor as part of an international UN force (INTERFET), has arrived.

with the Australian operational headquarters, a detachment from the United Nations Training and Advisory Team (UNTAT) flew out to Brunei from the UK to assist with pre-deployment training. This focused on urban patrolling, rules of engagement, situational awareness, and live firing and was informed by the training that UNTAT had recently delivered to 1RGR before it deployed to Kosovo as part of KFOR in June 1999.[113]

The company group flew to Darwin in northern Australia where it met up with the Australian component of INTERFET and was placed under tactical control (TACON) of the 2nd Battalion The Royal Australian Regiment (2RAR). Once preparations were complete, A Company Group departed Australia in Royal Australian Air Force (RAAF) C130s and, in the early hours of 21 September 1999, carried out a tactical air-land operation (TALO) onto Komoro

Commanders confirm their understanding of the tasks that they will carry out once they arrive in East Timor.

A final kit check in Darwin on 20 September 1999 before boarding RAAF C130s for a tactical air land operation (TALO) onto Komoro Airfield on the outskirts of Dili, the capital city of East Timor.

Gurkhas from A Company 2RGR man an impressively constructed sangar adjacent to the UN compound in Dili, the capital of East Timor.

Airfield just to the west of Dili, the capital of East Timor. The company group left the airfield at first light and, as the first contingent into Dili, had the task of securing the UNAMET compound. This key location had become a refuge for UN workers and others trying to escape the violence that had erupted on the streets after the election and securing it was therefore a high priority. A Company had expected to encounter some resistance but, as 2RGR noted after the event:

"The few Timorese who were still in the city reacted in an ambivalent way at first, before warming to the Gurkhas as they patrolled past. A professional but open and friendly manner, coupled with a few words of Malay (very similar to Indonesian) worked wonders, and applause greeted the tailenders. Fears of potential conflict at numerous TNI roadblocks did not materialise and the regular Indonesian soldiers adhered to the agreements made by their commanders and the Australian Commander of INTERFET, Major General Peter Cosgrove. On arrival the compound was secured and the dominating hills to the south picketed".[114]

Having secured the UNAMET compound, the company group then set about patrolling its area of responsibility, disarming militia, assisting Internally Displaced Persons (IDPs) to return to their homes, supporting the delivery of humanitarian aid, dealing with the ever-present media and doing their utmost to maintain a more stable and secure environment. Their patrolling activities brought the Gurkhas into contact with FALINTIL, the armed wing of the pro-independence movement. Outwardly at least, FALINTIL were working towards the same end as INTERFET and, with a few notable exceptions, good relations were quickly established. The TNI and pro-integration militia were less cordial in their dealings and it took a robust response at one of A Company Group's roadblocks to "make it irrevocably clear to both locals and the media just who was in charge in Area of Operations Kukri".[115]

As the TNI started to withdraw back to Indonesia, the company group pushed further out from Dili patrolling and escorting convoys of humanitarian aid. It was after escorting an aid convoy to the town of Los

Above: A different perspective of the sangar, this time from inside the sandbag wall.

Left: An observation post overlooking Dili.

Left: Some of the pro-Indonesian militia detained by 2RGR in Los Palos.

Below: Members of A Company Group 2RGR take a short break after a contact with a group of pro-Indonesian militia.

Palos, some 250km east of Dili, that the first shots of the entire campaign were fired. Arriving in Los Palos, the escort platoon were told of a militia group located not too far away in the port of Com. Colour Sergeant Rajan Rai and a small reconnaissance team went to investigate and came into contact with the group, an infamous outfit known as 'Team Alpha'. After a short firefight, Colour Sergeant Rajan and his men managed to capture the militia group and free approximately 3,500 refugees who were being held hostage. The incident attracted a great deal of positive media attention. The company group also did excellent work on the humanitarian front in Dili, rebuilding the capital's central market place so that it could once again become a hub for normal life.

Over the next few weeks, the company group settled into a routine of patrolling, organising training for INTERFET and conducting operations in increasingly remote areas of the country. A Company Group was then ordered to deploy to the Oekusi Enclave. This is a small but significant part of East Timor located 150km inside West Timor which, at the time, could only be reached by sea or helicopter. The company group deployed, led by 2 Platoon and Company Tactical Headquarters, and quickly established itself, setting up its headquarters in the

Buparti (or Mayoral) house, the only building in the entire enclave with a roof. Once an INTERFET presence had been established on the ground, the humanitarian aid effort commenced, bringing much needed relief to the local population. Patient and tactful negotiations also eventually led to thousands of abducted East Timorese being able to return to their homes in the enclave from camps inside West Timor.

In the final stages of the deployment, the company group was tasked to provide a strong platoon sized force to guard the INTERFET precinct in the centre of Dili. Heavily fortified, this contained all the key headquarters and installations and therefore the offices of a large number of important officials. It was a high profile role and, as 2RGR

A soldier from 2RGR dispensing medical aid to the East Timorese. During the course of the three-month deployment, the Regimental Aid Post treated nearly 5,000 patients. This remarkable effort considerably enhanced relationships with the locals and proved a key enabler in terms of winning the hearts and minds of the population.

noted afterwards, "hat felt Gurkha, Number 1 Kukri, ceremonial drill and sharp salutes were the order of the day".[116] The Commanding Officer of 2RGR, Lieutenant Colonel M M Lillingston-Price,[117] was also based in the precinct having taken over as Commander British Forces (COMBRITFOR) in mid-October 1999 from Brigadier D J Richards, the commander of the UK's high readiness Joint Force Headquarters (JFHQ). The JFHQ had deployed at the outset of the operation to support the UK contribution to INTERFET. Once the situation had stabilised, it returned to the UK. Having detached the guard force, the remainder of A Company Group deployed some 35km north of Dili to the island of Atauro. After a quick reconnaissance, it was apparent that the island had remained untouched by the troubles but that there was a need for considerable support to the population (which was no more than 8,000 people). Operations therefore concentrated on providing medical care and delivering humanitarian aid, particularly food. The company group stayed on the island for two weeks before being flown back to Dili. In early December the company group left Dili for the last time to the sound of the Pipes and Drums and headed back to Brunei.[118] Of note, Lieutenant Colonel Lillingston-Price was made an Officer of the Most Excellent Order of the British Empire (awarded an OBE) for his leadership during the operation.

A Company Group's deployment to East Timor was important for a number of reasons. Not only did the company make a significant contribution to establishing peace in the country as a key component of INTERFET but it was the first time that the Brunei based battalion had been deployed out of the country on UK operations. As Brigadier Christopher Bullock notes in his definitive history of Britain's Gurkhas, "hitherto it had been felt that since the Sultan was paying for the battalion, it should not be operationally deployed outside Brunei territory. The East Timor deployment, carried out with the agreement of the Brunei authorities, now created a precedent that left the door open for further operational deployments throughout the area".[119] Interestingly, although 2RGR was on high readiness in Brunei, this was a self-generated commitment, not one tasked by the UK Ministry of Defence. 2RGR was selected in preference to the UK's high readiness standby unit – which,

the year, that, with careful planning and a realistic view of what needs to be achieved, such operations can succeed. The common ingredient to both was the Gurkha soldier of the RGR. Whilst it might be stretching it too far to suggest that, without this, neither intervention would have been successful, it is worth pausing to consider the contribution made by the RGR so soon after its formation. Brigadier Christopher Bullock puts it rather neatly:

"The high-profile, swift and successful operations in Kosovo and East Timor carried out by both Royal Gurkha Rifles battalions – as well as, in the case of Kosovo, by Gurkha Engineers, Signals and Transport – sent out a clear message to the rest of the Army and the British public and media that Gurkhas could not only cope but were, in terms of speed of reaction and military professionalism, difficult to equal".[122]

at the time, was 45 Commando Royal Marines – because they were judged to be culturally and environmentally more acclimatised, as well as being geographically nearer. National decision making was also informed by a recent visit George Robertson, then Secretary of State for Defence, had made to 2RGR in Brunei.[120]

On 20 May 2002, East Timor achieved independence, becoming the first new sovereign state of the new millennium and, on 27 September 2002, it became the 191st member of the UN.[121] Although international interventions frequently have their critics, often for good reason, the case of East Timor demonstrates, as Kosovo did earlier in

The INTERFET (International Force East Timor) medal awarded to the members of 2RGR who deployed on Operation Langar.

95

RECRUITING AND BASIC TRAINING

Recruiting for all parts of the Brigade of Gurkhas, including The Royal Gurkha Rifles (RGR), takes place under the terms and conditions of the Tri-Partite Agreement signed between Britain, Nepal and India in November 1947. Every year, the Brigade of Gurkhas deploys teams into the hills of Nepal to conduct the initial phases of its recruit selection process. This begins with an advertising phase, which runs from April to May each year. Senior Recruit Assistants (SRAs – formally known as *'galah wallas'*) travel to as many of Nepal's 75 Districts as possible during this phase, briefing potential recruits as well as key people in the local community. During the briefings, the SRAs explain the selection procedure and the standards that candidates have to achieve in the various assessments, dispelling many of the myths that exist, particularly in the more remote areas.

The advertising phase is followed by a registration phase which takes place from May to July each year. During Registration, recruiting assistants carry out a basic assessment of each potential recruit to ensure that he meets the selection criteria. Some of the current entry criteria are:

- **Age.** Must be between 17 years and 6 months and 21 years as at January of the year in which selection is taking place.
- **Height.** Not less than 158cm (just over 5 ft and 2 in).
- **Body Mass Index.** Must have a Body Mass Index (BMI) between 17 and 30.
- **Dental.** No more than two dental corrections (fillings) or any dental problems.
- **Education.** Must have completed the Nepalese School Leaving Certificate in at least the 3rd Division (which approximately equates to having achieved three 'C' grades and two 'D' grades at GCSE).
- **Mid-Thigh Pull.** Able to pull 76kg from the ground to mid-thigh.
- **Heaves (Pull-Ups).** Achieve 6 over-arm heaves.

The transition from 'hill boy' to soldier in The Royal Gurkha Rifles (RGR) begins with the individual saying goodbye to his family and having the courage to put himself forward for the selection process that takes place across Nepal each year.

His Royal Highness The Duke of Edinburgh observing recruit selection in 1986. Although the 7th Gurkhas, one of the RGR's antecedent regiments, was known as The 7th Duke of Edinburgh's Own Gurkha Rifles, His Royal Highness was not its Colonel-in-Chief!

If an individual meets the required standard, he is called forward to Regional Selection. The dates for this vary slightly each year. In 2019, for example, this will take place from 19 August to 1 December 2019 at two locations in Nepal, Pokhara in the west (from 19 August to 20 September 2019) and Dharan in the east (6 November to 1 December 2019). The selection process lasts a day and includes

Above: The nature of the terrain in Nepal means that it takes Senior Recruit Assistants (SRAs) several months to visit villages high in the Himalayas to explain about the selection process for Britain's Brigade of Gurkhas.

Opposite: During the initial phase of recruit selection, Senior Recruit Assistants (SRAs) travel to towns and villages throughout Nepal to brief potential recruits, as well as members of the community, on the standards required for service in the British Army.

Right: Taken in 2012, this photograph of a young potential recruit being checked by a senior Gurkha officer during the selection process bears a striking resemblance to the one taken in 1986 with The Duke of Edinburgh.

Potential recruits have to be able to complete a minimum of 6 over-arm heaves at Registration and 8 over-arm heaves at Central Selection. This is not at all easy and the majority of young men will have practised this for a number of months prior to attempting recruit selection. Until recently, the requirement was a minimum of 12 under-arm heaves at Central Selection as shown in this photograph (image Crown copyright 2013).

an educational assessment, a medical examination, interviews with both a Nepali Gurkha officer and a British Gurkha officer and physical tests. The physical tests for Regional Selection in 2020 will consist of the following:[123]

- **Run**. 800 metre run in at least 2 minutes 40 seconds (best effort required).
- **Thigh Pull**. Mid-thigh pull to 100kg minimum but best effort required.
- **Medicine Ball Throw**. 4kg Medicine ball throw to 3.10 metres.
- **Burden Carry**. Repeated lift and carry of a 20kg burden over 30 metres. Applicants must run 30 metres five times with the burden and four times without in 1 minute 50 seconds. The faster they do it, the better they score.

Individuals are placed in an order of merit based on their performance. The final phase is Central Selection which lasts three weeks and takes place in the British Army's camp in Pokhara. Two candidates are called forward for every place that needs to be filled. In February 2020, for example, the British Army is looking to recruit 432 new soldiers for the Brigade of Gurkhas and therefore the best 864

Right: Until recently, potential recruits used to have to complete at least 70 sit-ups in 2 minutes during Central Selection. This test, and some of the others, have now been replaced by tests that more accurately reflect the sorts of physical tasks that soldiers might be required to carry out on the battlefield.

Below: Potential recruits warming up with an instructor prior to completing one of the physical assessments during recruit selection.

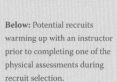

candidates will be called forward from Regional Selection to Central Selection.

The standards that potential Gurkha recruits have to achieve during recruit selection are particularly demanding. The Brigade of Gurkhas can set the highest of entry standards because there are many more applicants than places. In 2018, for example, there were 9,568 applicants for 270 places, an average of 35.5 applicants for each vacancy.

The current physical standards that potential recruits have to achieve during Central Selection are:

- **2,000 metre run**. Run 2,000 metres in no more than 8 minutes 15 seconds.
- **Jerry Can Carry**. Carry two 20kg jerry cans over a distance of 240 metres in no more than 2 minutes 10 seconds.
- **Heaves/Pull-Ups**. Perform not less than 8 over-arm heaves/pull-ups.
- **Repeated Lift and Carry of a 20kg Burden over 30 metres**. Run 30 metres 15 times with a burden of 20kg and 14 without in 6 minutes and 30 seconds.
- **Stamina Assessment**. Complete a 5.8km uphill route (height gain approximately 580 metres) carrying 15kg in no more than 50 minutes.

Potential recruits have to complete a number of physical tests during Central Selection. One of these is a 2,000 metre run which has to be completed in no more than 8 minutes 15 seconds. Numbers are painted on the recruits' chests to enable them to be identified

A potential recruit taking part in the stamina assessment conducted during Central Selection in Pokhara, West Nepal. During the assessment, which is conducted as a race, potential recruits have to carry a weight of 15kg in a 'doko', the rattan basket that the people of Nepal traditionally use to carry heavy loads along the mountain paths of the Himalayas (image Crown copyright 2010).

Potential recruits waiting to start the stamina assessment. Although the course is only 5.8km in length, it starts in the bottom of a river valley near the British Camp in Pokhara and climbs approximately 580 metres to the high ground shown in the picture. The footbridge in the background spanning the valley is typical of footbridges in Nepal. Traditionally made of hemp rope, these are often now made of steel wire. Notwithstanding this, crossing them, particularly at night and in bad weather, is not for the faint hearted! (image Crown copyright 2010).

During Central Selection in the British Army camp in Pokhara, potential recruits have to write essays and complete both reading and listening comprehension assessments (image Crown copyright 2010).

A potential recruit faces an interview panel during Central Selection. The panel is made up of Nepalese and British Gurkha officers (image Crown copyright 2010).

The stamina assessment is particularly challenging. Although the course is only 5.8km in length, the height gain and the weight that potential recruits have to carry make this is a formidable test. The weight has to be carried using the 'doko', a rattan basket that the hill people of Nepal traditionally use to carry loads along the mountain paths of the Himalayas.

Gurkha units have to operate within the wider context of the British Army. The working language within the Brigade of Gurkha is therefore English. Because of this, recruits are expected to have a reasonable grasp of the language before they join the British Army. Standards are assessed during Central Selection by means of an essay as well as reading and listening comprehension exercises.

At the end of the three week Central Selection, potential recruits are again placed in an order of merit. As two candidates are called forward for every vacancy, this means that those who finish in the top half will be offered places in the British Army. Over the last few years, 240 (of 480) have been offered places but recent decisions to expand the size of the Brigade of Gurkhas, and, in particular, to form a third battalion of the RGR, means that 432 (of 864) will be recruited in 2020. Once they have accepted a place, recruits are invited to swear allegiance to the British Crown, a process known as 'attestation', before being flown to the UK to begin a nine month training package at the Infantry Training Centre (ITC) in Catterick, North Yorkshire.

New recruits of the 3rd Gurkhas swearing their allegiance to the British Crown in 1944. This is known as attestation. Having 'attested', each recruit is given a kukri, the traditional fighting knife of the Gurkhas.

Left: The process of attestation has changed little over the last two hundred years. This photograph shows the then Chief of the General Staff (now the Chief of Defence Staff) taking part in the recruit Attestation Parade in 2018. They may be at the very start of their careers in the British Army and have done very little military training but new recruits are still expected to reach the highest standards of turnout and drill during their Attestation Parade (image copyright Ashess Shakya Photography 2018).

Below: An instructor from the RGR checks a young recruit's beret before the Attestation Parade.

The Brigade of Gurkhas aims to recruit 50% of its soldiers from the east of Nepal and 50% from the west. This mix has historical origins. Of the four Gurkha infantry regiments that transferred to the British Army in 1947, the 2nd and 6th Gurkhas were recruited from the west and the 7th and 10th from the east. Although some transfers between the infantry battalions do take place, the current battalions of the RGR perpetuate this geographic division with the soldiers in 1RGR being

Taken in January 2012, this photograph shows successful new recruits in their issued 'Regimental Mufti' at the end of course celebration. A few days later, these young men left Nepal for UK to begin their military training in earnest.

The Chief of the General Staff meets the family of a new recruit just after the Attestation Parade. For an individual to get through the rigorous selection process and be accepted into the British Army is a significant achievement. Families are immensely proud when this happens and celebrate with garlands of flowers, a Nepalese tradition.

His Royal Highness The Prince of Wales with Gurkha recruits in Malaya Lines, Hong Kong on 8 November 1994. This was the last batch of recruits to be trained at the Brigade of Gurkhas' Hong Kong Training Depot. All subsequent recruit intakes have been trained in the UK, initially in Church Crookham, where the resident UK-based Gurkha infantry battalion was located, and then in Catterick at the Infantry Training Centre. The recruits in the photograph were the first cohort to join the RGR direct from recruit training.

predominantly from the west whilst those in 2RGR are predominantly from the east. The supporting arms are completely mixed with all squadrons having approximately the same number of Gurkhas from the east and the west of Nepal.

All Gurkhas are trained as Infantry soldiers during the nine month training package at the Infantry Training Centre in Catterick, regardless of whether they will eventually serve in the RGR or not. This 'band of brothers' approach ensures that all Gurkhas have a basic understanding of Infantry tactics, widening their utility.

Like the majority of other regiments in the British Army, the RGR is officered by a mix of late entry officers (soldiers who have been promoted through the ranks and then commissioned) and direct entry officers (young men and women who have been specifically recruited as officers). Direct entry officers complete a nine month training programme at the Royal Military Academy Sandhurst before being

Taken in November 2018 and with snow still on the ground, these recruits prepare for another physical training event at the Infantry Training Centre in Catterick.

103

Top left: Recruits are taught to use the kukri during the training they receive at the Infantry Training Centre in Catterick (image Crown copyright 2013).

Top right: The spiritual needs of Gurkhas are well catered for in the British Army. All Gurkha units have a Hindu 'Pundit' permanently attached and Buddhist monks visit each of the RGR's battalions regularly, even on operations. This picture shows a Buddhist monk carrying out a religious ceremony for recruits (image Crown copyright 2012).

Above left: His Holiness The Dalai Lama visited the Infantry Training Centre in June 2012 to meet Gurkha recruits and staff.

Above right: At the end of the nine month training package at the ITC, those who have successfully completed the course take part in a Passing Out Parade that marks their formal transition from recruit to trained soldier in Britain's Brigade of Gurkhas. Recruits wear the uniform and cap badge of the regiments or corps that they will be joining after the parade. This photograph, taken in 2010, shows Lieutenant General Sir David Bill, the Reviewing Officer for the parade and the Colonel of The Queen's Own Gurkha Engineers, talking to a young recruit about to join the RGR and therefore wearing the Regiment's uniform for the first time.

Right: Taken in 1911, this photograph shows veterans from the Indian Mutiny and the Siege of Delhi of 1857. Despite their age, the Gurkha officers in the centre of the picture still exhibit the pride and discipline that was instilled into them during their basic training decades beforehand. Today's recruit training aims to develop the same enduring qualities in the soldiers of the RGR.

Left: The Colonel of the Regiment at the time (on the right) welcomes Officer Cadet Scott Sears to the RGR following his success at the Regimental Selection Board held earlier that morning. Officer Cadets are interviewed by regimental selection boards during the second term of their nine month commissioning course at the Royal Military Academy Sandhurst (RMAS). Two years after leaving Sandhurst, the 27 year old Lieutenant Sears would become the youngest person ever to reach the South Pole on his own and unsupported (on Boxing Day 2017), raising over £30,000 for the Gurkha Welfare Trust, the main Gurkha charity, and for schools destroyed in the 2015 Nepal earthquake.

Below left: His Royal Highness The Prince of Wales, the Colonel-in-Chief of the RGR, attaches the rank of captain to a newly commissioned Late Entry Officer in 2011 (image Crown copyright 2011).

commissioned. After Sandhurst, direct entry officers joining the RGR complete their infantry training, which gives them the professional skills they need to be effective as rifle platoon commanders, before joining their battalions. All officers serving with the Gurkhas, and the RGR in particular, are expected to speak Nepali. The Brigade of Gurkhas has a language school in Nepal which all officers attend before completing a month long trek. The aim of the trek is to enable officers to consolidate their new-found language skills as well as to improve their understanding of the environment from which their soldiers are recruited.

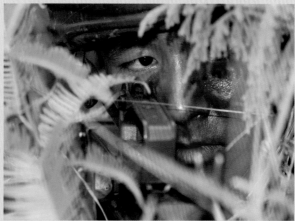

From recruit to trained soldier in the RGR takes nine months of hard work. Notably, the Brigade of Gurkhas maintains the British Army's highest pass rate during basic training, a tribute to the quality of the young men who join Britain's Gurkhas and to the quality of their instructors (image Crown copyright 2004).

SPECIALIST SKILLS

As a light infantry regiment, The Royal Gurkha Rifles (RGR) operates at the most physically demanding end of the spectrum of military operations, both in UK as a part of 16 Air Assault Brigade and in Brunei as the only battalion in the British Army that is fully trained and acclimatised for fighting in the jungle. At its starkest, its task is to close with the enemy, usually by covering long distances on foot over unforgiving terrain, and then kill them. This places a premium on a number of basic skills that the RGR works hard to maintain. Chief amongst these is the ability to shoot quickly and accurately, there being no point in pushing the limits of human endurance to get close to the enemy only to find that they are the better shots!

The RGR's antecedent regiments had a long tradition of exceptional marksmanship that the RGR has endeavoured to maintain. Much time is spent on the ranges refining basic skills before taking part in more demanding live firing exercises in increasingly

Above: Potential junior leaders carrying out a pairs advance to contact in 2006 under the watchful eye of an instructor. Having mastered the basics on the ranges, soldiers in the RGR are then put through their paces in increasingly complex and demanding environments.

Left: Soldiers in RGR battalions spend a great deal of time on the ranges, developing their skills until they can guarantee 'one shot, one kill'.

commissioned. After Sandhurst, direct entry officers joining the RGR complete their infantry training, which gives them the professional skills they need to be effective as rifle platoon commanders, before joining their battalions. All officers serving with the Gurkhas, and the RGR in particular, are expected to speak Nepali. The Brigade of Gurkhas has a language school in Nepal which all officers attend before completing a month long trek. The aim of the trek is to enable officers to consolidate their new-found language skills as well as to improve their understanding of the environment from which their soldiers are recruited.

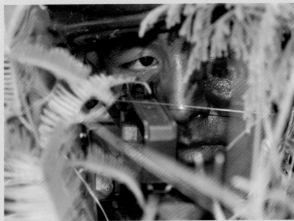

From recruit to trained soldier in the RGR takes nine months of hard work. Notably, the Brigade of Gurkhas maintains the British Army's highest pass rate during basic training, a tribute to the quality of the young men who join Britain's Gurkhas and to the quality of their instructors (image Crown copyright 2004).

CHAPTER 4

Sierra Leone

In March 1991, a group calling itself the Revolutionary United Front (RUF) tried to overthrow the government of Sierra Leone, initiating a civil war that continued for years. In July 1999, there was some hope of an end to the conflict when Foday Sankoh, the leader of the RUF, and President Ahmad Tejan Kabbah, the leader of the Sierra Leonean Government, signed a Peace Accord in Lomé, the capital of Togo. On 22 October 1999, the United Nations (UN) Security Council established the United Nations Mission in Sierra Leone (UNAMSIL) to "cooperate with the Government and the other parties in implementing the Lomé Peace Agreement and to assist in the implementation of the disarmament, demobilization and reintegration plan".[124] UNAMSIL set up disarmament camps throughout Sierra Leone with the intention of disarming the Sierra Leone Army (SLA), the RUF and various militia groups but, although the SLA and some of the militia groups began to enter the camps, the RUF refused to disarm.

Recognising the need for more robust measures, on 7 February 2000, the UN Security Council revised UNAMSIL's mandate and authorised UNAMSIL to "...take the necessary action to ensure the security and freedom of movement of its personnel and, within its capabilities and areas of deployment,

to afford protection to civilians under imminent threat of physical violence".[125] Although the revised mandate gave UNAMSIL greater powers, it had little impact on the RUF, largely because the under-resourced UNAMSIL had no real appetite for peace enforcement. Described by Tony Blair, the UK Prime Minister at the time, as "a collection of gangsters, madmen and sadists",[126] the RUF continued with its campaign of violence and, by early May 2000, had reached the outskirts of Freetown, the capital of Sierra Leone. The country had once been a British colony and, as the situation continued to deteriorate, the UK Government came under increasing international pressure to act. As Tony Blair notes in his memoirs, "when the RUF finally threatened to take over the whole country, there was a simple decision: did we leave it to the UN force, or did we decide to act ourselves?"[127] Following discussions with his key advisors, Blair decided that the UK should intervene unilaterally.

On 6 May 2000, Brigadier D J Richards, the Commander of the high readiness Joint Force Headquarters, deployed to Sierra Leone with an operational reconnaissance and liaison team (ORLT) to assess the situation and to begin planning the extraction of UK and other entitled personnel. Over the course of the next two days, the 1st Battalion The Parachute Regiment (1PARA) deployed to Sierra Leone and secured the main airport at Lungi,

GUINEA

Kabala

Makeni

SIERRA LEONE
Freetown

Kenema

Bonthe

LIBERIA

ATLANTIC
OCEAN

as well as the key routes to it. The 1PARA force included a significant component from C (Cassino) Company,[128] the Gurkha Reinforcement Company attached to 2PARA (which had stepped in to replace a 1PARA company away on an overseas exercise). The evacuation operation, which went under the UK name of Operation Palliser, began extracting people on 8 May 2000 and was a complete success, eventually ensuring that some 500 entitled persons were able to leave the country safely.

By 14 May 2000, a UK amphibious task force, known as the Amphibious Ready Group (ARG), had arrived off the coast of Sierra Leone. In addition to continuing to secure Lungi Airport, this enabled the UK force to provide assistance to the SLA and to support UNAMSIL as it began to build up its forces, as well as to prepare for the distribution of humanitarian aid should it be required. Undeterred, the RUF continued its operations, leading to the first contact between the RUF and British forces. This took place in a village near Lungi Airport on 17 May 2000 with

the RUF sustaining a significant number of casualties. Later that same day, Foday Sankoh was captured, leaving the RUF in disarray, at least temporarily. On 25 May 2000, the 1PARA battlegroup, complete with C (Cassino) Company, returned to the UK having handed over to 42 Commando Royal Marines, which had arrived with the ARG aboard HMS *Ocean*.[129]

Originally, British troops had been deployed to Sierra Leone to "...get British nationals out and help get UN reinforcements in".[130] As the situation around the capital began to stabilise and as UNAMSIL gained in capability, the UK focus switched to providing "... advice and training to help the Government of Sierra Leone rebuild new, effective and democratically accountable armed forces and a Ministry of Defence in line with the Lomé peace agreement".[131] The intention was to train the SLA, increasing its effectiveness so that it could take on the RUF. To do this, the UK's high readiness forces were replaced by regular infantry units which is why, in August 2000, the 1st Battalion The Royal Irish Regiment deployed to Sierra Leone on Operation Silkman, the UK codename given to this phase of operations in Sierra Leone. The battlegroup included D (Gurkha) Company, a Gurkha Reinforcement Company that had transferred to 1RIRISH from the 1st Battalion The Princess of Wales's Royal Regiment in December 1999, where it had been known as B (Sobraon) Company 1PWRR. 1RIRISH's deployment hit the headlines when, on 25 August 2000, 11 of the regiment's personnel were taken prisoner by a militia group known as the West Side Boys.[132] Negotiations led to five of the soldiers being released but the remaining six were only freed

Right: The Commanding Officer of 2RGR, Lieutenant Colonel M M Lillingston-Price, and the Gurkha Major lead the celebrations on Nepal Democracy Day in Sierra Leone on Operation Silkman. Colonel Lillingston-Price was awarded the OBE for his leadership during Operation Langar in East Timor (September to December 1999). He commanded 2RGR from April 1998 to May 2001.

Below right: A Gurkha officer delivers a lesson on Fighting in Built Up Areas (FIBUA) during 2RGR's deployment on Operation Silkman in 2001. The battalion deployed to help train the Sierra Leone Army (SLA).

after an operation on 10 September 2000 (known as Operation Barras) by UK special forces and a company from 1PARA. D (Gurkha) Company remained in Sierra Leone with 1RIRISH until October 2000.[133]

As the SLA gained in competence, it became increasingly successful against the RUF. This, combined with an international clampdown on the sale of the so-called 'blood diamonds' that had been largely funding the RUF, led to talks between the Sierra Leonean Government and the RUF being initiated and, on 10 November 2000, an initial cease-fire was agreed. Notwithstanding this, the UK's work to enhance the SLA's fighting ability continued and, from December 2000 to April 2001, 2RGR deployed a total of 320 men to provide short term training teams (STTTs). STTTs placed a premium on officers and non-commissioned officers with the result that the majority of the battalion's riflemen missed out on the deployment and had to remain in UK.[134]

Left: A senior non-commissioned officer from 2RGR gives a lesson to help prepare members of the battalion for their Junior Leaders Cadre (JLC) whilst deployed on Operation Silkman in 2001.

Opposite: Clearing weapons after range practice.

Left: Troops from the SLA on their way to lessons with their instructor from 2RGR during Operation Silkman in 2001.

Below left: An instructor from 2RGR teaching marksmanship principles on the ranges during Operation Silkman.

Below: President Kabbah of Sierra Leone shakes hands with a non-commissioned officer from 2RGR following a graduation parade held to celebrate a cohort of the SLA completing their training. The parade marked the end of a training programme delivered by 2RGR in 2001.

In spring 2001, the RUF began the process of disarmament, demobilisation and reintegration (DDR) in earnest. The last UK STTT rotation ended in September 2001 and was replaced by an International Military Assistance and Training Team (IMATT). The UK continued to provide the largest contingent, as well as an infantry company for force protection, but Australia, Canada and the United

A soldier from 1RGR with a member of the Republic of Sierra Leone Armed Forces (RSLAF) during Operation Silkman (January 2002 to July 2002). 1RGR provided Short Term Training Teams (STTT) to help train the RSLAF on Military Reintegration Programmes (MRP).

States also contributed instructors. Support Company and D Company were the first 1RGR sub-units to be involved in this. Support Company deployed in early January 2002 to support Military Reintegration Programme 2 (MRP 2) being run in Benguema Training Camp. The company's mission was to "advise and assist the Republic of Sierra Leone Armed Forces (RSLAF) with basic training, in order to provide fully integrated and well-trained individual reinforcements ready to take their place in RSLAF units".[135] That same month, the SLA had unified with the "tiny Sierra Leone Air Force and the moribund Sierra Leone Navy to form a reconstituted force known as the Republic of Sierra Leone Armed Forces (RSLAF)",[136] which is why the company's mission referred to the RSLAF rather than the SLA. While Support Company focused on delivering training support, D Company 1RGR, which arrived towards the end of January 2002, provided force protection in Freetown. The following extract from an article written by one of the RGR instructors in Support Company gives an insight into what the reintegration programme was like:

"MRP 2 started on 8 January with a total strength of 647 recruits, all ex-combatants (rebels and pro-government factions, including a company from the previous Sierra Leone Army). They were grouped into seven companies. Each company had a minimum of three Gurkha instructors in order to shadow their SLAF counterparts responsible for their particular companies. In addition, a team consisting of one Gurkha officer and two senior non-commissioned officers was formed to conduct a Short Commissioning Course (SCC). The

MRP 2 itself was very tight and busy. The programme was set from 0800hrs to 1700hrs daily from Monday to Saturday. The RSLAF instructors were entirely responsible to their trainees for lessons and activities throughout training, however, their lessons and activities had to be closely supervised and monitored by our instructors...The entire training was mainly focused on basic military skills and tactics at platoon level and up to company level at some stages. It included weapon handling using the SLR,[137] individual foot drill, first aid, fieldcraft, short ranges and infantry tactics for the first four weeks of the training and progressed to various tactical exercises. The Gurkhas and the RSLAF instructors worked closely during the progressive exercises and throughout the training...The MRP 2 finally ended successfully on 7 March 2002 with a passing out parade, reviewed by President Ahmed Tejan Kabbah. This parade is regarded as a big ceremony in Sierra Leone. Thousands of people from all over the country gathered to watch this event".[138]

Right: Members of the Republic of Sierra Leone Armed Forces (RSLAF) on the ranges during a Military Reintegration Programmes (MRP) run by 1RGR on Operation Silkman.

Below: Members of 2RGR on Operation Keeling with HMS *Iron Duke* in the background. A joint task force deployed to deter a possible coup when the Special Court for Sierra Leone indicted a number of key political figures for crimes committed during the civil war.

On completion of MRP 2, A Company 1RGR replaced Support Company 1RGR in March 2002 and B Company 1RGR replaced D Company 1RGR at the end of April 2002.[139] These two companies then supported the IMATT's next Military Reintegration Programme (MRP 3). By the end of July 2002, 1RGR was complete back in Brunei having deployed over 280 soldiers to Sierra Leone, either as part of the force protection company in Freetown or running the Military Reintegration Programme in Benguema Training Camp.[140]

In February 2003, approximately half of 2RGR, which was 'on duty' as the UK's high readiness Spearhead Land Element (SLE) battalion at the time, deployed to Sierra Leone as part of a Joint Task Force (JTF) to deter a possible coup when the international Special Court for Sierra Leone indicted key Sierra Leonean political figures (including the Minister of Internal Affairs) for crimes committed during the civil war.[141] The deployment, which was called Operation Keeling, was led by Headquarters 19 Brigade and

Right: The Commanding Officer of 2RGR, Lieutenant Colonel I N A Thomas, in Sierra Leone during Operation Keeling.[144]

Below: Never miss a training opportunity! A member of 2RGR teaches self-defence to a member of the Republic of Sierra Leone Armed Forces (RSLAF) during Operation Keeling.

included HMS *Iron Duke*. It was judged to be a success as no coup attempt was made. To some extent, this might be because at the time the press were reporting that a force of some 3,000 Gurkhas had deployed to Sierra Leone;[142] in reality, the force comprised only two rifle companies, plus supporting elements and a small tactical battalion headquarters.

2RGR's contribution on Operation Keeling was the RGR's last deployment to Sierra Leone. Given this, it is worth reflecting on the battalion's view of the deployment:

"The situation in Sierra Leone was both complex and fragile. In a time of heightened threat and a palpable feeling of anxiety locally, the purposeful and timely committal of the Spearhead Group, as part of the JTF, had an unquestionably beneficial, stabilizing effect. It demonstrated the UK's continued commitment

Members of 2RGR working with members of the Republic of Sierra Leone Armed Forces (RSLAF) during Operation Keeling in March 2003.

Right: Members of 2RGR on patrol in Sierra Leone during Operation Keeling in March 2003.

Below right: Two officers from 2RGR with Commander 19 Mechanised Brigade, Brigadier 'Bill' Moore CBE, in Sierra Leone during Operation Keeling.

Below: Soldiers from 2RGR applying camouflage cream on Operation Keeling. The photograph was taken in March 2003.

to Sierra Leone, reassured the local population and deterred all potential threats. As such, it achieved results totally disproportionate to the size of the force deployed and much of the success can be directly attributed to the professionalism of Gurkha soldiers".[143]

Looking back on the UK's intervention in Sierra Leone, Tony Blair observed that "it is one of the least discussed episodes of my ten years as prime minister, but it's one of the things of which I am most proud".[145] Whatever one's view of Tony Blair, there is no doubt that the UK's intervention in Sierra Leone, both in May 2000 to stabilise the country and in the years that followed to enhance the government's military capacity, made a significant contribution to the country's longer term stability, security and prosperity. The RGR can therefore be immensely proud of the role it played in such a worthwhile endeavour.

HMS *Iron Duke*, part of the Joint Task Force that deployed to Sierra Leone during Operation Keeling.

SPECIALIST SKILLS

As a light infantry regiment, The Royal Gurkha Rifles (RGR) operates at the most physically demanding end of the spectrum of military operations, both in UK as a part of 16 Air Assault Brigade and in Brunei as the only battalion in the British Army that is fully trained and acclimatised for fighting in the jungle. At its starkest, its task is to close with the enemy, usually by covering long distances on foot over unforgiving terrain, and then kill them. This places a premium on a number of basic skills that the RGR works hard to maintain. Chief amongst these is the ability to shoot quickly and accurately, there being no point in pushing the limits of human endurance to get close to the enemy only to find that they are the better shots!

The RGR's antecedent regiments had a long tradition of exceptional marksmanship that the RGR has endeavoured to maintain. Much time is spent on the ranges refining basic skills before taking part in more demanding live firing exercises in increasingly

Above: Potential junior leaders carrying out a pairs advance to contact in 2006 under the watchful eye of an instructor. Having mastered the basics on the ranges, soldiers in the RGR are then put through their paces in increasingly complex and demanding environments.

Left: Soldiers in RGR battalions spend a great deal of time on the ranges, developing their skills until they can guarantee 'one shot, one kill'.

Above: Corporal Bishal Rai of 2RGR, winner of the Queen's Medal for being the best shot in the 2018 Army Operational Shooting Competition, being carried by Colonel Brigade of Gurkhas, the Commanding Officer of 1RGR and other members of the RGR to celebrate his victory. Two members of the RGR, Captain Dharmendra Gurung and Warrant Officer Second Class Lalitbahadur Gurung, have each won the medal a remarkable three times.

Below: The RGR maintains its shooting edge by taking every opportunity to practise, even when deployed on operations. This photograph was taken in early 2019 during 1RGR's tour on Operation Toral 7 (November 2018 to May 2019).

complex environments. The end result is a soldier who is highly competent with both his primary and secondary personal weapon systems in a wide variety of different circumstances.

Although competition shooting is different to engaging an enemy in a combat zone, the results of Army level competitions give an indication of the importance that regiments accord to their shooting. It will therefore come as no surprise that the RGR's record in the Army's annual Operational Shooting Competition is exceptional; in 14 of the last 25 years, the Queen's Medal, which is awarded to the top shot in the competition, has been won by a member of the RGR.

Officers and soldiers within the RGR are highly competitive, and one way to ensure that their basic military skills are finely developed is to exploit this competitiveness by holding competitions. Unless deployed on operations, both battalions therefore run annual inter-platoon or inter-company military skills competitions, which contribute to the broader Champion Company Competitions.

Leading from the front! A sergeant in 1RGR leads his platoon during an event in the battalion's inter-platoon 'Bullock Trophy' Competition in 2011.

Because the majority of Gurkhas grow up in a rural environment, many of them are able to read the ground with an expert eye. In particular, those who spent much of their youth in the Middle Hills of the Himalayas looking after their families' sheep or goat herds in the high pastures have an ability to interpret 'ground sign' that far exceeds that of the majority of Europeans. This makes them highly effective at tracking. The value of this skill has long been appreciated in jungle warfare. Indeed, in one incident during the Malayan Emergency (1948 to 1960), a company of soldiers from 6GR, one of the RGR's antecedent regiments, spent over a week tracking an infamous group of communist terrorists (CT) through dense jungle before successfully engaging them.[146] The Gurkhas' talent for tracking has proven to be invaluable in Afghanistan, often

enabling them to detect when the ground has been disturbed by an IED being placed in their path.

The combination of exceptional shooting skill and a highly developed understanding of field craft makes soldiers in the RGR ideal as snipers. During their multiple tours in Afghanistan, both RGR battalions deployed snipers to help defeat the threat posed by the Taliban.

Given the high standards of basic infantry skills that the RGR maintains, it is not surprising that the Regiment's soldiers make excellent paratroopers. Lieutenant Colonel (later Major General) F J Loftus-Tottenham, who formed 153 (Gurkha) Parachute Battalion, the first Gurkha parachute unit, in India in October 1941 believed that:

"The nastiest part about parachuting is landing, and in this, with his compact light body and strong hill legs,

Left: Soldiers in the RGR will often push themselves to their absolute limits to reach the highest of standards, particularly in a competition. This places a duty of care on officers, non-commissioned officers and the more experienced soldiers to ensure that younger Gurkhas do not over-reach themselves, especially in hot climates.

Below left: A soldier on a field firing exercise in Brunei during a Junior Leaders Cadre in 2017. The RGR places a great deal of emphasis on exercising in a live environment, developing soldiers' confidence as well as their military skills.

Below: Soldiers from 2RGR clearing a route in Afghanistan on Operation Herrick 14 (April to October 2011). The soldier in front is using a device that detects some of the materials routinely found in IEDs whilst the soldier behind is using his eyes, and his years of tracking experience, to identify any 'ground sign' that might indicate whether an IED has been buried on the route.

Above: A Gurkha sniper from 2RGR on patrol in Afghanistan during Operation Herrick 14 (April to October 2011).

Left: A Gurkha sniper from 1RGR in Afghanistan during Operation Herrick 7 (September 2007 to April 2008).

117

Right: A Gurkha sniper and his spotter from D (Tamandu) Company blending into the background in Afghanistan on Operation Herrick 4 (April to October 2006)

Below right: A Gurkha sniper from 1RGR taking aim from a vehicle. Note the Army 100 badge on his left sleeve. This means he finished in the top 100 in the annual Army Operational Shooting Competition at Bisley, making him one of the best 100 shots in a Regular Army of over 80,000 personnel (image Crown copyright 2006).

he [the Gurkha] has a distinct advantage over other races. For this reason I would say that, along with the Japanese who is similarly built, he is probably the best natural parachutist in the world".[147]

3/7th Gurkhas became the second Gurkha parachute unit in May 1942, changing its name to 154 (Gurkha) Parachute Battalion on 4 August 1943. Both 153 and 154 (Gurkha) Parachute Battalions saw active service during the Burma Campaign and were disbanded after the end of the Second World War.

The next Gurkha parachute organisation to be formed was the Gurkha Independent Parachute

Above: Snipers are trained to blend in with their surroundings. It is highly unlikely that the enemy would be able to see this sniper from more than a few metres away. Given a sniper would aim to achieve a first-round hit at 600 metres, there is little chance of him being spotted by his target (image Crown copyright 2007).

Field Marshal Lord Wavell being introduced to officers and soldiers of 153 (Gurkha) Parachute Battalion during the Second World War. Formed in October 1941, the battalion was disbanded in November 1947.

Company. Raised on 2 January 1963, it served with distinction during the Borneo Confrontation (1963 to 1966) and was disbanded on 2 December 1971. For the next 25 years, there was no formal Gurkha parachuting capability until C (Cassino) Company, a Gurkha Reinforcement Company, was raised in November 1996 for service with the 2nd Battalion The Parachute Regiment (2PARA). The company deployed on numerous operations, serving in Bosnia and Herzegovina on Operation Palatine, in Sierra Leone on Operation Palliser, in Macedonia on Operation Bessemer and in Afghanistan on Operation Fingal, before being disbanded in May 2002.

Left: Tense faces as members of the Gurkha Independent Parachute Company await the signal to prepare to jump. Formed in January 1963, the company disbanded in December 1971.

Far left: A Gurkha sniper from 2RGR on sentry duty in Afghanistan during Operation Herrick 9 (September 2008 to April 2009).

Third from left, a young Gurkha non-commissioned officer (NCO) about to complete one of his first parachute descents on the famous 'jumps' course that follows successful completion of the All Arms Pre-Parachute Selection Course, otherwise known as 'P Company', one of the toughest and most physically demanding courses in the Army. The NCO went on to pass the course, earning the right to wear the blue wings of the qualified military parachutist on his uniform (image copyright Sean Statham).

From its formation in July 1994, the UK-based RGR battalion served as part of 5 Airborne Brigade. This was a natural home for its talents but, in September 1999, 5 Airborne Brigade was re-roled to become 12 Mechanised Brigade. Not being a mechanised unit, the UK-based RGR battalion was transferred to 2 Infantry Brigade, which subsequently became 2 (South East) Brigade in 2007. After much hard work by Headquarters Brigade of Gurkhas, and in recognition of its exceptional ability in the light infantry role, the UK-based RGR battalion was transferred to 16 Air Assault Brigade on 1 June 2015. The occasion was marked by a parade held in Sir John Moore Barracks, the home of the UK-based RGR battalion which, at the time, was 2RGR. During the

Gurkha paratroopers from C (Cassino) Company 2PARA in Afghanistan on Operation Fingal in January 2002. The company was formed in November 1996 and disbanded in May 2002.

120

parade, Brigadier (now Major General) Nick Borton DSO, the Commander of 16 Air Assault Brigade, noted that the Gurkhas' "characteristics of high standards, physical fitness and fierce fighting spirit perfectly match those of the Army's very high readiness brigade, and we are looking forward to working with them".[148]

The same qualities and characteristics that make RGR officers and soldiers highly effective at the more demanding end of the spectrum of military operations also make them well suited to service with the Special Forces. The RGR continues to provide a steady stream of officers and soldiers to the Special Air Service, the Special Boat Service and the Special Reconnaissance Regiment. Having passed the rigorous selection process, some remain with these organisations for the majority of their service but others, keen to progress in their Gurkha careers, return to the RGR after a few years, bringing a wealth of experience from which others can learn.

CHAPTER 5

Afghanistan

On the morning of Tuesday 11 September 2001, Al Qaeda, the terrorist group led by Osama bin Laden, launched a series of spectacular and devastating attacks against the United States of America. Using hijacked airliners, they managed to destroy the iconic Twin Towers of New York's World Trade Centre, as well as part of the Pentagon, the headquarters of America's Department of Defense. In all, 2,996 people died and more than 6,000 were injured, making the attacks the world's most deadly terrorist atrocities. On 21 September 2001, President George Bush addressed the US Congress. Declaring a "war on terror", he identified bin Laden as the man responsible for the attacks and demanded that the Taliban leadership of Afghanistan hand over the leaders of Al Qaeda or "share their fate".[149] In a show of solidarity, British Prime Minister Tony Blair addressed the House of Commons and urged action:

"We must bring bin Laden and other Al Qaida leaders to justice and eliminate the terrorist threat they pose. And we must ensure that Afghanistan ceases to harbour and sustain international terrorism. If the Taliban regime will not comply with that objective, we must bring about change in that regime to ensure that Afghanistan's links to international terrorism are broken."[150]

Mullah Omar, the Taliban's leader, refused to cooperate and on 7 October 2001, US and UK operations against the Taliban began in Afghanistan with the bombing of training camps and other military installations. This was quickly followed by ground deployments in support of the Northern Alliance, the Taliban's arch rival in the north of the country. On 20 December 2001, the UN passed Resolution 1386 calling for the establishment of an International Security Assistance Force (ISAF) in Afghanistan to be led by the North Atlantic Treaty Organisation (NATO).[151] The UK's initial contribution to this force came from 16 Air Assault Brigade which is why C (Cassino) Company, a Gurkha Reinforcement Company (GRC) from the RGR

Left: A Rifleman from C (Cassino) Company, 2PARA in Kabul on Operation Fingal in February 2002. Note the parachute wings on the soldier's right upper arm which denote that he is a trained and qualified Gurkha Paratrooper. The snow-capped mountains in the background are the foothills of the famous Hindu Kush.

Below: A sentry stands guard with a medium machine gun during the deployment of C (Cassino) Company, 2PARA to Kabul during Operation Fingal in January 2002.

then attached to the 2nd Battalion The Parachute Regiment (2PARA),[152] found itself in a snowy Kabul in January 2002, wearing the newly-designed ISAF insignia. Although the overarching name for the US deployment was Operation Enduring Freedom, UK deployments to Afghanistan initially went under the name of Operation Fingal. 2PARA's task on Operation Fingal was to help the fledgling Afghan Interim Authority provide security in and around the Kabul area.[153] The role was interesting but, from a Gurkha perspective, it was also highly significant as it marked a return to Gurkha operations in Afghanistan after a break of more than fifty years.

Despite Afghanistan's well-deserved reputation as a graveyard for intervening powers, the UK Government was optimistic that its operations in the country would be short-lived. However, this has not been the case and in the seventeen years that have elapsed since that first deployment, soldiers from the RGR have completed multiple tours in Afghanistan. The nature of the tasks they have undertaken has changed over the years. When 2RGR first deployed on Operations Tarrock and Fingal in October 2003,[154] the battalion had three distinct roles. The first was to

help provide security in and around Kabul as part of the NATO security force; the second was to assist the US military with training the Afghan National Army; and the third was to deploy Provincial Reconstruction Teams (PRTs) 'up country' to the north of Kabul. This latter task was particularly challenging as it required small groups of soldiers to deploy out into the countryside with development experts to provide support to rural communities. The aim was to help

Below: The Officer
Commanding C (Cassino)
Company 2PARA (left) discusses
the deployment with a young
officer from 2PARA. Note the
press presence to the left of the
company commander.

Below: The Officer
Commanding C (Cassino)
Company 2PARA (left) discusses
the deployment with a young
officer from 2PARA. Note the
press presence to the left of the
company commander.

Right: A Gurkha officer from
2RGR with members of the Afghan
National Army during Operation
Fingal in October 2003. The battalion
formed the heart of the UK Afghan
National Army Training Team
(UKANATT) throughout their tour.

empower local leaders so that they were able to
govern their constituents more effectively, providing
the increased stability and security that would
make it difficult for the Taliban to gain support. It
was dangerous work; but so was providing security
in Kabul, as Sergeant Kajiman Limbu discovered
on 12 October 2003 when, despite being under
effective enemy fire, he ran forward and rescued a
wounded US Army colonel from a vehicle that had
been ambushed by the Taliban. Sergeant Kajiman
was awarded the Military Cross (MC) for his heroic
actions, the first medal to be awarded to a Gurkha
soldier for gallantry since 1979.[155]

Less than a year later, 2RGR returned to
Afghanistan on the second rotation of the now renamed Operation Herrick.[156] As well as providing
a Kabul Patrols Company (KPC), a PRT and an
Afghan National Army Training Team (ANATT),
the battalion also fielded an operations company and
a national support element. They had little option
but to hit the ground running as within hours of
taking over command of the KPC, the command

The Commanding Officer of 2RGR talking to an officer from the
Afghan National Army during Operation Fingal in December 2003.

team from A Company 2RGR found themselves
having to deal with the first strike by an improvised
explosive device (IED) for six months. The main
focus during the deployment was the National
Assembly Provincial Council Elections (NACPE)
which took place in September 2005. This was the
first time that parliamentary elections had taken
place in Afghanistan since the fall of the Taliban,

Soldiers from 2RGR take a break during Operation
Fingal in February 2004.

and the battalion therefore had a key role to play
in ensuring that the security situation encouraged
as many people as possible to turn out and vote.
The role of the operations company was interesting
but demanding. Working alongside two platoons
from the Swedish Army, they conducted long-range
patrols, self-sufficient for up to ten days, deep into
the countryside to try to disrupt the Taliban.

Top: A detachment of soldiers from the Afghan
National Army practise stop and search operations
under the watchful eye of instructors from 2RGR
during Operation Fingal in March 2004.

Above: A British officer from 2RGR with an
Afghan officer taking a break during a training
exercise in February 2004 during Operation Fingal.

The ever-present threat from improvised explosive devices (IED) and small arms fire mean that helicopters are the preferred mode of transport in Afghanistan, particularly for long distance moves. This photograph shows members of 2RGR deploying by helicopter in May 2005 during Operation Herrick 2.

Although they have good off-road mobility on dry land, Land Rovers are not known for their ability to float, as this patrol from 2RGR found out to its cost in June 2005 during Operation Herrick 2.

In early 2006, both 1RGR, which was deployed on Operation Oculus in Bosnia and Herzegovina at the time, and 2RGR contributed soldiers to form D (Tamandu) Company. This composite company, which formed up in Risborough Barracks in Shorncliffe, deployed with 16 Air Assault Brigade in April 2006 on Operation Herrick 4. Although initially tasked with providing force protection at Camp Bastion, the combined British/American base deep in the desert of Helmand Province, it was not long before the company's role changed. In addition to providing the security force for Camp Bastion and supporting combat operations in Sangin, D (Tamandu) Company was also tasked with defending the district centre in Now Zad. However, with the British force now so thinly spread across Helmand Province, the Taliban sensed an opportunity to seize the isolated outpost and inflict a severe, and potentially irrecoverable, humiliation on the British. With greater numbers and relative freedom of movement, the Taliban launched multiple direct assaults on the base, often supported by heavy machine guns, snipers and mortars. For

Vehicles have their limitations! A non-commissioned officer (NCO) from 2RGR makes best use of the available modes of transport during Operation Herrick 2 in June 2005.

A senior non-commissioned officer (SNCO) from 2RGR demonstrating his Himalayan surefootedness. The photograph was taken in August 2005 during Operation Herrick 2 and shows the inhospitable nature, as well as the scale, of Afghanistan's mountains.

Even when deployed on operations, exercises continue to maintain the extreme fitness that soldiering in Afghanistan requires. This photograph shows two soldiers from 2RGR taking part in Exercise Gallipoli Gallop in September 2005 during the battalion's deployment on Herrick 2.

over two months, the small Gurkha force in Now Zad resisted multiple attempts to overrun its position, inflicting heavy casualties on the attackers in what became known as 'the siege of Now Zad'.

That D (Tamandu) Company managed to achieve so much during its six month tour in this highly contested environment is testament to the quality of the soldiering exhibited by all ranks and the leadership of the officers and non-commissioned officers. In some ways, this was a defining tour for the RGR in that it demonstrated to the wider British Army, and to their enemy, that the RGR could take on the Taliban in close quarter ground combat and win. The company returned from Afghanistan in October 2006 and disbanded in January 2007, its soldiers returning to their parent battalions with much useful

The Commander-in-Chief of Land Forces, General Sir Mike Jackson, visits D (Tamandu) Company RGR in Helmand during Operation Herrick 4. He is shown here talking to the Company Commander.

A sniper pair from D (Tamandu) Company, comprised of the sniper and his spotter, are well camouflaged to blend in with the sandy environment of Afghanistan. The photograph was taken in 2006 during Operation Herrick 4.

Soldiers from D (Tamandu) Company take a well-earned break from the rigours of desert patrolling in Helmand Province during Operation Herrick 4. The photograph was taken in April 2006, early in their six month deployment.

Left: Troops from D (Tamandu) Company providing protection for a convoy move in Helmand Province during Operation Herrick 4.

Below: The tension is obvious on the faces of these soldiers from 1RGR as they deploy by helicopter at the start of an operation in February 2008 during Operation Herrick 7.

experience, particularly of how the Taliban could be defeated at their own game.

In 2006, ISAF began to expand its mandate beyond the Kabul area.[157] As part of this, the UK assumed responsibility for the security of Helmand Province, arguably the most insecure of Afghanistan's thirty four semi-autonomous provinces. British responsibility for this region meant that the majority of British units that deployed to Afghanistan from 2006, at least until NATO transitioned to its Resolute Support Mission on 1 January 2015, operated in Helmand under the command of Task Force Helmand, a UK-led 1* formation headquarters. However, this was not the case with 1RGR when it deployed on Operation Herrick 7 in September 2007.[158] Rather than being deployed in the south to hold ground, the bulk of 1RGR had the task of acting as a divisional-level manoeuvre strike force,[159] able to penetrate deep behind enemy lines in order to hit the Taliban where it least expected. Placed directly under Headquarters Regional Command (South) (RC(S)), a 2* headquarters then commanded by Major General 'Jacko' Page, the 1RGR battlegroup deployed throughout the whole of southern Afghanistan, conducting strike operations with the Dutch/Australian

Task Force in Uruzgan, with the Canadians in Kandahar, as well as with US special forces in Kandahar and Zabul, and with the British in Helmand. It was at the end of one such operation during a road move back to Kandahar on 4 October 2007 that Major Lex Roberts, the Officer Commanding Support Company, was killed when his vehicle hit an improvised explosive device (IED). Major Roberts' death was a real blow for the battalion. Popular, brave and hugely competent, he was the first member of a Gurkha infantry battalion to be killed in action since Rifleman Lachhuman Rai of 1/10th Gurkhas lost his life on 26 March 1966 during the Borneo Confrontation.

Below: Major Lex Roberts (on the right) and two officers from 1RGR deploying to Afghanistan on 1 September 2007 at the start of the battalion's tour on Operation Herrick 7. Major Roberts was killed by an IED during a road move on 4 October 2007 after a battalion offensive operation. Major Roberts was the first member of the RGR to be killed by enemy action since the Regiment's formation on 1 July 1994. The officer on the left, Major Leigh Roberts (no relation) was seriously injured in an IED strike later in the tour but went on to make a full recovery.

Bottom: An example of the sort of prepared defensive position that, given time, the Taliban construct to protect against attack. This photograph was taken in October 2007 shortly after the position had been cleared of enemy by 1RGR during Operation Herrick 7.

During the course of its tour, the battalion conducted eleven major battlegroup-level operations. These usually involved air assault and were often carried out at night against defended, and well prepared, enemy positions. Success in this environment placed a premium on exceptional basic infantry skills, physical fitness, determination, teamwork and, perhaps above all, courage. Although the Gurkha infantry has traditionally excelled in all of these, the fact that five members of the RGR battlegroup were awarded Military Crosses (MCs) for their actions during the tour, and another three were Mentioned in Despatches (MiD), gives an indication of just how tough the fighting was during Operation Herrick 7.

Above: Orders! The Commanding Officer of 1RGR and his command group during Herrick 7, October 2007.

Right: A heavily-armed vehicle from 1RGR leading a convoy in January 2008 during Operation Herrick 7.

Below: A foot patrol from 1RGR takes a moment to reorganise during Operation Herrick 7.

His Royal Highness Prince Harry with Gurkhas from B Company 1RGR during Operation Herrick 7. His Royal Highness got to know Gurkhas well as he worked alongside them for several months during his two tours in Afghanistan.

During its pre-deployment training for Operation Herrick 7, the battalion worked with Mastiff armoured vehicles driven by soldiers from The King's Royal Hussars (KRH). This fortuitous arrangement enabled the battalion to rekindle the affiliation that exists between the RGR and this famous armoured regiment. Formed in Italy in 1945 during the battle for the town of Medicina when 6GR (one of the RGR's antecedent regiments) fought alongside the 14th/20th King's Hussars (one of the KRH's antecedent regiments), the affiliation was carried forward by the RGR on its formation. The affiliation explains why the eagle of the KRH adorns the cross-belts of RGR officers and why members of the KRH wear a kukri badge on their arm. Interestingly, Afghanistan has provided a number of other opportunities to consolidate this affiliation. For example, when 1RGR deployed on Operation Herrick 12 in April 2010, two KRH officers joined them for the duration of the tour. Herrick 7 also

Below: The Commanding Officer of 1RGR (on the right) receiving the 'Canadian Forces Unit Commendation' from the Canadian High Commissioner in London. This prestigious award, which is rarely presented to 'foreign' units, was presented to 1RGR for its service with the Canadian-led Task Force in Kandahar during Operation Herrick 7. The Commanding Officer is accompanied by the Gurkha Major of 1RGR and three members of the battalion wounded during the tour (image Crown copyright 2008).

Above: Some of the recipients of operational honours and awards from Operation Herrick 7 after their Investiture at Buckingham Palace on 4 November 2008. From left to right: Lieutenant Colonel Jonny Bourne, the Commanding Officer of 1RGR during Operation Herrick 7, who was made an Officer of the Most Excellent Order of the British Empire (OBE), and Rifleman Bhimbahadur Gurung, Lance Corporal Mohansing Tangnami, Lance Corporal Agnish Thapa and Major Paul Pitchfork who all received Military Crosses (MC) (image Crown copyright 2008).

provided an opportunity for the RGR to get to know His Royal Highness Prince Harry who was based in Garmsir with B Company for much of his tour in Afghanistan. B Company's tour was just as demanding as the rest of the battalion's; as the Regimental Newsletter notes, "…there was hardly a single day of their 6 month deployment when the company was not in contact with the Taliban".[160]

At the end of the deployment, 1RGR was awarded a 'Canadian Forces Unit Commendation' by the Canadian Chief of Defence Staff in recognition of the battalion's service in support of the Canadian Task Force. This was a particular honour as the award is rarely given to non-Canadian units. Interestingly, the first 'foreign' unit to receive the award was the KRH in 1996 for their service in Bosnia and Herzegovina as part of a Canadian-led multi-national brigade.

In September 2008, 2RGR returned to Afghanistan on Operation Herrick 9. Although the battalion's 'centre of mass' was located in Musa Qal'eh, elements of the battalion were dispersed across a wide geographical area. For example, A Company was located in the south in Lashkar Gah in the police mentoring role. B Company was based in its own forward operating base (FOB Delhi) in Garmsir, which, only six months earlier, had been the home of B Company 1RGR during Operation Herrick 7, and D Company was deployed in the south under the command of the Queen's Dragoon Guards (QDG). The Quartermaster's Department was based in Camp Bastion and two platoons operated

A sniper from 2RGR observes the ground to his front in January 2009 during Operation Herrick 9.

independently, one in the Danish area of operations and one with the Commando Logistic Regiment (CLR). This latter role brought numerous challenges as the platoon's task was to provide force protection to logistics convoys as they delivered materiel to the many bases spread throughout Helmand Province. Not surprisingly, the platoon soon became "...the force of choice amongst commanders and crews when it comes to protecting the CLR's large and vulnerable convoys (often comprising up to 80 logistics vehicles and as long as 77km)".[161] Working in conjunction with the Afghan National Army, the 2RGR battlegroup conducted several deliberate operations, all of which succeeded in seizing the initiative from the enemy and limiting their freedom of action. But the battalion's successes came at a significant cost. On 4 November 2008, Rifleman Yubraj Rai, of B Company, died after receiving a gunshot wound from enemy fire and, on 15

November 2008, Colour Sergeant Krishnabahadur Dura, the commander of the battalion's Sniper Platoon, was killed when the Warrior Infantry Fighting Vehicle in which he was travelling was struck by an explosive device.

Life in a Patrol Base! Soldiers from 2RGR get on with the routine of living in a patrol base during Operation Herrick 9. A network of such bases was established to enable the battalion to dominate ground previously controlled by the Taliban. An aggressive programme of patrols launched from these patrol bases, both in vehicles and on foot, enabled the battalion to seize the initiative by taking the fight to the enemy.

Although the patrol bases were reasonably well protected from ground attack, they were effectively nothing more than defended compounds. As such, they were vulnerable to indirect fire from mortars. This image is of a piece of shrapnel from a Taliban mortar bomb that fortunately landed just to the north of one of 2RGR's patrol bases during Operation Herrick 9. There were no casualties as a result of this attack.

Right: Gordon Brown took over as Prime Minister from Tony Blair on 27 June 2007 and remained in this appointment until 11 May 2010. This photograph was taken during a visit the Prime Minister made to Afghanistan in December 2008 whilst 2RGR was deployed on Operation Herrick 9. You can just see the head of the Commanding Officer of 2RGR beyond the Prime Minister's right shoulder!

Opposite: Weapons need to be kept ready for action at all times. This image shows a Gurkha soldier from 2RGR sharpening his kukri during Operation Herrick 9. Some might think that there is no place for a traditional weapon like the Gurkha kukri on the modern battlefield. They would be wrong, as Lance Corporal Tuljung Gurung demonstrated when, ammunition expended, he used his kukri to beat off an attack by Taliban fighters on 22 March 2013. He was awarded the Military Cross for his bravery.

Left: To avoid the threat from IEDs and to move large numbers of troops across the country, maximum use is made of helicopters in Afghanistan. This photograph shows members of 2RGR crammed into an ISAF helicopter in March 2009.

Above left: A company commander from 2RGR (on the right) and his second-in-command (in the middle) share a joke with their Brigade Commander during Operation Herrick 9. One of the most defining characteristics of the RGR is the close relationship that exists between British and Gurkha officers.

Above: A soldier from 2RGR wading across a wadi in April 2009 whilst on patrol in the green zone of Helmand Province during Operation Herrick 9 (image copyright Richard Pohle 2009).

Above: The Officer Commanding B Company 2RGR lowers the company's flag in front of assembled Gurkhas and Fusiliers in Patrol Base Woqab as the company hands over responsibility for its area at the end of Operation Herrick 9 to the 2nd Battalion The Royal Regiment of Fusiliers (image copyright Richard Pohle 2009).

Right: D Company 2RGR pose for a group photograph towards the end of their tour in March 2009 on Operation Herrick 9.

Soldiers from 2RGR prepare to board a Chinook helicopter to take them to Camp Bastion for the last time as they begin their journey back to the UK at the end of their six month deployment on Operation Herrick 9 (image copyright Richard Pohle 2009).

When 2RGR began its preparation for Operation Herrick 9, much of the manpower from C Company was taken to reinforce the other companies. However, reinforcements from 1RGR arrived during the course of 2008 to bring C Company up to strength before it deployed on Operation Herrick 10 under the direct command of 19 Light Brigade. In recognition of its composite nature, the company was given the title 'Foxtrot (Tavoleto) Company'[162] after Ferret Force, a composite Gurkha company that saw service, and considerable success, during the Malayan Emergency. The company deployed to Afghanistan in April 2009 and took over the police mentoring role from A Company 2RGR in the Lashkar Gah area of Helmand Province. It operated throughout Helmand, often on deliberate operations with up to 300 ANSF members under command.[163]

It was a dangerous task and, on 7 May 2009, tragedy struck when Corporal Kumar Pun was killed by a suicide bomber whilst out on patrol in Gereshk town bazaar. Having completed its tour in October 2009, the company returned to the UK before being disbanded in March 2010.

Below: Soldiers from 2RGR enjoy a pizza in Camp Bastion in April 2009 at the end of their six month deployment on Operation Herrick 9 (image copyright Richard Pohle 2009).

Right: Conditions deteriorate during 1RGR's in-theatre training at the start of their tour on Operation Herrick 12 in April 2010. This training, which was conducted in Camp Bastion in Helmand Province, enabled incoming troops to acclimatise and hone their skills before venturing beyond the relative safety of the UK's main operating base. Interestingly, 1RGR completed their in-theatre training wearing the 'old' desert combats but switched to the newly issued multi-terrain pattern (MTP) combats when they arrived in their operational area of responsibility.

Although it imposed considerable strain on the Regiment, the RGR's ability to form Gurkha Reinforcement Companies (GRCs) was greatly appreciated by the wider Army, mainly because many British infantry battalions were struggling to recruit and retain sufficient soldiers to man their operational establishments. In December 2008, the RGR was tasked to form another GRC to support the 1st Battalion, The Mercian Regiment (Cheshire) (1MERCIAN) on Operation Herrick 12. GRC 2 (G (Tobruk) Company 1MERCIAN), as the company was titled, deployed to Afghanistan from April until October 2010.[164] It was in good company whilst there as 1RGR was also deployed on the same Herrick. In an interesting twist of fate, the brigade level of command for Operation Herrick 12 was originally due to be provided by 52 Infantry Brigade, the brigade that the author was commanding at the time. However, reductions in UK force levels in Iraq meant that instead of deploying on Operation Telic, 4 Mechanised Brigade was rerouted to Afghanistan, removing the need for 52 Infantry Brigade to deploy.

A soldier from 1RGR on patrol during Operation Herrick 12. Although much of Afghanistan is comprised of mountains and arid plains, the terrain either side of its rivers tends to be lush and fertile. Fighting in this complex environment places a real premium on basic infantry skills, something the RGR excels at (image Crown copyright 2010).

Below: Given the ferocity of the fighting, many people might be surprised at how young some of the battlegroup's officers and soldiers are. But while they might lack experience, at least at the start of their first tour, they make up for this with enthusiasm, grit and determination. As these members of the 1RGR battlegroup show, a ready smile goes a long way when the pressure starts to mount.

1RGR therefore deployed to the Nahr-e-Saraj area of Afghanistan in April 2010 under the command of Headquarters 4 Mechanised Brigade. The battalion sustained its first casualty of the tour before the handover/takeover with the outgoing unit[165] had been completed when Corporal Haribahadur Budha Magar was struck by an IED whilst on a familiarisation patrol. That he survived is quite remarkable and a tribute to the immediate trauma care he received, both from members of his own patrol and from the medical services, as well as to his own determination.

There is no doubt that the battalion had a demanding tour, sustaining many other casualties. Perhaps the most galling incident occurred on the night of the 12/13 July 2010 when a sergeant from the Afghan National Army (ANA) opened fire on the operations room in Patrol Base 3, killing Major Josh Bowman, the officer commanding A Company,[166] Lieutenant Neil Turkington and Corporal Arjun Purja Pun. This incident could easily have destroyed

the trust that the battalion had built up with their ANA partners; something which, had it happened, would have undermined what the battalion was trying to achieve. But as the 1RGR Newsletter from June to December 2010 notes:

"It was a shocking event that none of us had anticipated. We had built up a good rapport with our Afghan partners, and there had been no indications that anything like this might happen. The only consolation is that all of our soldiers accepted that partnering must go on, and they continued to act in a highly professional manner. They might have been forgiven for doing otherwise, but to their credit they showed not only restraint, but also understanding."[167]

The aggressive operations carried out by both 1RGR and G (Tobruk) Company 1MERCIAN during Operation Herrick 12 did a great deal to erode the enemy's capabilities and to put ISAF on the front

A patrol from 1RGR takes a few minutes to pose for a photograph during Operation Herrick 12. Note the quad bike in the centre of the photograph. These were used to carry ammunition and stores during foot patrols, as well as to help evacuate the wounded. Note also the head of the hand-held metal detector above the soldier on the extreme left of the picture. These are used to try and locate IEDs in the path of the patrol.

foot. However, as the attack in July had demonstrated, conducting such operations against a well-trained and determined enemy was not without considerable risk and the RGR suffered further losses as a result. On 10 August 2010, a Chinook helicopter landing at a patrol base to conduct a resupply struck the edge of a sangar. The building then collapsed and fell on an accommodation block, seriously injuring Rifleman Remand Kulung from G (Tobruk) Company. Although Rifleman Remand received immediate treatment before being evacuated to UK, via the Role 3 Hospital in Camp Bastion, he died of his injuries on 12 August 2010. On 2 October 2010, Rifleman Suraj Gurung, serving with 1RGR, was killed by a suicide bomber whilst out on patrol following an attack on his patrol base. Rifleman Sachin Limbu was badly wounded on 24 June 2010 when an IED exploded as he moved into a fire position to provide protection to his comrades. He was evacuated to the UK for specialist care and, for over eighteen months, he fought hard to overcome his devastating injuries. But, despite his heroic efforts, this was a battle he could not win and on 2 January 2012 he passed away.

A soldier on patrol at night during Operation Herrick 12
(image Crown copyright 2010).

Left: The RGR places a premium on maintaining the highest standards of basic infantry skills, including shooting. Every year, it produces some of the finest shots in the Army, with members of the Regiment often winning the Queen's Medal at Bisley. This pays real dividends on operations as it enables the battalions to deploy teams of highly effective snipers. This photo shows a sniper on Operation Herrick 12 acting as a sentry during a temporary halt.

Both the battalion and G (Tobruk) Company received many accolades for their outstanding performances during Operation Herrick 12, with every member of the RGR working hard to maintain the highest of professional standards. Throughout the tour, there were numerous instances of individuals behaving with utter disregard for their own safety. Some received formal awards for their actions but, as in any conflict, many others went unrecognised. One of those whose exploits led to a formal gallantry award was Acting Sergeant Dipprasad Pun. On 17 September 2010, Acting Sergeant Dipprasad Pun was one of four men left guarding a compound after the remainder of his platoon had deployed to set up checkpoints to the east of a remote village.[168] Sergeant Dipprasad was on duty manning a single sangar on a roof in the middle of the compound. He detected a noise and immediately suspected that his lightly manned position was about to be attacked. Having warned his commander by radio, he fired a weapon-launched grenade at the assaulting enemy and then, single-handedly, beat off attacks from multiple directions, "…killing three assailants and causing the others to flee".[169] He was awarded the Conspicuous Gallantry Cross (CGC) for his actions. As his citation notes, he "…could never have known how many enemies were attempting to overcome his position, but he sought them out from all angles despite the danger, consistently moving towards them to reach the best position".[170]

Another member of the battalion whose conduct under fire received formal recognition was Rifleman Sunil Limbu. Despite being the most junior

141

Left: Commander ISAF, General David Petraeus, congratulating Acting Sergeant Dipprasad Pun on his gallant actions defending his patrol base against a determined attack by insurgents on 17 September 2010. Sergeant Dipprasad was subsequently awarded the Conspicuous Gallantry Cross.

Below: Members of 1RGR take a short break during a foot patrol on Operation Herrick 12. The photograph was taken towards the end of the tour in October 2010 (image Crown copyright 2010).

rifleman in his patrol, Rifleman Sunil demonstrated remarkable courage and determination during a Taliban attack on 21 June 2010. This extract from the citation for the Military Cross that he was subsequently awarded for his actions describes what happened:

"Despite sustaining injuries to his legs and hands from shrapnel during a direct enemy mortar attack, resulting in injuries to several of his team, Rifleman Limbu seized the initiative and staggered forward through the area to drag his Platoon Commander into the relative cover of a nearby compound.

Limbu then exposing himself to the continuing intermittent and highly unpredictable weapon launched grenade fire, returned to the area to reach an Afghan interpreter who was also hit, removing him to safety. It was only once he was satisfied that the other casualties were safe that he succumbed to his own injuries, which by this time were so serious that

he could no longer stand. The fire fight lasted over forty minutes, and it was not until the enemy were beaten back by an attack helicopter that Sunil and his other wounded colleagues could be evacuated, and he could receive surgery".[171]

Below: Operational honours and awards from Operation Herrick 12. From left to right: Acting Sergeant Dipprasad Pun with the Conspicuous Gallantry Cross; Lieutenant Colonel G M Strickland with the Distinguished Service Order; and Rifleman Sunil Limbu with the Military Cross (MC).

Bottom: The members of 2RGR in discussion with officers from the Afghan Uniformed Police (AUP) during Operation Herrick 14. The photograph was taken in June 2011 and illustrates the close relationship that existed between the battalion and the police during the tour (image Crown copyright 2011).

2RGR's next deployment to Afghanistan took place on Operation Herrick 14 in April 2011. Throughout this tour, 2RGR formed the core of ISAF's Police Mentoring and Advisory Group (PMAG), which meant that the battalion's primary focus was on improving the capability of the Afghan National Police (ANP). In addition to helping the Afghan Uniformed Police (AUP) develop their effectiveness, the summer of 2011 saw the PMAG's responsibilities expand to include working with the newly created Afghan Local Police (ALP) and the Afghan National Civil Order Police (ANCOP). The former has a key role to play in providing security within rural communities, a traditional target of Taliban activity. The latter provides a pan-Afghanistan capability in responding to civil disorder. Sadly, on 15 October 2011, Rifleman Vijay Rai, of A Company 2RGR, was killed by enemy small arms fire whilst manning a temporary check point with members of the AUP in an area known to have a strong insurgent presence. Although he received immediate medical care, he later died of his wounds in the Role 3 Hospital in Camp Bastion.

A soldier from 2RGR takes up a fire position during a patrol on Operation Herrick 14. The photograph was taken in June 2011 (image Crown copyright 2011).

A soldier from 2RGR shaking hands with a member of the Afghan National Security Forces (ANSF) in September 2011 during Operation Herrick 14. The Gurkhas' ability to build good relations with their Afghan partners made a strong contribution to the success of the battalion's tour (image Crown copyright 2011).

Soldiering in Afghanistan requires high levels of physical fitness – one reason why members of 2RGR never missed an opportunity to squeeze in a quick workout during Operation Herrick 14! One member of the battalion cools another down as he pushes out the press-ups, using the tyre of an armoured vehicle to elevate his legs and make it more difficult.

The battalion's Hindu Pundit and Buddhist religious teacher take part in a 'shura', or meeting, with key members of a local Afghan community. A Company Commander and the Gurkha Major look on. The photograph was taken in June 2011 during a visit to the battalion by the battalion's two religious leaders.

GRC3[172] was formed in July 2009 for service in the 1st Battalion The Yorkshire Regiment (1YORKS) as its C Company. It deployed to Afghanistan with 1YORKS in October 2011 on Operation Herrick 15, changing its name to D (Delhi) Company when it was placed under the command of a Danish battlegroup in theatre. Based in Khar Nikah (KNK) in the Upper Gereshk Valley throughout its tour, one of the most kinetic regions of Afghanistan, its primary focus was on developing the ALP's capabilities. It was highly successful in this and, when it departed Afghanistan in April 2012, it had succeeded in developing the local ALP cohort to the extent that they were able to man their own checkpoints, "…pushing the Forward Line of Own Troops (FLOT) to the north and to the south by about 400 metres in each direction, whilst providing enhanced security for central KNK…"[173] Working in small groups with the ALP was an immensely rewarding experience but it was also dangerous; on 27 January 2012, Lance Corporal Gajbahadur Gurung was killed by enemy small arms fire whilst out on patrol.

Below: A patrol from C Company 1RGR doing
final checks and having a last cigarette before
going out on patrol during Operation Herrick 17.

Two years after its last tour in Afghanistan, 1RGR returned in October 2012 on Operation Herrick 17. It was originally intended that the battalion would deploy as a battlegroup and that it would occupy its own area of operations. However, changes to the force laydown in theatre meant that there was no need for five ground-holding units. Headquarters 4 Mechanised Brigade, which was providing the one-star level of command for the deployment, therefore decided that 1RGR's sub-units would be attached to other battlegroups dispersed across the brigade area, with the commanding officer (CO) and his headquarters team filling roles in the headquarters of the task force. This decision was a huge disappointment, particularly for battalion headquarters, but the battalion took it in its stride, maintaining the highest of professional standards wherever they were deployed. In some respects, it was an opportunity for elements of the battalion to master a variety of different roles, operating alongside

Lance Corporal Tuljung Gurung from 1RGR who was awarded a Military Cross (MC) for his actions in defence of a sangar in Lashkar Gah, Helmand Province on 22 March 2013. The photograph shows Lance Corporal Tuljung at Buckingham Palace having just received his medal from His Royal Highness The Prince of Wales, Colonel-in-Chief of The Royal Gurkha Rifles.

or as part of British units. C Company, for example, had a particularly diverse tour working in small teams across the whole area of operations as part of the Police Mentoring Advisory Group headed up by The Royal Dragoon Guards (RDG). For many, it was also a return to familiar territory. For example, A Company, attached to 40 Commando Royal Marines, and B Company, attached to 1MERCIAN, redeployed to the areas they had operated in during Herrick 12.

Sadly, tragedy struck early in the tour on 30 October 2012 when Lieutenant Ed Drummond-Baxter and Lance Corporal Siddhanta Kunwar, both from A Company, were killed in an incident involving a suspected member of the Afghan police. As the battalion newsletter notes, "these were the only fatalities of the tour, and the manner of their death greatly shocked everybody. However, within days A Company were back supporting the Afghan National Security Forces (ANSF)".[174] By the time A Company handed over its area of responsibility at the end of the tour in April 2013, it was very much under the control of the ANSF, a testament to the hard work done by the company in improving local security and developing its Afghan partners.

There were many instances of real bravery during the tour as the members of 1RGR sought to take the fight to the enemy. Although many of these went unrecorded, some were documented and it is helpful

to consider one of these as it gives an idea of the type of conflict that the battalion was involved in.[175] In the early hours of 22 March 2013, Lance Corporal Tuljung Gurung was on sentry duty on the front gate of a patrol base near the town of Lashkar Gah in Helmand Province. At 0345 hours, two insurgents attacked his sangar. He returned fire but was knocked to the floor when a bullet hit his helmet. As he stood up, he saw a grenade land on the floor next to him. Showing remarkable coolness, he picked it up and threw it back. It exploded outside the sangar but the blast knocked him off his feet. As he started to stand up, he saw an insurgent climbing over the wall and into the sangar. Given the close range, he was unable to bring his rifle to bear so he drew his kukri, slashing at the insurgent. The citation for the Military Cross that he was subsequently awarded for his actions explains what happened next:

"Exposed to possible further insurgent firing positions, he aggressively and tenaciously continued to fight with his kukri. The two insurgents, defeated, turned and fled. Gurung then quickly climbed back into the sangar by which time the Quick Reaction Force had arrived. Gurung reported the incident calmly and bemoaned the fact he had not been able to prevent the insurgents escaping".[176]

On 31 December 2014, Operation Herrick officially ended and was replaced by Operation Toral which began on 1 January 2015.[177] The change in name reflected a transition in the nature of the operations conducted by NATO in Afghanistan. Its ISAF mission

A Gurkha officer from 1RGR hands out notebooks to
Afghan school children in November 2012. This was just one
of the many small initiatives carried out by 1RGR designed
to win hearts and minds during Operation Herrick 17.

A Gurkha medic from 1RGR giving a lesson to Afghan police
officers on how to treat an IED injury during Operation
Herrick 17. IEDs are so prevalent in Afghanistan that all
personnel, whatever their nationality, need to understand how
to stabilise a casualty until they can be evacuated for expert care.
Knowing what to do can be the difference between life and death.

was replaced by its Resolute Support mission with, as
the name implies, the emphasis shifting from combat
operations against the Taliban to supporting the
ANSF as it took the lead in the provision of security.
Commenting on the change, the Secretary of State for
Defence, Sir Michael Fallon, said:

*"It is with pride that we announce the end of UK
combat operations in Helmand, having given
Afghanistan the best possible chance of a stable future.
Our Armed Forces' tremendous sacrifice laid the
foundations for a strong Afghan Security Force, set
the security context that enabled the first democratic
transition of power in the country's history, and
stopped it being a launch pad for terrorist attacks in
the UK....Although we are ending a significant chapter
in our shared history, the UK's commitment to support
Afghanistan will continue through institutional
development, the Afghan National Army Officer
Academy, and development aid."*[178]

Operation Herrick 17 was the last Herrick that
the RGR would deploy on but it was not the last
tour that the Regiment would do in Afghanistan. In
April 2016, 2RGR deployed on Operation Toral 3,
protecting and enabling NATO forces as part of the
Kabul Security Force. In many ways, the tour was very
different to the multiple Herrick deployments that the
battalion had completed in the past but it remained
the same in one important respect. Namely, that the
Taliban were still the main threat and they remained
determined to inflict as much damage as possible on
the ANSF and their NATO allies. It was therefore
still a dangerous tour and it placed a premium on the
high levels of determination and professionalism that
characterise the RGR. Interestingly, Operation Toral
3 was the second iteration of the split-tour construct
with battalion headquarters completing eight months
in theatre and each of the companies doing only
four. But although two months shorter than the six
month tours that the companies were accustomed to
on Operation Herrick, the four month tours were no
less dangerous.

The Adjutant of 2RGR raises the battalion flag at the start of their tour on Operation Toral 3 in April 2016.

Left: A soldier from 2RGR on patrol during Operation Toral 3 in the remains of the famous Bala Hissar, the old fortress that once dominated the skyline of Kabul.

Below: The Commanding Officer of 2RGR (on the right) talking to US members of NATO's Resolute Support Mission during Operation Toral 3 (image Crown copyright 2016).

Above: Members of 2RGR meet up with an old friend, Brigadier Ian Thomas, who was serving in Kabul as Commander British Forces Afghanistan when the battalion was on Operation Toral 3. Brigadier Thomas commanded 2RGR from May 2001 to November 2003.

Right: A soldier preparing 'extra messing' during a break on Operation Toral 3. Note the ubiquitous Gurkha kukri in the top right of the picture, used for everything from chopping up meat to fighting the Taliban in hand-to-hand combat.

The last elements of 2RGR departed Afghanistan in December 2016 on completion of their tour. Many members of the battalion were fortunate enough to receive their operational service medals from His Royal Highness The Prince of Wales in March 2017 at a parade which also celebrated His Royal Highness' 40 years as Colonel-in-Chief of Gurkha infantry

Following in 2RGR's footsteps, 1RGR deployed on Operation Toral 7 in November of 2018. On arrival in theatre, the battlegroup doubled in size when it took under command a company from the

1st Battalion The Royal Anglian Regiment, a Danish Company and platoons from Estonia and Australia. Interestingly, one of the most challenging aspects of the pre-deployment training for what is effectively

Left: Members of 2RGR reunited with their families in Sir John Moore Barracks at the end their deployment on Operation Toral 3.

Below left: Members of 2RGR at Buckingham Palace on 14 March 2017 to receive operational service medals for their deployment on Operation Toral 3. Their Royal Highnesses The Prince of Wales and Prince Harry presented the medals. The parade was also an opportunity to celebrate His Royal Highness The Prince of Wales' 40 years as the Colonel-in-Chief of Gurkha Infantry, a quite remarkable achievement (image Crown copyright 2017).

Below: Taken in November 2018, this photograph shows soldiers from 1RGR deploying to Afghanistan at the start of their deployment on Operation Toral 7.

a protected mobility role was qualifying sufficient men to drive the nine-tonne Foxhound armoured vehicles used to transport personnel around Kabul. As well as providing protected mobility for NATO advisors, the 2RGR battlegroup also had to provide a quick reaction force (QRF) capable of responding to incidents that required an armed NATO presence, such as a large scale insurgent attack. It was in this capacity that elements of both B and C Companies found themselves deploying to support the ANSF when, only a few weeks after the battalion's arrival in theatre, the Taliban mounted a concerted attack on Camp Anjuman in Kabul.[179] As a result of their quick deployment, the 1RGR battlegroup were able to rescue over 200 personnel, many of them injured ex-Gurkha security guards.

As this chapter explains, the RGR's tasks over the seventeen years that it has been deploying to Afghanistan have ranged from aggressive operations

Two soldiers from 1RGR in December 2018 comparing notes during a training exercise on Operation Toral 7. Although deployed on operations, the battalion worked hard to maintain its skills throughout the tour.

A soldier from 1RGR explains
the finer points of the Kukri
to two British soldiers during
Operation Toral 7.

A soldier from 1RGR explains the finer points of the Kukri to two British soldiers during Operation Toral 7.

against hardened Taliban fighters down in Helmand Province through to, more recently, the provision of protected mobility for NATO personnel in Kabul. However, whatever the task, the RGR has taken the same professional approach to its execution, firmly establishing itself as one of the most capable and versatile of the British Army's infantry units and proving beyond any doubt that it is every bit as competent as its antecedent regiments. The dedication shown by officers and soldiers of the Regiment in Afghanistan, whether serving with the battalions, in GRCs, with special forces or in individual appointments, has been outstanding and has resulted in the award of a Conspicuous Gallantry Cross, eight Military Crosses and one Distinguished Service Order (DSO), as well as numerous other awards and commendations. The recipients of these and other awards are listed in Appendix 2. But as this chapter has also tried to highlight, such commitment has come at a significant cost. To date, the RGR has lost fourteen killed in action, with many more officers and soldiers sustaining injuries, both mental and physical, that have changed their lives forever. Some of these have gone on to achieve remarkable things. Lower limb amputees Corporal Netra Rana and Rifleman Kushal Kumar Limbu, for example, won a number of gold and silver medals at the 2018

Invictus Games and Corporal Haribahadur Budha Magar, the first above-the-knee double amputee to summit a peak of more than 19,000 feet, now has his sights set firmly on Everest in 2019, though whether the Nepalese Government will grant authority for his climb to go ahead remains to be seen. Others have just tried to get on with their lives, overcoming their disabilities with dignity and courage through hard work, dedication and the support of their friends and families. All of them are inspirational people and fine examples of what it means to be a member of the RGR. Not surprisingly, the Regiment is immensely proud of them all.

Reflecting on the RGR's time in Afghanistan, the Colonel of the Regiment, Major General Gez Strickland, who was awarded a Distinguished Service Order in recognition of his "flawless judgement"[180] and leadership during 1RGR's tour on Operation Herrick 12, offered the following thoughts:[181]

"The insurgency in southern Afghanistan evolved constantly throughout the RGR's commitment there. The Taliban proved an adaptable adversary, battling to win and retain the support of the people. Tactically, they were astute, conducting hit and run attacks with small arms, rocket propelled grenades and occasionally mortars and rockets. They mastered the

The Colonel of The Regiment (on the right), as the
Commanding Officer of 1RGR during Operation
Herrick 12, talking with Commander ISAF,
General David Petraeus, on 23 September 2010.

Below: The operational service medal
for Afghanistan awarded to members of
the RGR who served in the theatre. The
qualifying period for the medal is 30 days
continuous service, or 45 days of service on
working visits within Afghanistan aggregated
over a period of one calendar year.

*production of improvised explosive devices, reducing
the metal content and offsetting battery packs so as
to minimise the chances of detection by the metal
detectors carried by all our patrols. They set up
alternative government structures, most importantly
offering local justice that the Afghan government was
failing to provide. But at its heart, the insurgency was
a power struggle between different Afghan factions
tied up in tribal rivalries, all vying for control of the
various levers of power. The central core of Helmand,
including the towns of Lashkar Gah and Gereshk, was
the prize. The rest of the Helmand River valley was
the battleground on the periphery. The Taliban aimed
to limit the coalition's freedom to operate, just as the
coalition sought to do the same back to the Taliban.
But of course the UK's operations were only a part of*

*the overall battle for the Pashtun South. Kandahar
remained the centre of control throughout, but with
the exceptions of 1RGR's tour in 2007–08 and the
company-level tours before 2006, the bulk of the RGR
effort went into the Helmand River Valley. During the
many deployments there, Gurkhas were involved in a
range of activities; fighting to clear the Taliban from
areas under their control, building relationships to
win the battle of the narrative, patrolling to dominate
the area, establishing checkpoints and patrol bases,
defending against Taliban attacks, and partnering and
training the Afghan National Army and Police. The
work was slow and painstaking, involving much risk
and the need for strategic patience, but our soldiers
revelled in it, understanding as few others do, the
human nature of the conflict."*

SPORTS AND ADVENTUROUS TRAINING

Sport and adventurous training play an important role in The Royal Gurkha Rifles (RGR). Not only do they provide an interesting way of maintaining the highest levels of physical fitness but they also help develop team spirit, leadership ability, personal determination and many other individual qualities. This short Special Interest Section provides an insight into some of the sports and adventurous training successes that the RGR has achieved in recent years.

SPORT

The British Army believes that sport provides the following benefits:[182]

1RGR being awarded the Nepal Cup for winning the Brigade of Gurkhas' annual football competition in 2011.

- Promotes development of the Army's Core Values and Standards.
- Promotes development of the Army Leadership Code.
- Development of teamwork, team spirit, determination and esprit de corps.
- Development of physical and mental fitness, general health and well-being.
- Development of military skills.
- Provision of welfare, a healthy work/life balance and an opportunity to foster and improve morale.
- Recruiting and retention positive.
- Direct contribution to the achievement of the aims and objectives set out in the International Defence Engagement Strategy (IDES).
- Provides opportunities for Civilian Engagement.
- Provides opportunities for 'decompression' from prolonged military tasks.

- Provides opportunities to facilitate recovery, rehabilitate from injury and provide activity for Wounded, Injured and Sick (WIS) personnel.
- Provides opportunities for positive media communication.
- Provides opportunities for personal development through the learning of new skills or the gaining of sports officiating and coaching qualifications in order to ensure sport is delivered safely.

The Army's view is that "the benefits listed above all combine to produce officers and soldiers who are more motivated, physically robust and better able to withstand the physical and psychological stresses of operations and capable of projecting the British Army as a collaborative organisation".[183]

Right: 1RGR in the final of the Nepal Cup 2011 which took place in July during the annual Brigade 'Bhela'.

Below right: A senior Gurkha officer reads out the results of the Nepal Cup. This key event, which takes place in Aldershot each year, is attended by hundreds of spectators, including many retired Gurkhas and their families.

The RGR recognises these benefits and plays a wide variety of both team and individual sports to a high level. For example, the Regiment has won the Brigade of Gurkhas' annual football competition, the Nepal Cup, many times over the last 25 years, most recently in 2018 when 2RGR secured victory in a nail-biting final against 1RGR. The RGR's sporting success is not just confined to the more 'traditional' Gurkha sports; as well as winning the Army Volleyball Championships numerous times, the RGR has also won the Army Canoe Polo Championships and the Army Squash Championships in recent years.

Pipes and Drums from 1RGR and The Queen's Own Gurkha Logistic Regiment (QOGLR) at the final of the 2011 Nepal Cup.

Above: The Commanding Officer and Gurkha Major of 2RGR with the battalion's football team after winning the Nepal Cup in 2018.

Above right: Colonel Brigade of Gurkhas offering advice to 2RGR's cricket team. 2RGR reached the final of the Army Major Inter-Unit Cup in 2015, losing narrowly to the 4th Battalion The Rifles.

Right: During the final of the Army Major Inter-Unit Cricket Competition in 2015, 2RGR managed to score 148 runs. Unfortunately, it was not quite enough to beat 4 RIFLES.

Left: Although unlikely to become a mainstream sport in the Regiment, an RGR officer tries his hand at wrestling a Mongolian soldier during 1RGR's tour on Operation Toral 7 in Afghanistan.

Top left: A member of 1RGR taking first place in a table-tennis competition organised by the Romanian contingent during the battalion's recent tour in Afghanistan on Operation Toral 7.

Top right: Soldiers from 1RGR in March 2008 doing a spot of fishing in Afghanistan during the battalion's tour on Operation Herrick 7.

Above: Leading by example! The Commanding Officer of 2RGR taking part in a Rugby 7s competition on Boxing Day 2008 in Afghanistan on Operation Herrick 9.

Rugby has always been popular in Brunei, with the Flying Kukris taking part in competitions across Asia, but cricket is also gaining momentum, with 2RGR reaching the finals of the Army Major Inter-Unit Competition in 2015. The Regiment has also had considerable success in tennis, table-tennis, boxing, tae kwon do, sports climbing, Trailwalker and a range of other sports.

Above: A member of the RGR taking part in Exercise Frosted Blade, the Infantry Skiing Championships in Val D'Isere, France.

Right: All sport in the RGR is taken seriously – even a tug-of-war against the British Officers during Regimental Birthday celebrations. Taken on 1 July 2011, the Gurkha team in this photograph demolished the British team!

Top: The final of the 2019 Army Volleyball Championships was an all RGR affair with 2RGR beating eight time champions 1RGR to win the title.

Above: The RGR has enjoyed considerable success in Army running competitions over the last 25 years, winning a number of individual and team championships. This photograph shows the 1RGR cross-country team which came second in the Army Cross-Country Championships in 2016.

Right and below right:
Members of 1RGR (Rifleman Rakesh Sunwar) nd 2RGR (Corporal Umesh Gurung) with their battalion flags at an altitude of 8,848 metres above sea level on the summit of Everest in May 2017. Four members of the Regiment reached the top of the world as part of the Gurkha Everest Expedition's 13 man summit team. The expedition's first attempt in 2015 had to be abandoned when severe earthquakes shook Nepal.

Adventurous Training

The UK Joint Services define adventurous training as: "challenging outdoor training for Service personnel in specified adventurous activities that incorporates controlled exposure to risk, in order to develop: leadership; teamwork; physical fitness; moral and physical courage; as well as other personal attributes and skills that are vital to the delivery of Operational Capability".[184]

The RGR has been extremely active on the adventurous training front throughout its 25-year history, pushing the limits of human endurance in activities ranging from scuba diving through to mountaineering. Most recently, the RGR succeeded in putting soldiers on the summit of Everest, a magnificent achievement by any standards. In addition, officers from the Regiment have rowed across the Atlantic Ocean and completed a solo expedition across the Antarctic to the South Polo. The only constraint appears to be the imagination of the officers and soldiers who take part in these activities.

Left: Lieutenant Scott Sears RGR at the South Pole on Boxing Day in 2017, becoming the youngest person ever to reach the South Pole on his own and unsupported in only 38 days.

Left: In January 2018, Captain John Armstrong RGR and his teammate won the pairs category in the Talisker Whisky Atlantic Challenge by rowing across the Atlantic Ocean in 37 days 8 hours and 8 minutes, setting a new world record.

Below: Adventurous training can be a team activity as well as an individual one as this photograph of members of 2RGR mountain biking in Bali in 2018 shows.

CHAPTER 6

Other Operational Deployments

As well as completing multiple operational tours in the Balkans, Sierra Leone and Afghanistan, and deploying to East Timor in September 1999 as part of an international force (INTERFET) to restore peace and security, The Royal Gurkha Rifles (RGR) has also taken part in numerous other short-term operational deployments over the last 25 years. These have been diverse in nature and have ranged from, for example, a non-combatant evacuation operation (NEO) in the Ivory Coast through to assisting with flood defences and helping to contain foot and mouth disease in the UK. This chapter does not aim to provide an exhaustive examination of these deployments, but seeks to provide an insight into some of them in order to demonstrate just how versatile and adaptable the RGR is.

OPERATION DETERMINANT, ZAIRE (THE DEMOCRATIC REPUBLIC OF THE CONGO) – APRIL 1997

In early 1997, the situation in Zaire started to deteriorate as the rebel forces of General Laurent Kabila began to move from the east of the country towards the capital city of Kinshasa. Kabila's intention was to replace the repressive regime of President Sese Seko Mobuto with a democratically elected government. However, it was assumed that Mobuto would not go peacefully and that the

rebels would therefore try to oust him in a coup. The UK's response, which was known as Operation Determinant, was to position very high readiness forces in Brazzaville, the capital of the neighbouring country of the Republic of the Congo, and then deploy them forward to Kinshasa to evacuate British nationals and other entitled personnel should the city erupt in violence. The high readiness forces included the 1st Battalion The Princess of Wales's Royal Regiment (1PWRR), which was on duty as the Spearhead Land Element (SLE) at the time.

B (Sobraon) Company, a Gurkha Reinforcement Company that had joined 1PWRR in December

The Company Command team of B (Sobraon) Company 1PWRR in Brazzaville waiting to deploy forward to Kinshasa to evacuate entitled personnel if the situation in the city deteriorated when General Laurent Kabila attempted to seize power from President Sese Seko Mobuto.

Soldiers from B (Sobraon) Company 1PWRR training whilst waiting to deploy forward to Kinshasa. Note the Russian made fighter aircraft in the background.

Inside one of the hovercraft that would have been used to help evacuate British nationals and other entitled personnel had the situation in Kinshasa turned violent.

Although most of the time that B (Sobraon) Company 1PWRR spent waiting to see whether there would be a need to evacuate people from Kinshasa was spent training, there was some downtime!

1996, deployed to Brazzaville with its parent battalion on 28 April 1997 and waited. Attempts to negotiate a peaceful solution to the problem eventually failed and, as Kabila's forces came ever closer to Kinshasa, people feared the worst. However, as soon as it became apparent that his days were numbered, Mobuto fled the country. This caught everyone by surprise but ensured that the rebels took Kinshasa peacefully. There was therefore no need for 1PWRR to conduct a NEO. This came as something of a disappointment to B (Sobraon) Company as its mission, had the evacuation been required, was to secure the British Embassy, as well as the routes to it. These were exciting tasks and would have "guaranteed a prominent role in the operation".[185] Putting a brave face on it, B (Sobraon) Company noted that "our deterrent presence in Brazzaville was judged to have been a restraining influence on all parties to the conflict, so we can take comfort that we made a positive contribution – albeit in an indirect manner!"[186] The company returned to UK on 22 May 1997.[187]

OPERATION TELIC, IRAQ – 2003

In 2003, the UK joined a US-led coalition to overthrow Saddam Hussein in Iraq. The UK's contribution to this included 16 Air Assault Brigade with the 1st Battalion The Royal Irish Regiment (1RIRISH) under command. One of 1RIRISH's rifle companies was D (Gurkha) Company, the GRC originally formed in November 1996 for service with 1PWRR as B (Sobraon) Company that had transferred to 1RIRISH in December 1999. Brigadier Christopher Bullock describes D (Gurkha) Company's role on Operation Telic:

"D (Gurkha) Company, the reinforcement company with 1st Battalion The Royal Irish Regiment, was preparing to disband when it was warned to accompany its parent battalion on 'Operation Telic,' the invasion of Iraq. After a training period in Wales, Gurkha Company accompanied 1st Royal Irish to Kuwait, crossing the border into Iraq on 21 March 2003.[188] Their first task was to secure the vital oilfields at Rumailah and ensure there were no enemy forces still in the area, as well as conducting

Top: A soldier from D (Gurkha) Company 1RIRISH in Iraq during Operation Telic. Note the respirator in the carrying case strapped to the soldier's leg. The threat from chemical and biological weapons was considered to be high during the deployment and all ranks therefore had to carry their respirators with them at all times.

Above: Preparing hasty defensive positions during a road move. The threat from enemy indirect fire and the possibility of an enemy airstrike meant that hasty defensive positions had to be prepared whenever the company stopped for more than a few minutes.

Below: Waiting for action. Soldiers from D (Gurkha) Company 1RIRISH wait for orders to move out during Operation Telic. The company was in Iraq from 21 March 2003 until mid May 2003 as part of the UK's contribution to the US-led coalition.

Bottom: A Gurkha soldier stands in the foreground whilst behind him oil wells burn during Operation Telic in 2003.

vehicle checkpoints around the periphery of Basra. The Gurkhas and their comrades were then ordered to push on up the River Euphrates to El Medina and Al Amarah, following the footsteps of their predecessors 87 years before. There, in spite of harassment and abuse, by continual patrolling they restored order and stopped looting. By the time the Gurkhas left three months later, they had instilled sufficient confidence in the local police to be able to conduct joint patrols with them. On return to Britain they disbanded and the personnel returned to their parent units."[189]

OPERATION PHILLIS, THE IVORY COAST – NOVEMBER 2004

On 11 November 2004, C Company 1RGR, supported by a small team from battalion headquarters headed up by the Commanding Officer, deployed to Accra in Ghana to prepare to conduct a NEO in the Ivory Coast. Once in Accra, 1RGR met up with lead elements from the UK's high readiness Joint Force Headquarters (JFHQ), commanded by Brigadier Barney White-Spunner, and a squadron of Special Forces (SF). The NEO had been requested by the British Ambassador to the Ivory Coast because of the increasing level of civil unrest in the country caused by a group calling itself the *Jeune Patriotes* (Young Patriots). As well as being anti-government, the *Jeune Patriotic* were also anti-French as they perceived the French forces based there to be supportive of the regime.

After a night of planning and preparation in a quiet corner of Accra airport, C Company Group deployed to Abidjan in the Ivory Coast on the morning of 12 November 2004 in RAF C130s. The situation that greeted them when they landed at the airport was chaotic as many different nations had despatched military teams to evacuate their own nationals from the country. With no overall coordination, it was every nation for itself and C Company came tearing out of the C130s in Land Rovers and disappeared into Abidjan to try to get ahead of the other military rescue teams. C Company's primary tasks were to secure the Embassy, releasing members of the SF to go up-country, and then escort British nationals and other entitled personnel from the Embassy to the airport in order

165

The Operations Officer of 1RGR briefing C Company Group on the outline plan for the evacuation of entitled personnel from the British Embassy in the Ivory Coast. The photograph, one of very few from the operation, was taken on the night of 11 November 2004 in a hangar on an airfield in Accra, Ghana.

that they could be evacuated to Ghana. The battalion headquarters team deployed to a nearby French camp and set up alongside the lead elements from the JFHQ. By last light, the operation was complete and the company group was back in Ghana, having helped evacuate 220 British nationals and other entitled personnel.[190]

Although short in duration, the deployment to the Ivory Coast, which went under the name of Operation Phillis, served to remind the battalion that being on standby as the UK's very high readiness SLE brought with it the very real possibility of deploying on operations at extremely short notice. This understanding brought additional focus to the battalion's training, as well as a degree of excitement whenever it was the battalion's turn to be the SLE.

Six months after the earthquake of 25 April 2015, much of the village of Barpak, which was the epicentre of the first earthquake to hit Nepal, remains in ruins. Although the large building in the centre of the photograph appears untouched, fractures to its supporting structures meant that it was extremely unsafe to use.

Below: The earthquakes of April and May 2015 were felt across much of Nepal and caused extensive damage in Kathmandu as well as in the countryside.

Right: Before the earthquake this was a thriving community school near the epicentre of the first earthquake in Barpak. Pages from school books can be seen mixed in with rubble from the walls and roof that collapsed. Fortunately, the first earthquake struck on a Saturday so the schools were largely empty.

Operations Layland and Marmat, Nepal – 2015 and 2016

On 25 April and 12 May 2015, Nepal was hit by devastating earthquakes that killed nearly 9,000 people and injured 22,000. The earthquakes destroyed 600,000 homes and damaged a further 288,000, affecting the lives of nearly 8 million people and making them the worst natural disasters to hit Nepal since 1934.[191] The UK's immediate response to this, which went under the name of Operation Layland, was aimed at providing emergency support and humanitarian relief to those most affected by the earthquakes. Operation Marmat, which followed, was focused on post-earthquake reconstruction. The RGR contributed to both, deploying teams on Operation Layland in 2015 and Operation Marmat in 2016.

The immediate priority in the aftermath of the earthquakes was to make what remained of the buildings safe; often this meant pulling them down.

Reaching some of the communities affected by the earthquakes was hard work. Many of the more remote villages still do not have road access and even those that do frequently found their roads blocked by landslides caused by the earthquakes.

167

Left: A non-commissioned officer from 2RGR giving a lesson on model making to a group of Kenyan soldiers in October 2017.

Below: Taken in 2014 during Operation Newcombe, this photograph shows the relaxed yet respectful relationship that existed between the Gurkhas and Malian troops. The Gurkhas' natural ability to empathise with other cultures helps make them highly effective on operations and in training teams.

Overseas Training Teams

Over the last 25 years, the RGR has been tasked to deploy short term training teams (STTT) to numerous different countries. One of the RGR's first tasks of this sort was in August 1996, when 1RGR deployed a 10-man team to Nepal for three weeks to help teach low-level tactics to a cadre of army instructors. More recently, both battalions have deployed teams to Mali on Operation Newcombe, the name for the UK's contribution to the EU training mission (EUTM) in the country. This is a particularly interesting and important task as the training being delivered is to prepare members of the Malian Armed Forces for operations in the north of the country. Other teams have deployed to Lebanon, Gabon, Kenya, Canada, Cyprus, Saudi Arabia, Malawi and Uganda to name but a few of the countries that the RGR has helped. Soldiers from the RGR are particularly effective at delivering these training tasks, not just because of their own high standards and wealth of operational experience, but also because Gurkhas appear to have higher levels of cultural empathy than their British counterparts.

A non-commissioned officer from 2RGR giving a lesson on survival to members of the Kenyan Army in 2017.

Left: Leading by example! The Commanding Officer and Adjutant of 2RGR in Mali in 2014 setting the pace with their Brigade Commander who was visiting from the UK.

Below: Poised for action, an instructor from 2RGR waits in the treeline with Malian soldiers for the training serial to start. The photograph was taken in 2014 during Operation Newcombe, the UK contribution to the EU training mission in Mali.

A Gurkha instructor from 2RGR on the ranges on Operation Newcombe in early 2015. As the best shots in the British Army (*see* Special Interest Section 4), members of the RGR are well placed to teach other soldiers how to shoot. Note the blue badge on the instructor's left arm, the tactical recognition flash of the EU Training Mission (EUTM).

Above: The Falkland Islands provides superb training opportunities for an infantry company. This photograph shows a soldier from G (Tobruk) Company taking part in field firing on Onion Range.

Below: G (Tobruk) Company's deployment to the Falkland Islands in Spring 2009 provided an ideal opportunity for the company to carry out field firing before deploying to Afghanistan on Operation Herrick 12 from April until October 2010.

THE FALKLAND ISLANDS

Although not an operational deployment in the sense that troops deploying to the Falkland Islands might expect to be in combat, as they would in Afghanistan, their presence undoubtedly has a deterrent effect and it is therefore worth mentioning them in this chapter. Beginning with B Company 3RGR's deployment in late November 1995, many RGR companies and GRCs have deployed to the Falklands as the Roulement Infantry Company (RIC) over the last 25 years. A (Gallipoli) Company, a GRC attached to the 1st Battalion The Highlanders (Seaforth, Gordons and Camerons) deployed there in July 2000 and had this to say about the RIC task:

"The 18 week RIC tour is perhaps one of the best-kept secrets of the Army. Based in Mount Pleasant Complex with platoon locations a few miles south at Mare Harbour and a well-established training camp at Onion

Range to the north, it offers unrivalled opportunities for training and in particular field firing. For the initial 10 weeks of the tour, platoons rotate between Mare Harbour, patrols and field firing at Onion Range".[192]

In commenting on the Mare Harbour task, the Company reported that "the most enjoyable aspect was the fishing – the record of 68 White Mullet on a single evening was achieved by 2 Platoon".[193]

Members of G (Tobruk) Company, a GRC attached to the 1st Battalion The Mercian Regiment (Cheshire), in the Falkand Islands in 2009 on Exercise Cape Bayonet.

The Prime Minister, David Cameron, visiting members of 2RGR deployed on Operation Pitchpole in February 2014. As part of this, 2RGR deployed two companies to the Chertsey area to support those affected by the floods. 2RGR's deployment on this task lasted from 16 to 22 February 2014.[194]

UK Operations

The UK-based RGR battalion is frequently called upon to provide support to the civilian authorities. As well as adding value, these tasks are invariably interesting and help keep the RGR in the public eye. The RGR's first major commitment of this sort occurred in April and May 1997 when B (Gallipoli) Company, the GRC attached to the 1st Battalion The Royal Scots (1RS), took part in Operation Fresco, the provision of a fire fighting capability during industrial action by the fire and rescue services. More recent commitments have included deploying two rifle companies to help those affected by floods in February 2014 (on Operation Pitchpole) and assisting with the provision of key point security at the 2014 Commonwealth Games in Glasgow (on Operation Comet).

A soldier from the RGR helps prepare flood defences during Operation Pitchpole, the name given to support to the civilian authority during the floods of February 2014.

Above: No task too complex! A soldier from 2RGR demonstrating his mastery of the scanner at one of the fixed locations during the 2014 Commonwealth Games. The name given to support to the games was Operation Comet.

Left: The RGR can be relied upon to do the job properly, whatever the task. This photograph, which was taken in July 2014, shows a soldier from 2RGR searching a vehicle before granting access to one of the sports locations used during the 2014 Commonwealth Games in Glasgow.

THE GURKHA KUKRI

The Gurkhas are famous for their fighting knife, known as the kukri or 'khukuri'. Short, broad-bladed and with a distinctive curve, the kukri is widely used in the hills of Nepal for chopping wood, killing animals, opening cans, clearing undergrowth and indeed any other task that requires a strong blade. Young men learn to use the kukri from a very early age, and it is this deep familiarity with the weapon that makes it so effective in the hands of a Gurkha soldier. By the time a young man joins the Army in his late teens or early twenties, the kukri has effectively become an extension of his dominant arm. This short Special Interest Section looks at the background to the kukri and examines why, even after hundreds of years, the kukri remains a key part of a Gurkha soldier's personal armoury – indeed, the prospect of a soldier from the RGR deploying on operations without his kukri remains as unthinkable today as it was over 200 years ago, when Gurkhas were first recruited into the service of the British Crown.

Above right: This painting shows the Gurkhas of one of the RGR's antecedent regiments using their kukris in battle during the Anglo-Sikh Wars of the 1840s. Note the pun on the Gurkhas' knife in the caption: "the Nusseree Battalion teaching the Sikhs the art of cookery".

Right: Gurkhas from The Royal Gurkha Rifles (RGR) on guard at Buckingham Palace in 2015 during the celebrations to mark 200 years of Gurkha Service to the British Crown. Soldiers in the RGR have two kukris, a ceremonial one, as shown in this photograph, which is carried on parades and other formal occasions, and a 'working' one, which is carried on operations and exercises (image copyright Richard Pohle 2015).

A modern military kukri is usually about 30cm in length. The scabbard contains two pockets at the back to hold a pair of small knives. One of these, the *chakmak*, is for sharpening the kukri and can be used with a flint to create a spark. The other, the *karda*, is used as a penknife for skinning animals.

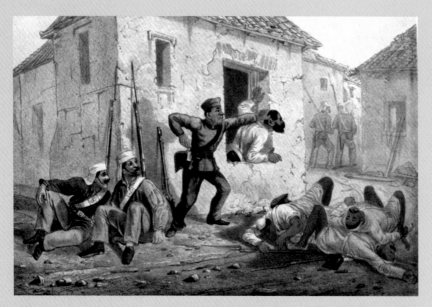

Left: A painting of the storming of Delhi in 1857 showing 'the incident at Subjee Mundi'. A soldier from the Sirmoor Battalion (later the 2nd Gurkhas, one the RGR's antecedent regiments) is about to draw his kukri and decapitate a mutineer.

Below: A painting by Jason Askew of the Sirmoor Battalion (later 2nd Gurkhas) defending Hindu Rao's house against an assault by mutineers during the Indian Mutiny of 1857. The kukri carried by today's soldiers is little different to that carried by the Gurkha in the centre of the painting. Then as now, it is a lethal weapon in the hands of a Gurkha.

There are a number of different theories about the origin of the kukri. One theory is that it is a descendent of the *machaira*, the curved cavalry sword of the ancient Macedonians carried by Alexander's horsemen when he invaded north-west India in the Fourth Century BC.[195] Another not necessarily contradictory theory is that it originates from a form of knife used by the Mallas who came to power in Nepal in the Thirteenth Century.[196] Arguably the most credible theory is that it was developed in isolation by the peasants of Nepal. Its size and dimensions may have been shaped by the environment, as a longer weapon would have been impractical given the very steep hillsides that characterise much of Nepal.

A rifleman of the 3rd Gurkhas taken in the Regimental home of Almorah in India circa 1907. The kukri is worn on the soldier's right hip with the handle free of obstruction, enabling the kukri to be easily drawn when required.

A group of Gurkhas from the 3rd Gurkhas circa 1890. Note the kukris being held by the two soldiers bottom right.

Although the picture was taken about a hundred years ago during the First World War, the kukris that Gurkhas use on contemporary operations remain virtually unchanged from those shown in the photograph. The caption reads: "The Great European War: Gurkhas sharpening their kukris so dreaded by the Huns".

Although all kukris have a similar basic shape, there are a number of different variations on the theme. Historically, kukris from the west of Nepal tended to be short and 'round-bellied' whilst those from the eastern districts had longer, more slender blades.[197] Kukris used for ceremonial or sacrificial purposes, such as chopping the head off a water buffalo during the Hindu festival of 'Dashera' or 'Dashain', are necessarily bigger and heavier. *Kothimora* kukris, which are frequently given as gifts to esteemed people, are highly polished and often have intricate silver designs on the scabbard. Within the RGR, *Kothimora* kukris are given as awards in recognition of outstanding service. For example, the winners of both the Prince of Wales' Kukri (see Appendix 8) and the Tuker Award (see Appendix 9) both receive *Kothimora* kukris.

A soldier from the 9th Gurkhas demonstrates the use of the kukri to incapacitate an adversary as a group of senior officers approach. Although this photograph was taken in 1945, young Gurkha soldiers are still taught the same slashing action during recruit training.

A rifleman of the 10th Gurkhas, one of the RGR's antecedent regiments, smiles as he tests the edge of his kukri. The photograph was taken in Italy in 1945.

Soldiers from RGR practising their kukri drills in Bosnia in 2005. Its size and shape make the kukri an ideal weapon for close quarter fighting (image Crown copyright 2005).

Modern military kukris tend to be about 30cm in length. The blades are made of steel[198] and have a distinctive notch near the handle known as the *kaura*. There are numerous interesting explanations of its presence.[199] One of these is that it is an ingenious aiming sight for when the kukri is thrown at a target. Another is that it is to stop blood running down the blade and onto the handle. Yet another is that it is to catch and then neutralise an enemy blade. Whilst the latter two explanations might contain an element of truth, the reality is that the *kaura* is a decorative Hindu religious and phallic symbol.

Gurkhas from The Royal Gurkha Rifles in Afghanistan.

When in the field, the kukri's scabbard is usually covered in camouflage material as in this photograph taken in Afghanistan on Operation Herrick.

The handle of the modern military kukri is usually made of dense wood. It is secured to the blade by rivets through the hilt or by flattening the end of the hilt over the bottom of the handle. On more expensive kukris, such as the *Kothimora* kukris described earlier, the handle might be made of bone, horn, ivory or even metal.

The scabbard is traditionally made of wood with a leather covering. There are two small pockets at the back of the scabbard to hold a pair of small knives, one for sharpening the kukri and one for skinning animals. The tip of the scabbard is protected by a metal cap. When worn in the field, the kukri is normally covered with camouflage material and attached to the soldier's combat belt or load-bearing system.

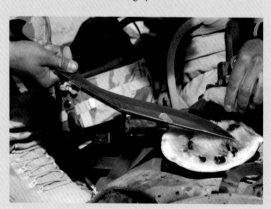

Above: As well as being a fearsome and effective weapon, Gurkhas use their kukris for everyday tasks. This photograph, taken in Afghanistan on Operation Herrick, shows a kukri being used to carve up a watermelon (image Crown copyright 2007).

Right: Young Nepalese men grow up using the kukri as a general utility tool in Nepal. During their basic training in the UK, they are taught how to turn this familiarity with the kukri into a lethal capability.

A soldier from 2RGR serving in a Provincial Reconstruction Team in Afghanistan on Operation Fingal in 2003. Note that his kukri is easily accessible, and ready for action, on his left hip (image Crown copyright 2003).

Bottom: Gurkhas using a kukri to prepare meat by candlelight in a remote Patrol Base on Operation Herrick in Afghanistan in 2010 (image Crown copyright 2010).

The ceremonial kukri (known as the *konra*) is usually about twice the size of the military kukri and has a large handle to allow the user to take a double-handed grip. Traditionally, the konra will be used to sacrifice a water buffalo during the Hindu festival of Dashain (or 'Dashera'). The soldier selected to do this is under real pressure. If he decapitates the animal with a single blow, then his unit will be blessed with good luck in the year ahead; if he fails to do this, then bad luck will follow. Although this practise still takes place in Nepal, it is not permitted in the UK.

The kukri is ubiquitous in Britain's Brigade of Gurkhas and, in particular, within the RGR. It has a prominent position on the Regiment's cap badge and features in the intricate design of the Queen's Truncheon, a magnificent silver and bronze staff

A Gurkha soldier in Afghanistan with a ceremonial kukri (known as a 'konra'). Note the two handed grip necessary to wield this kukri.

An RGR soldier in contemplative mood with his kukri drawn in Afghanistan (image Crown copyright 2009).

presented to one of the RGR's antecedent regiments in 1863 in recognition of its loyal and courageous service during the Indian Mutiny of 1857 (*see* Special Interest Section 1). But the kukri is not just an historic symbol. Although the basic design of the kukri has changed little over the centuries, it remains a potent weapon in the hands of a Gurkha, delivering lethal effect even on today's contemporary battlefield. As described in Chapter 5, its continued utility was demonstrated in Afghanistan when Lance Corporal Tuljung Gurung used his kukri to defeat two Taliban fighters who attacked his sangar position, an act of bravery for which he received the Military Cross (MC).

A soldier from 3rd Gurkhas about to decapitate a water buffalo in 1945 or 1946 as a sacrifice during the Hindu festival of Dashain. Severing the head with a single blow will bring the Battalion good luck in the year ahead – anything less will bring bad luck.

Soldiers from the Band of the Brigade of Gurkhas performing a kukri display to music.

A Gurkha soldier and his kukri. In 1948, the Prime Minister and Supreme Commander of Nepal, Maharaja Padma Shamsher Jangabahadur Rana, wrote that the kukri "is the national as well as the religious weapon of the Gurkhas. It is incumbent on a Gurkha to carry it while awake and to place it under the pillow when retiring"[200] (image copyright Amrit Thapa 2018).

Above middle: Gurkha paratroopers from the RGR with their kukris (image copyright Amrit Thapa 2018).

Below: Ready for action! A Gurkha in Afghanistan in March 2019 with his kukri clenched firmly between his teeth.

CHAPTER 7

The Jungle

During the Second World War, Colonel F Spencer Chapman DSO spent more than three years living in the jungles of Malaya, working with Malayan tribesmen and training Chinese guerrillas in order to disrupt the Japanese war effort. It was a remarkable achievement comparable, in many ways, to T E Lawrence's exploits with Arab irregulars during the First World War.[201] In 1949, Colonel Chapman wrote a book about his ordeal. A best-seller at the time, it remains the definitive authority on jungle operations. Its title, *The Jungle is Neutral*,[202] neatly summarised Chapman's view of this most demanding environment, having got to know it so intimately. In the book's foreword, Field Marshal Earl Wavell commented that, "the title of Colonel Spencer Chapman's work implies that if human beings have the fortitude to bear the malevolence and hazards of the jungle and the resource to use what benefits it produces, it has no particular objection to their living in it".[203]

Over the last seven decades, Gurkhas have repeatedly demonstrated that not only do they have the 'fortitude' and 'resource' to live in the jungle, but that they also have a natural affinity for it. Perhaps

A Gurkha soldier from 2RGR on exercise in the jungle of Brunei in 2017.

Left: An early morning shot of the Brunei jungle from high ground. Stretching for miles in all directions, it is easy to see why soldiering in this environment is so challenging.

Below: Junior soldiers being trained to operate in the jungle during their Junior Leaders Cadre (JLC). The Brunei based RGR battalion spends much of its time in the jungle, refining its skills so that it remains the world's most capable jungle force.

A detailed model being used to help explain the route that a patrol intends to follow to reach its objective deep in the jungle. This technique, which has changed little over the last 70 years, remains invaluable as modern satellite-based GPS systems often do not work in the jungle because of the heavy canopy.

surprisingly, over thirty percent of the world's land surface is still covered by forest or jungle and the ability to master this formidable and unforgiving environment therefore remains as important today as it always has been.[204] As 2RGR's rapid deployment to East Timor (in September 1999 – see Chapter 3) demonstrated, having a unit that is both trained and acclimatised for jungle operations can have strategic, as well as tactical, impact and it is for this reason that the Brunei based RGR battalion works so hard to maintain its edge. Understanding where and how the Gurkha infantry first established, and then consolidated, its jungle reputation is important as it helps explain why the RGR is almost fanatical in ensuring that it remains able to live and fight in this environment better than anyone else. Extreme proficiency in jungle warfare is, in many ways, a golden thread that connects the RGR to its famous antecedent regiments.

The Gurkha infantry's natural aptitude for jungle operations became widely apparent during the Burma Campaign of 1942 to 1945. As part of General 'Bill' Slim's 14th Army, the so-called 'Forgotten Army', they made a vital contribution to the overall success of the

Left: Brigadier (later Major General) Orde Wingate who commanded the Chindits. He was killed when his aircraft crashed during a visit to one of the strongholds established behind enemy lines during the Second Chindit Offensive.

Below: Taken at Imphal in 1943, this picture shows the Viceroy of India inspecting Gurkha survivors of the first Chindit operation.

Bottom: The parachute drop at Elephant Point by a composite Gurkha parachute battalion on 1 May 1945. The parachute insertion was part of Operation Dracula, the air, land and sea operation to seize Rangoon from the Japanese at the end of the Burma Campaign.

campaign and, specifically, to numerous operations conducted deep behind the enemy's front lines in the thickest of Burma's jungles. Their role in the two Chindit Operations led by Brigadier Orde Wingate deserves particular mention. The first of these began on 6 February 1943 and involved the deployment of seven columns into the jungle to disrupt Japanese lines of communication.[205] Of the 3,000 men involved, 1,289 were ethnic Gurkhas, the majority of whom were from the 3rd Battalion of the 2nd Gurkhas (3/2nd), one of the RGR's antecedent regiments. Although the operation arguably achieved little at the tactical level, with the force sustaining some 800 casualties, it was 'beyond price' as propaganda as it helped destroy the myth that the Japanese could not be beaten in the jungle.[206] The Gurkha contribution to the second Chindit Operation, which commenced in early March 1944, was equally as impressive. Four Gurkha units were involved in this ambitious operation (3/4th, 3/6th,

Below left: Rifleman Bhanbhagta Gurung who was awarded the Victoria Cross for single-handedly clearing five heavily defended enemy positions on the Snowden East feature near the village of Tamandu in Burma on 5 March 1945. Nine Victoria Crosses were awarded to Gurkhas for their bravery in the jungles of Burma during the Second World War.

Below right: A jungle river patrol being carried out by 10th Gurkhas in Malaya during the Emergency. Because the jungle is so dense, rivers act as main arterial routes through the jungle.

3/9th and 4/9th) which saw forces being air-landed by glider deep in the jungle to establish strongholds from which to harass the Japanese. This time, the operation was a tactical success as well as a public relations one.

Gurkhas continued to play a significant role in the remainder of the campaign, with a composite jungle trained Gurkha parachute battalion even taking part in Operation Dracula, the land, air and sea assault to recapture Rangoon, the capital of Burma, on 1 May 1945.[207] Given their contribution in Burma, it is no surprise that nine Gurkhas received Victoria Crosses for their bravery during the campaign, with many others receiving other honours and awards for their courage and leadership.

In 1948, the Gurkha infantry was again committed to operations in the jungle, this time fighting against the communist terrorists (CT) of the Malayan Races Liberation Army (MRLA), the action arm of the Malayan Communist Party (MCP),

during the so-called Malayan Emergency. For 12 years, the Gurkha infantry fought a "deadly game of hide and seek" in the jungles of Malaya,[208] often deploying for weeks at a time in order to track their quarry deep into the jungle. It was hard work and, as well as mental and physical robustness, it required a great deal of patience as John Cross, a Gurkha officer who served in Malaya, notes: "…for every million hours of security force endeavour in the Federation of Malaya the enemy was in the sight of a soldier's weapon for 20 seconds".[209] The conflict eventually ended on 1 August 1960. The Gurkha contribution to the outcome of the campaign was apparent to all involved: not only did they account for "…over a quarter of all eliminations during the Emergency" but they conducted themselves in a manner that earned the respect and gratitude of the Malayan people.[210] They also proved beyond any doubt that, when it came to jungle operations, they were second to none.

Below: Although the boats might have changed, rivers remain important as a way of penetrating the deepest parts of the jungle. This photograph, taken in June 2006, shows the RGR practising their river patrolling technique in a modern Hard Hulled Raiding Craft (HHRC). The Brunei based RGR battalion continues to maintain a highly effective riverine capability (image Crown copyright 2006).

Right: Belvedere helicopters were used throughout the Brunei Revolt to deploy troops deep into the jungle.

The next opportunity to demonstrate their jungle ability began on 8 December 1962 when the North Kalimantan National Army (TNKU) launched a rebellion in the British Protectorate of Brunei. The British responded quickly, deploying a force comprised of Gurkhas, Royal Marines and British infantry. By 17 December 1962, order had largely been restored but it was 2/7th Gurkhas who, having deployed into the jungle to track down the remaining insurgents, brought the Brunei Revolt to a conclusion by capturing the TNKU's military commander, Yassin Affendi, on 18 May 1963.[211]

The Borneo Confrontation, which began in April 1963, again provided an opportunity for the Gurkha infantry to demonstrate their mastery of this unique environment. It was a vicous war, fought at close quarters in the deepest jungles of Sarawak, Sabah and across the border in Indonesia. The enemy were Indonesian Border Terrorists (IBT) and regular Indonesian soldiers, including highly capable paratroopers and marines. As General Sir Walter Walker, who was Commander Land Forces and Director of Operations in Borneo, noted, they were "...very bright, a first-class enemy".[212] The British only really started to get the upper hand when British troops were eventually allowed to cross the border and conduct clandestine operations in Indonesia. These 'Claret' operations began in May 1964 and fell into two basic categories: either an ambush on a route known to be used by the enemy or an attack on a known base. They were extremely effective as they enabled the British forces to seize the initiative, depriving the enemy of the secure bases and routes they had become accustomed to; almost overnight, the hunter became the hunted. However, they required a high level of skill in jungle warfare, not least because helicopters were not allowed to cross the border and patrols therefore had to be inserted by foot. Water, food, ammunition, radios, first aid equipment and spare clothing all had to be carried for each 10 day operation, a significant task given the nature of the terrain and the extreme climate. In was on one such 'Claret' operation that Lance Corporal Rambahadur Limbu of 2/10th Gurkhas became

Far left: Lance Corporal Rambahadur Limbu of 2/10th Gurkhas who was awarded a Victoria Cross for his actions on 21 November 1965 during a secret cross border 'Claret' operation to try and capture an Indonesian prisoner.

Left: Captain Rambahadur Limbu VC MVO (on the left) on parade in June 2015, 50 years after being awarded the Victoria Cross for his bravery in the jungles of Borneo. Captain Rambahadur's Victoria Cross was the 26th to be awarded to members of the Gurkha infantry – he is the only surviving recipient (image Crown copyright 2015).

the last Gurkha soldier to be awarded the Victoria Cross, bringing the total number of Victoria Crosses awarded to Gurkhas for jungle operations to 10. The Borneo Confrontation ended on 11 August 1966. For three years and nine months, the RGR's antecedent regiments had been carrying the lion's share of the operational burden in some of the most inhospitable jungle in the world.

To maintain its competence in jungle operations, the RGR spends a great deal of its time on exercise in the jungles of Brunei. The following images aim to provide an insight into what this is like.

Although helicopters were used to great effect throughout the Borneo Confrontation, the nature of the terrain, and the fact that British helicopters were not allowed to cross the border into Indonesia, meant that soldiers had to patrol on foot as they played a deadly game of hide-and-seek against the Indonesian forces of President Sukarno.

Right: Gurkhas practising their river crossing technique in a swimming pool. Heavy rainfalls in the jungle often lead to flash floods that can turn even the smallest of streams into real obstacles. But rehearsing in the benign environment of a pool is a very different proposition to crossing a raging torrent in the middle of the jungle. This is far more dangerous; in 2004, Corporal Desbahadur Rai from C Company 2RGR sadly lost his life whilst carrying out a river crossing during a company level exercise in Brunei (image copyright Dharam Prakash Limbu 2018).

Below: Members of 2RGR take part in a military swimming test. Because water obstacles can prove to be so dangerous in the jungle, it is important that every member of the RGR is able to swim. Given Gurkhas come from Nepal, where there are very few opportunities to develop this skill at an early age, the PT staff have to work hard to ensure that everybody reaches the required standard. For this reason, all Gurkha infantry barracks have traditionally had their own swimming pool, a consequence of the Malayan Emergency (1948 to 1960) when more Gurkha infantry soldiers reputedly lost their lives through drowning than as a result of enemy action.

Below right: Water is a hazard but it also presents an opportunity in the jungle as this soldier from 1RGR, emerging from a jungle river with his rifle at the ready, demonstrates,.

Below: 1RGR on exercise in the jungle in 2007.

Bottom left: A Gurkha applies 'cam cream' before going on a patrol. The ability to blend into the jungle remains as important today as it did over 70 years ago during the Burma Campaign of the Second World War (image copyright Dharam Prakash Limbu).

Bottom right: Soldiers from 2RGR practise jungle patrolling during an exercise in Brunei in December 2017 (image copyright Dharam Prakash Limbu).

Right: The Commanding Officer of 1RGR (in the lighter-coloured jungle combats) briefs his brigade commander on a jungle exercise being conducted by the battalion in Brunei in September 2006. In September 1999, the officer, Lieutenant Colonel T C StJ Warrington MBE, commanded 2RGR's lead company group (based on A Company 2RGR) when it deployed at short notice to the island of East Timor on Operation Langar (see Chapter 3).

Below: Jungle operations place a premium on physical fitness, one reason why the Brunei-based Gurkha battalion carries out hard physical training almost every day. This photograph shows members of the 2RGR Junior Leader's Cadre in March 2018 taking part in a log race along the beach near Tuker Lines, the battalion's base in the south of Brunei.

Above: A soldier from A Company 2RGR in Afghanistan during Operation Herrick 14 (April 2011 to October 2011). As this image suggests, the RGR's jungle experience has proven to be extremely useful in trying to seize the initiative from the Taliban.

Left: River crossing skills learnt in the jungles of Brunei are invaluable in Afghanistan. This image was taken in May 2011 during 2RGR's tour on Operation Herrick 14 (April 2011 to October 2011).

Opposite: A Corporal from A Company 1RGR taking a well-deserved break in the cover of a cornfield during a patrol in Helmand Province, Afghanistan. 1RGR deployed on Operation Herrick 17 from October 2012 to April 2013, the battalion's second Afghan tour in 30 months. As they did during their first tour, the soldiers found their jungle skills were highly transferable to the Afghan environment (image Crown copyright 2012).

Left: Soldiers from 2RGR occupy a hasty defensive position during a jungle exercise in Brunei.

Below: Members of 2RGR finish a run with a quick dip in the sea in Brunei. Note the caption on the back of the soldiers' T-shirts. As Colonel F Spencer Chapman noted, the jungle is neutral, but it favours those who spend time understanding its ways and who prepare themselves for its hardships, including by maintaining an extreme level of physical fitness.

Some of the skills essential in jungle warfare, such as tracking, have proven to be transferable to other theatres. For example, in Afghanistan (see Chapter 5) RGR soldiers have used their ground sign awareness training to spot when Taliban fighters have placed IEDs on roads or paths. In addition, much of the terrain running alongside the main rivers in Afghanistan, which is where the rural populations tend to be located, is similar to jungle. The RGR's tracking skills have also been in demand in non-operational theatres.

In 2017, for example, a tracking instructor from 1RGR deployed to Gabon to teach park rangers how to track poachers through the dense jungle of the West-African country as the government sought to protect what remains of its wild elephant population.[213]

Above: Of the 26 Victoria Crosses awarded to members of the Gurkha infantry, 10 have been for acts of gallantry during jungle operations, nine during the Burma Campaign of the Second World War (1942–45) and one during the Borneo Confrontation (1963–66).

CHAPTER 8

Parades and Visits

Over its 25-year history, The Royal Gurkha Rifles (RGR) has taken part in numerous parades and hosted several hundred visitors. Many of these are described in other chapters and sections of this book, such as Special Interest Section 2 which covers visits by members of the Royal Family. This Chapter aims to provide an insight into some of the others, starting with visits by politicians and ending with unusual visits by, or to, members of the Regiment.

Above: In December 2008, the Prime Minister, Gordon Brown, visited 2RGR in Afghanistan. The battalion was midway through its tour on Operation Herrick 9 and, as this photograph shows, morale was high!

Left: The Pipes and Drums of the two RGR battalions have taken part in nearly all of the RGR's parades over the last 25 years. 1RGR's Pipes and Drums are shown here in January 2011 leading their battalion onto the parade square in Sir John Moore Barracks in order that His Royal Highness The Prince of Wales, the Regiment's Colonel-in-Chief, could present operational service medals to members of the battalion following their deployment in Afghanistan on Operation Herrick 12. With their fine music and precision marching, the Pipes and Drums can always be relied upon to bring a sense of occasion to any RGR event.

Left: Philip Hammond, Secretary of State for Defence, visited Afghanistan in February 2013 and met members of 1RGR deployed on Operation Herrick 17. During the visit, Mr Hammond observed that: "transition is proceeding very well – it is on track, the Afghans are taking more and more responsibility for planning and executing operations and British forces are more and more in an advising and assisting role".[215]

Visits by Secretaries of State for Defence

Soldiers from the RGR first deployed to Afghanistan in January 2002. Since then, RGR battalions and sub-units have completed numerous tours. It is therefore not surprising that they have hosted several visits by different Secretaries of State for Defence over the years.

In August 2010, Liam Fox, Secretary of State for Defence, met members of 1RGR during his second visit to Afghanistan. At the time, the battalion was deployed on Operation Herrick 12. A few weeks after his visit, one UK newspaper carried the headline: "Gurkha regiment faces axe as Liam Fox insists on £20bn Trident replacement".[214] Fortunately, this transpired not to be the case, as the proposal was just one of a range of measures being considered by the Ministry of Defence to meet savings targets.

It is not just British Defence Secretaries who find the RGR interesting, as this photograph of Ron Mark, New Zealand's Defence Minister, shows! The photograph was taken in September 2018 when A Company 2RGR were taking part in Exercise Pacific Kukri 18 in Tekapo, New Zealand.

Visit of Nicholas Soames MP, Minister of State for the Armed Forces

Nicholas Soames MP, the Armed Forces Minister at the time, was one of the first ministers to meet officers and soldiers of the newly formed RGR when he visited Hong Kong in late 1994. Speaking in the House of Commons several weeks after his visit, he stated that: "more recently, I returned from a visit to Hong Kong and Brunei, where I was able to see in detail how our garrisons go about their business and get a feel for the reality of the tasks that they perform. I am pleased to report that morale is high and one cannot fail to be struck by the energy and dedication on display".[216]

Visits by the Deputy Chief of the General Staff and the Army Sergeant Major

Top: The Gurkha officer commanding the Honour Guard awaits the arrival of the Deputy Chief of the General Staff and Army Sergeant Major at the start of their visit to 2RGR in Brunei in November 2017.

Above: The Army Sergeant Major, Warrant Officer Class 1 Glenn Haughton, signs the visitor's book in the Warrant Officers' and Sergeants' Mess during his visit to 2RGR in Brunei.

Below: The Deputy Chief of the General Staff, Lieutenant General Nick Pope, inspecting the Honour Guard at the start of his visit to 2RGR in Brunei. General Pope, who was Colonel Commandant Brigade of Gurkhas at the time, wears a garland in RGR colours presented by the Gurkha Major to welcome him to the battalion.

The Minister of State for the Armed Forces, Nicholas Soames MP, being briefed about the battalion's radios during his visit in late 1994. The RGR was only a few months old when this image was taken.

Right: The Mayor of Folkestone, Janet Andrews, presenting 2RGR with the Freedom of Folkestone on 18 June 2009. Stood on the Mayor's left are Joanna Lumley, actress and daughter of a Gurkha officer, and Michael Howard, the Member of Parliament for Folkestone and Hythe (image Crown copyright 2009).

Below: Local children cheer as 2RGR marches through the streets of Folkestone having received the Freedom of the Town (image Crown copyright 2009).

Freedom of Folkestone and visit of General Sir David Richards KCB CBE DSO ADC

On 18 June 2009, 2RGR marched through the town's streets to celebrate receiving the Freedom of Folkestone. After the parade, the battalion formed up in Sir John Moore Barracks and the Commander-in-Chief Land Forces, General Sir David Richards, presented members of the battalion with the operational service medal for Afghanistan. It was particularly fitting that General Richards

The Commander-in-Chief presenting the operational service medal for
Afghanistan on 18 June 2009 (image Crown copyright 2009).

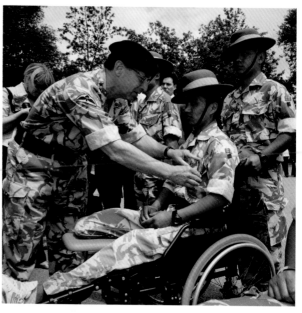

was able to present the medals as he was also
Colonel Commandant of the Brigade of Gurkhas
at the time. The battalion deployed to Afghanistan
from September 2008 to April 2009 on Operation
Herrick 9.

Above: The Commander-in-Chief
presenting the operational service
medal to Rifleman Anil Gurung,
who was injured by an IED whilst
in Afghanistan. Rifleman Anil
went on to win a gold medal as
a member of the Great Britain
Sitting Volleyball Team in the
2014 Invictus Games (image
Crown copyright 2009).

Left: A close-up of the operational
service medal for Afghanistan,
awarded to members of 2RGR
following their deployment on
Operation Herrick 9 (image
Crown copyright 2009).

Soldiers from G (Tobruk) Company meet two ladies from the Sun newspaper during a march through Chester in June 2009 by the 1st Battalion The Mercian Regiment (Cheshire) to exercise its Freedom of the City (image Crown copyright 2009).

FREEDOM OF CHESTER

On 3 June 2009, 350 soldiers from 1st Battalion The Mercian Regiment (Cheshire) (1MERCIAN) exercised their Freedom of the City of Chester by marching through the City. Marching with the battalion were members of G (Tobruk) Company, a Gurkha Reinforcement Company formed with soldiers from 1RGR in December 2008 to deploy with 1MERCIAN to Afghanistan on Operation Herrick 12 (from April to October 2010). Following its return from Afghanistan, G (Tobruk) Company was reattributed to 1RGR on 31 March 2011 to become D (Kandahar) Company 1RGR, deploying on Operation Herrick 17 with 1RGR in October 2012.

GURKHA 200 – 2015

From 1814 to 1816, the British East India Company fought two wars against Nepal to try to contain the country's expansionist aspirations. Impressed by the fighting qualities of their enemy, the British began

The Commanding Officer leading 1RGR on a parade in Brunei to mark the Gurkhas' 200 years of service to the British Crown. The Queen's Truncheon is carried by the Truncheon Jemadar and escorted by the Truncheon Party. The parade, which took place in October 2015, was reviewed by His Majesty The Sultan of Brunei.

recruiting Gurkhas into the ranks of the East India Company before the first war was even over. As explained in Appendix 17, the first three battalions of Gurkhas were formally raised on 24 April 1815 and were known as: the 1st Nusseree Battalion (later to become the 1st Gurkha Rifles); the Sirmoor Battalion (later 2nd Gurkha Rifles); and the Kumaon Battalion (later 3rd Gurkha Rifles). In 2015, the Gurkhas had served the British Crown for 200 years, a magnificent achievement that was celebrated in a number of parades.

Top: A Company Commander from the RGR leads his company during the Changing of the Guard at Buckingham Palace. During May 2015, the RGR took part in public duties in London as part of the Gurkha 200 celebrations (image copyright Richard Pohle 2015).

Above left: Gurkhas and Guards! The RGR take over from the Welsh Guards during the Changing of the Guard at Buckingham Palace (image copyright Richard Pohle 2015).

Above right: A Gurkha non-commissioned officer from the RGR gives orders during the Changing of the Guard at Buckingham Palace in May 2015 (image copyright Richard Pohle 2015).

Other Visits and Television

As well as hosting visits to the two battalions, serving and retired members of the RGR have also taken part in visits, such as the visit of Alan Titchmarsh and the team from *Love Your Garden* to the home of Corporal Haribahadur Budha Magar. Although Corporal Hari, who was wounded in an IED strike in Afghanistan on Operation Herrick 12, is actively involved in numerous charitable activities, he and his family were finding it difficult to manage their garden. Alan Titchmarsh and the *Love Your Garden* team therefore transformed it into a more easily managed "colourful and private sanctuary for the whole family".[217]

Above: In 2015, Lance Corporal Tuljung Gurung MC won the Uniformed and Civil Service category at the Asian Achievers Awards in London. Lance Corporal Tuljung was awarded the Military Cross (MC) for his bravery in defending his patrol base in Afghanistan against an attack by Taliban fighters on 22 March 2013. Lance Corporal Tuljung attended the awards ceremony with his wife.

Below: Corporal Haribahadur Budha Magar and his family with Alan Titchmarsh and members of the RGR after the *Love Your Garden* team had transformed Corporal Hari's garden. The programme showing the transformation was screened as Episode 3 of Series 6 of 'Love Your Garden' on Tuesday 12 July 2016.

APPENDIX 1

The Roll of Honour

551359	**Major A M Roberts**	1RGR	Afghanistan	4 October 2007
21170127	**Rifleman Yubraj Rai**	2RGR	Afghanistan	4 November 2008
21168855	**Colour Sergeant Krishnabahadur Dura**	2RGR	Afghanistan	15 November 2008
21169587	**Corporal Kumar Pun**	1RGR	Afghanistan	7 May 2009
551249	**Major J J Bowman**	RIFLES/1RGR[218]	Afghanistan	13 July 2010
25154732	**Lieutenant N Turkington**	1RGR	Afghanistan	13 July 2010
21169379	**Corporal Arjun Purja Pun**	1RGR[219]	Afghanistan	13 July 2010
21171487	**Rifleman Remand Kulung**	1RGR[220]	Afghanistan	12 August 2010
30047633	**Rifleman Suraj Gurung**	1RGR	Afghanistan	2 October 2010
30085734	**Rifleman Vijay Rai**	2RGR	Afghanistan	15 October 2011
30048322	**Rifleman Sachin Limbu**	1RGR	Afghanistan[221]	2 January 2012
21171410	**Lance Corporal Gajbahadur Gurung**	2RGR[222]	Afghanistan	27 January 2012
25194218	**Lieutenant E A Drummond-Baxter**	1RGR	Afghanistan	30 October 2012
21171435	**Lance Corporal Siddhanta Kunwar**	1RGR	Afghanistan	30 October 2012

Far left: His Royal Highness The Prince of Wales, Colonel-in-Chief of The Royal Gurkha Rifles, laying a wreath at the Memorial Wall in Sir John Moore Barracks, Shorncliffe on 28 January 2011 (image Crown copyright 2011).

Left: The wreath laid, and personally signed, by His Royal Highness The Prince of Wales at the Memorial Wall in Sir John Moore Barracks, Shorncliffe (image Crown copyright 2011).

Right: The Secretary of State for Defence, the Right Honourable Gavin Williamson CBE MP, pays his respects to the Regiment's Fallen during a visit to 2RGR in May 2018.

Below: The Colonel-in-Chief, Colonel Commandant of the Brigade of Gurkhas, Colonel of the Regiment, Commander 4 Mechanized Brigade and the Commanding Officer, Gurkha Major and Regimental Sergeant Major of 1RGR pay their respects to the Regiment's Fallen on 28 January 2011 at the Memorial Wall in Sir John Moore Barracks, Shorncliffe (image Crown copyright 2011).

Below right: Her Majesty The Queen paying her respects at the Armed Forces Memorial in the National Memorial Arboretum. The wall immediately in front of where Her Majesty is stood includes the names of some of the officers and soldiers from The Royal Gurkha Rifles who lost their lives on operations whilst serving with the Regiment (image Crown copyright).

2007

CBE	Colonel D G Hayes MBE
MBE	Major C R Boryer
MVO	Captain (QGO) Umeshkumar Pun

2008

MVO	Captain[223] Khusiman Gurung
OBE	Lieutenant Colonel A J P Bourne MBE
MC	Rifleman Bhimbahadur Gurung
MC	Major P R G Pitchfork
MC	Lance Corporal Mohansingh Tangnami
MC	Lance Corporal Agnish Thapa
MID	Rifleman Omprakash Ale
MID	Lieutenant J A E E Jeffcoat
QCVS	Major G M Strickland MBE

2009

MBE	Major J P Davies
MBE	Major W R Kefford
MBE	Major Guptaman Gurung MVO
MVO	Major Yambahadur Rana
MC	Lance Corporal Gajendra Rai
MID	Captain R T Anderson
MID	Rifleman Darshan Chamling Rai
MID	Major R J Daines
MID	Rifleman Manju Gurung
MID	Corporal Basanta Rai
MID	Sergeant Bikash Rai
MID	Corporal Bishwahang Rai
MID	Rifleman Gopal Rai
MID	Captain T W Rose
QCVS	Lieutenant Colonel C B Darby

2010

CB	Lieutenant General P T C Pearson CBE
MID	Lance Corporal Buddhibahadur Gurung
MID	Rifleman Prakash Pun
MID	Lance Corporal Tilakkumar Rai
QCVS	Lieutenant A C Connolly
QCVS	Colonel I A Rigden OBE
QCVS	Major A G Alexander-Cooper
MVO	Captain Dhyanprasad Rai

2011

MBE	Major T C M-K Jackman
DSO	Lieutenant Colonel G M Strickland MBE
CGC	Acting Sergeant Dipprasad Pun
MC	Rifleman Sunil Limbu
MID	Rifleman Maniraj Gurung
MID	Captain P A Houlton-Hart
MID	Lance Corporal Nabin Rai
MID	Captain Shureshkumar Thapa
QCVS	Corporal Manoj Gurung
MBE	Lance Corporal Ambarbahadur Khadka

2012

MBE	Major W J Hughes
MID	Corporal Baljit Limbu
MVO	Captain Chinbahadur Thapa
MID	Corporal Dhanbahadur Gurung
MID	Colour Sergeant Lakhbahadur Gurung
MID	Major S C Marcandonatos
MBE	Major A G Alexander-Cooper
MID	Rifleman Suman Rana Magar

Right: The Secretary of State for Defence, the Right Honourable Gavin Williamson CBE MP, pays his respects to the Regiment's Fallen during a visit to 2RGR in May 2018.

Below: The Colonel-in-Chief, Colonel Commandant of the Brigade of Gurkhas, Colonel of the Regiment, Commander 4 Mechanized Brigade and the Commanding Officer, Gurkha Major and Regimental Sergeant Major of 1RGR pay their respects to the Regiment's Fallen on 28 January 2011 at the Memorial Wall in Sir John Moore Barracks, Shorncliffe (image Crown copyright 2011).

Below right: Her Majesty The Queen paying her respects at the Armed Forces Memorial in the National Memorial Arboretum. The wall immediately in front of where Her Majesty is stood includes the names of some of the officers and soldiers from The Royal Gurkha Rifles who lost their lives on operations whilst serving with the Regiment (image Crown copyright).

APPENDIX 2

Honours and Awards

This Appendix lists the Honours and Awards received by members of The Royal Gurkha Rifles from its formation in 1994 to July 2019. The rank shown against an individual denotes the rank held at the time of the award, noting that many recipients went on to achieve higher rank later in their careers. Within each year, recipients are listed in the order in which they were published in successive editions of the *London Gazette*, not alphabetically nor by the precedence of their award. The initial research for this Appendix was done by Captain Michael Barney RGR.

1995

OBE	Lieutenant Colonel W F Shuttlewood
MBE	Major Ombahadur Chhetri BEM
MBE	Captain (Acting Major) Lalbahadur Gurung
MBE	Staff Sergeant Rachhabahadur Gurung
MBE	Staff Sergeant Shivakumar Limbu
MVO	Captain (QGO) Balkrishna Gurung
MVO	Captain (QGO) Prabin Gurung
MBE	Major (QGO) Khagendrabahadur Limbu MVO

1996

MBE	Major J G H Corrigan
MBE	Sergeant Kamalbahadur Nepali
MVO	Captain (QGO) Chittrabahadur Rai
QCVS	Lance Corporal Shailendra Shrestha
MBE	Major (GCO) Udaibahadur Gurung
MBE	Major (GCO) Chandraprasad Limbu

1997

MBE	Captain (QGO Dharmendra Gurung
MBE	Major (QGO) Lilbahadur Gurung
MBE	Major L A Holley
MBE	Major G R J Glanville
MVO	Captain (QGO) Narbahadur Gurung BEM

1998

MBE	Major (QGO) Deoman Limbu
CBE	Colonel D R Willis
MBE	Lieutenant Colonel R M Venning
MBE	Lieutenant (GCO) Balkrishna Gurung MVO
MVO	Captain (QGO) Khemkumar Limbu
MVO	Captain (QGO) Narainbahadur Gurung

1999

MBE	Lieutenant (QGO) Rajendra Sherchan
MBE	Colour Sergeant Yambahadur Khatri
MVO	Captain (QGO) Dharambahadur Gurung
MID	Captain F J Rea

2000

OBE	Lieutenant Colonel S D Crane
MBE	Major M P H Gouldstone
MVO	Captain (QGO) Bhimbahadur Gurung
CBE	Brigadier P T C Pearson
OBE	Lieutenant Colonel M M Lillingston-Price
MBE	Warrant Officer Class 2 Bijaykumar Limbu
MBE	Major T C St.J Warrington
QCB	Corporal Kumar Ghale

2001

MBE	Captain (QGO) Hitman Gurung
MBE	Major J C Lawrence
MVO	Captain (QGO) Chandrabahadur Gurung
QCVS	Colonel D G Hayes MBE

2002

MBE	Major N D Wylie-Carrick
MID	Corporal Yakchharaj Limbu
QCVS	Captain L E Fowkes
QCVS	Major J G Robinson

2003

| MVO | Captain (QGO) Harkaraj Rai |

2004

OBE	Lieutenant Colonel I N A Thomas
MBE	Major (QGO) Laxmibhakta Bantawa
MBE	Major J P Bourne
MBE	Major Q W M Naylor
QCVS	Corporal Dhanbahadur Dura
MVO	Captain (QGO) Guptaman Gurung
MC	Sergeant Kajiman Limbu
QCVS	Lieutenant Colonel J C Lawrence MBE

2005

MBE	Major T D P O'Leary
MVO	Captain (QGO) Bhaktabahadur Thapa
MVO	Captain (QGO) Padambahadur Limbu

2006

MBE	Major G M Strickland
MBE	Lieutenant (QGO)/(Acting Captain (QGO)) Daniel Lama
QCVS	Lieutenant Colonel C D Wombell
Bronze Star Medal	Major J G Robinson
QCVS	Captain S W M Chandler
MBE	Major S J P Gilderson
QCVS	Lance Corporal Buddhibahadur Gurung
OBE	Lieutenant Colonel I A Rigden
MVO	Captain (QGO) Shivakumar Limbu MBE
MID	Rifleman Ganesh Gurung
MID	Warrant Officer Class 2 Trilochan Gurung
MID	Lieutenant P R Hollingshead
MID	Corporal Kailash Khebang
MID	Rifleman Nabin Rai

2007

CBE	Colonel D G Hayes MBE
MBE	Major C R Boryer
MVO	Captain (QGO) Umeshkumar Pun

2008

MVO	Captain[223] Khusiman Gurung
OBE	Lieutenant Colonel A J P Bourne MBE
MC	Rifleman Bhimbahadur Gurung
MC	Major P R G Pitchfork
MC	Lance Corporal Mohansingh Tangnami
MC	Lance Corporal Agnish Thapa
MID	Rifleman Omprakash Ale
MID	Lieutenant J A E E Jeffcoat
QCVS	Major G M Strickland MBE

2009

MBE	Major J P Davies
MBE	Major W R Kefford
MBE	Major Guptaman Gurung MVO
MVO	Major Yambahadur Rana
MC	Lance Corporal Gajendra Rai
MID	Captain R T Anderson
MID	Rifleman Darshan Chamling Rai
MID	Major R J Daines
MID	Rifleman Manju Gurung
MID	Corporal Basanta Rai
MID	Sergeant Bikash Rai
MID	Corporal Bishwahang Rai
MID	Rifleman Gopal Rai
MID	Captain T W Rose
QCVS	Lieutenant Colonel C B Darby

2010

CB	Lieutenant General P T C Pearson CBE
MID	Lance Corporal Buddhibahadur Gurung
MID	Rifleman Prakash Pun
MID	Lance Corporal Tilakkumar Rai
QCVS	Lieutenant A C Connolly
QCVS	Colonel I A Rigden OBE
QCVS	Major A G Alexander-Cooper
MVO	Captain Dhyanprasad Rai

2011

MBE	Major T C M-K Jackman
DSO	Lieutenant Colonel G M Strickland MBE
CGC	Acting Sergeant Dipprasad Pun
MC	Rifleman Sunil Limbu
MID	Rifleman Maniraj Gurung
MID	Captain P A Houlton-Hart
MID	Lance Corporal Nabin Rai
MID	Captain Shureshkumar Thapa
QCVS	Corporal Manoj Gurung
MBE	Lance Corporal Ambarbahadur Khadka

2012

MBE	Major W J Hughes
MID	Corporal Baljit Limbu
MVO	Captain Chinbahadur Thapa
MID	Corporal Dhanbahadur Gurung
MID	Colour Sergeant Lakhbahadur Gurung
MID	Major S C Marcandonatos
MBE	Major A G Alexander-Cooper
MID	Rifleman Suman Rana Magar

2013

CBE	**Brigadier J C Lawrence MBE**
MVO	**Captain Trilochan Gurung**
MC	**Rifleman Tuljung Gurung**
MID	**Rifleman Bikash Gurung**
MID	**Corporal Govinda Gurung**
MBE	**Major D T Pack**

2014

MVO	**Captain Shureshkumar Thapa**

2015

MVO	**Captain Prakash Gurung**

2016

QCB	**Sergeant Dhaniram Rai**
MBE	**Major Yambahadur Rana MVO**
MBE	**Major A P Todd**
MVO	**Captain Muktiprasad Gurung**

2017

QCVS	**Corporal Mahesh Gurung**
QCVS	**Major E P Oldfield**
MVO	**Captain Lalitbahadur Gurung**
MBE	**Major Prembahadur Gurung**
MBE	**Sergeant Dhaniram Rai**

2018

MVO	**Captain Dillikumar Rai**
MBE	**Major P A Houlton-Hart**

2019

MBE	**Lieutenant S Sears**
CBE	**Colonel J G Robinson**
MBE	**Corporal Netrabahadur Rana**
MSM	**Sergeant Rameshkumar Limbu**

Members of 1RGR on parade in January 2011 in Sir John Moore Barracks in order that His Royal Highness The Prince of Wales, the Regiment's Colonel-in-Chief, could present operational service medals to members of the battalion following their deployment in Afghanistan on Operation Herrick 12. Note the Military Cross (MC) worn by the non-commissioned officer standing second from right next to the Buddhist Lama. Corporal Agnish Thapa was awarded the MC for his actions in Afghanistan in October 2007 during Operation Herrick 7 (see Chapter 5).

Sergeant Dipprasad Pun CGC and the actress Joanna Lumley in April 2015. Sergeant Dipprasad was awarded the Conspicuous Gallantry Cross (CGC) for his actions in Afghanistan on 17 September 2010 (see Chapter 5 for the detail of what happened).

The Queen's Medal

The importance that the RGR attaches to shooting was explained in the 'Specialist Skills' section of the book, as was the fact that members of the RGR have won the coveted Queen's Medal, the medal awarded each year to the best shot in the Army Operational Shooting Competition at Bisley, 14 times in the 25 years that the Regiment has existed. This is such a remarkable achievement that the RGR winners of the medal, which is worn alongside an individual's other medals in dress uniform, are listed below:

Colonel William Shuttlewood, second in from the right, who was one of the RGR's first recipients of an award when, in 1995, he received the OBE (Officer of the Most Excellent Order of the British Empire) for his services to the Brigade of Gurkhas. The Gurkha officer third in from the left, Major (QGO) Khusiman Gurung, is wearing the Queen's Medal (third medal from the right) having won it in 1985 as a young lance corporal serving with 6GR, one of the RGR's antecedent regiments. Michael Howard, then the MP for Folkestone and Hythe and leader of the Conservative Party, is stood between him and the Regimental Sergeant Major of 1RGR

Rifleman Dilip Gurung	1RGR	1994
Captain (QGO) Dharmendra Gurung	1RGR	1995
Lance Corporal Biendrakumar Magar	2RGR	1997
Corporal Dilip Gurung	1RGR	1998
Sergeant Lalitbahadur Gurung	1RGR	2000
Colour Sergeant Manbahadur Garbuja	2RGR	2002
Corporal Prembahadur Baral	2RGR	2003
Sergeant Biendrakumar Magar	2RGR	2004
Rifleman Hirabahadur Pun	1RGR	2005
Warrant Officer Class 2 Lalitbahadur Gurung	1RGR	2006
Corporal Sombahadur Chhantel	1RGR	2013
Sergeant Sanjib Rai	2RGR	2014
Corporal Ashok Thapa	1RGR	2017
Corporal Bishal Rai	2RGR	2018

The table above does not tell the full story of the incredibly high standard that some of the RGR's shots actually achieve. For example, both Captain (QGO) Dharmendra Gurung and Warrant Officer Class 2 Lalitbahadur Gurung won the Queen's Medal three times during their service. Warrant Officer Class 2 Lalitbahadur won it in 1992 whilst serving with 6GR, as well as in 2000 and 2006 whilst with the RGR. Captain Dharmendra won it in 1982 and 1993 whilst also serving with 6GR, as well as in 1995 with the RGR. Interestingly, he came very close to winning it again in 1985, losing by one point in a tied shoot to Lance Corporal Khusiman Gurung, the Gurkha officer in the photograph with Michael Howard!

In addition to the honours and awards described in this Appendix, most members of the RGR now have several operational service medals, evidence of the operational experience that now resides in the RGR's battalions. Taken in January 2011 after Operation Herrick 12, this photograph shows members of 1RGR having just received their operational service medals for Afghanistan from His Royal Highness The Prince of Wales (image Crown copyright 2011).

It is right to celebrate the honours and awards received by members of the RGR but we must not forget that operations exact a very human cost. This image shows officers from 1RGR and the 1st Battalion The Mercian Regiment (Cheshire) at the funeral of Rifleman Remand Kulung at Aldershot Military Cemetery. Rifleman Remand was seriously injured on Operation Herrick 12 whilst serving with G (Tobruk) Company, a GRC attached to 1MERCIAN, when a Chinook helicopter landing at a patrol base to conduct a resupply struck the edge of a sangar, causing it to collapse onto the soldiers' accommodation block. Although Rifleman Remand received immediate treatment before being evacuated to UK, he died of his injuries on 12 August 2010 (image Crown copyright 2010).

Colonels of The Regiment

Lieutenant General Sir Peter Duffell KCB CBE MC	1 July 1994–1 July 1999
Lieutenant General P T C Pearson CB CBE	1 July 1999–1 July 2009
Major General J C Lawrence CBE	1 July 2009–1 February 2016
Major General G M Strickland DSO MBE	1 February 2016–

Lieutenant General Sir Peter Duffell KCB CBE MC inspecting 1RGR's Pipes and Drums in Hong Kong in February 1995, the year after the Regiment was formed. General Duffell was the first Colonel of the Regiment and held the appointment from 1 July 1994 until 1 July 1999.

Above: Major General J C Lawrence CBE who was the third Colonel of the Regiment and held the appointment from 1 July 2009 until 1 February 2016. This photograph was taken at a parade on 28 January 2011 held in Sir John Moore Barracks, Shorncliffe at which the Colonel-in-Chief awarded operational service medals to members of 1RGR following their deployment on Operation Herrick 12.

Below right: This photograph was taken on 4 November 2008 following an investiture at Buckingham Palace during which members of the RGR were awarded a remarkable four Military Crosses (MC) and an OBE for their actions in Afghanistan on Operation Herrick 7. From left to right: Field Marshal Lord Bramall, Field Marshal Sir John Chapple, Lieutenant General Peter Pearson (the Colonel of the Regiment at the time), Rifleman Bhimbahadur Gurung, Lance Corporal Mohansing Tangnami, Lance Corporal Agnish Thapa, Major Paul Pitchfork, Lieutenant Colonel Jonny Bourne and Lieutenant General Sir Peter Duffell. The lunch was organised by the Regiment and held at the Travellers Club to celebrate the awards (image Crown copyright 2008).

Above: Lieutenant General P T C Pearson CB CBE who was the second Colonel of the Regiment and held the appointment from 1 July 1999 until 1 July 2009.

Left: Major General G M Strickland DSO MBE the fourth, and current, Colonel of the Regiment who assumed the appointment on 1 February 2016. This photograph was taken at a commissioning parade in Brunei in November 2018.

Commanding Officers

THE FIRST BATTALION

Lieutenant Colonel N J H Hinton MBE	July 1994–December 1995
Lieutenant Colonel Bijaykumar Rawat	December 1995–March 1998
Lieutenant Colonel S D Crane OBE	April 1998–January 2001
Lieutenant Colonel N D J Rowe	January 2001–February 2003
Lieutenant Colonel J C Lawrence MBE	February 2003–July 2005
Lieutenant Colonel T C StJ Warrington MBE	July 2005–July 2007
Lieutenant Colonel A J P Bourne OBE	July 2007–July 2009
Lieutenant Colonel G M Strickland DSO MBE	August 2009–August 2011
Lieutenant Colonel D J Robinson	August 2011–January 2014
Lieutenant Colonel J P Davies MBE	January 2013–August 2016
Lieutenant Colonel C N A Crowe	August 2016–August 2018
Lieutenant Colonel C Conroy	August 2018–

Lieutenant Colonel D T Pack MBE receives a formal welcome back to the battalion in July 2018 on taking over as the Commanding Officer of 2RGR in Brunei.

THE SECOND BATTALION

Lieutenant Colonel D G Hayes MBE	July 1994[224] –November 1996
Lieutenant Colonel M W L Theobald	November 1996–April 1998
Lieutenant Colonel M M Lillingston-Price	April 1998–May 2001
Lieutenant Colonel I N A Thomas OBE	May 2001–November 2003
Lieutenant Colonel I A Rigden	November 2003–April 2006
Lieutenant Colonel C D Wombell	April 2006–April 2008
Lieutenant Colonel C B Darby	April 2008–October 2010
Lieutenant Colonel F J Rea	October 2010–April 2013
Lieutenant Colonel M H Reedman	April 2013–August 2015
Lieutenant Colonel J C Murray	August 2015–July 2018
Lieutenant Colonel D T Pack MBE	July 2018 –

THE THIRD BATTALION

Lieutenant Colonel P T C Pearson	July 1994[225] – December 1995
Lieutenant Colonel M W L Theobald	December 1995[226] – November 1996

Below: Lieutenant Colonel J C Murray receives a traditional farewell from 2RGR on handing over command of the battalion in July 2018.

Right: Lieutenant Colonel A J P Bourne, the Commanding Officer of 1RGR, speaks to the troops before an operation in Afghanistan during Operation Herrick 7 (September 2007 to April 2008).

APPENDIX 5

Gurkha Majors

THE FIRST BATTALION

Major (QGO) Lalbahadur Gurung MBE	July 1994–February 1996
Major (QGO) Balkrishna Gurung MVO MBE	February 1996–March 1998
Major (QGO) Kulbahadur Thapa	March 1998–March 2000
Major (QGO) Dharambahadur Gurung MVO	March 2000–March 2002
Major (QGO) Narkaji Gurung	March 2002–April 2004
Major (QGO) Khusiman Gurung	April 2004–April 2006
Major (QGO) Guptaman Gurung MVO	April 2006–August 2008
Major Khusiman Gurung MVO	August 2008–November 2010
Major Dhyanprasad Rai MVO	November 2010–December 2012
Major Rambahadur Pun	December 2012–January 2015
Major Chandrabahadur Pun	January 2015–February 2017
Major Shureshkumar Thapa MVO	February 2017–

Major Khusiman Gurung MVO, Gurkha Major of 1RGR, with the Regimental Sergeant Major, Warrant Officer Class 1 Kushal Kumar Gurung, in Afghanistan on Operation Herrick 12 (April 2010 to October 2010). Major Khusiman was the Gurkha Major of 1RGR from August 2008 to November 2010.

The Second Battalion

Major (QGO) Hansraj Magar	July 1994–October 1995
Major (QGO) Deuman Limbu	October 1995–October 1997
Major (QGO) Ashokbahadur Tamang	October 1997–November 1999
Major (QGO) Indrakumar Limbu	November 1999–December 2001
Major (QGO) Laxmibhakta Bantawa MBE	December 2001–January 2005
Major (QGO) Harkaraj Rai MVO	January 2005–May 2007
Major (QGO) Shivakumar Limbu MVO MBE	May 2007–July 2009
Major Yambahadur Rana	July 2009–January 2012
Major Dammarbahadur Shahi	January 2012–June 2014
Major Prembahadur Gurung	July 2014–July 2016
Major Gajendrakumar Angdembe	July 2016–July 2018
Major Rajkumar Rai	July 2018–

The Third Battalion

Major (QGO) Chandraprasad Limbu	July 1994[227] – November 1996

Left: Major Gajendrakumar Angdembe, Gurkha Major of 2RGR from July 2016 to July 2018, inspecting the guard of honour during his formal farewell having handed over as Gurkha Major.

Above: Major Guptaman Gurung MVO, Gurkha Major of 1RGR, leading proceedings during the Festival of Dashain in 2006. Major Guptaman was the Gurkha Major of 1RGR from April 2006 to August 2008.

APPENDIX 6

Regimental Sergeant Majors

THE FIRST BATTALION

21160724	Warrant Officer Class 1 Dipakbahadur Chand	July 1994–August 1995
21161890	Warrant Officer Class 1 Lokbahadur Pun	August 1995–March 1997
21162418	Warrant Officer Class 1 Bhagwankumar Mall	March 1997–July 1999
21162981	Warrant Officer Class 1 Rajkumar Gurung	July 1999–July 2001
21165826	Warrant Officer Class 1 Kusang Kumar Gurung	July 2001–June 2002
21166886	Warrant Officer Class 1 Chinbahadur Thapa	June 2002–March 2003
21166737	Warrant Officer Class 1 Ghanasyam Pun	March 2003–March 2005
21167354	Warrant Officer Class 1 Prakash Gurung	April 2005–January 2007
21168180	Warrant Officer Class 1 Dolbahadur Gurung	January 2007–June 2008
21168275	Warrant Officer Class 1 Jitbahadur Chungbang	June 2008–June 2010
21168466	Warrant Officer Class 1 Kushal Kumar Gurung	June 2010–June 2011
21168464	Warrant Officer Class 1 Ganesh Kumar Gurung	June 2013–December 2014
21169475	Warrant Officer Class 1 Giriprasad Gurung	December 2014–April 2016
21169495	Warrant Officer Class 1 Bahadur Budha Magar	April 2016–May 2017
21169698	Warrant Officer Class 1 Bikash Gurung	May 2017–August 2018
21170275	Warrant Officer Class 1 Narbir Galami	August 2018–

The Second Battalion

21161281	**Warrant Officer Class 1 Bhaktabahadur Gurung**	July 1994–December 1996
21162043	**Warrant Officer Class 1 Madanbahadur Thapa**	December 1996–February 1998
21163802	**Warrant Officer Class 1 Suryabahadur Khapung**	February 1998–March 2000
21163149	**Warrant Officer Class 1 Dewansing Gurung**	March 2000–March 2002
21165542	**Warrant Officer Class 1 Yubaraj Rai**	March 2002–September 2004
21166995	**Warrant Officer Class 1 Raghubir Rai**	September 2004–September 2006
21168271	**Warrant Officer Class 1 Gajendrakumar Angdembe**	September 2006–September 2007
21168223	**Warrant Officer Class 1 Maniram Rai**	September 2007–July 2009
21168601	**Warrant Officer Class 1 Dhalindrabahadur Khatri Chhetri**	July 2009–July 2011
21168682	**Warrant Officer Class 1 Yakchharaj Limbu**	July 2011–January 2014
21169154	**Warrant Officer Class 1 Krishnaprasad Loksam**	January 2014–April 2015
21169352	**Warrant Officer Class 1 Nawalkiran Yakha**	April 2015–April 2016
21169693	**Warrant Officer Class 1 Sangam Rai**	April 2016–March 2018
21169963	**Warrant Officer Class 1 Lakhbahadur Gurung**	March 2018–July 2019
21169835	**Warrant Officer Class 1 Bhupendra Gaha**	July 2019–

The Third Battalion

21160849	**Warrant Officer Class 1 Gyan Raj Limbu**	July 1994–October 1995
21162043	**Warrant Officer Class 1 Madanbahadur Thapa**	October 1995–November 1996

Right: Warrant Officer Class 1 Dolbahadur Gurung, Regimental Sergeant Major of 1RGR, in Afghanistan on Operation Herrick 7 (September 2007 to April 2008).

Far right: Warrant Officer Class 1 Krishnaprasad Loksham, Regimental Sergeant Major of 2RGR from January 2014 to April 2015, watches on as the Secretary of State for Defence, Sir Michael Fallon, discusses tactics during Operation Comet, the name given to support to the 2014 Commonwealth Games.

Regimental Secretaries

Lieutenant Colonel G C J L Pearson	1994–1998
Lieutenant Colonel C N Fraser	1998–1999[228]
Lieutenant Colonel W J Dawson OBE	1999–2001
Major P H Gay	2001–2011
Major B McKay MBE	2011–

The Regimental Headquarters of the RGR was formally established on 3 April 1995[229] and was initially based in Church Crookham with Headquarters Brigade of Gurkhas.

Opposite: One of the Regimental Secretary's key responsibilities is to ensure that The Royal Gurkha Rifles only selects young British officers who will be able to form strong relationships with the older and more experienced Gurkha officers with whom they will live and work when they join the Regiment. Another key responsibility is to ensure that the traditions and practices of the Regiment, such as the procedure for a Regimental Dinner Night, are not lost.

Recipients of the Prince of Wales' Kukri

The Prince of Wales' Kukri is awarded on 1 January annually to the outstanding Warrant Officer Class 2 or below who has, in the opinion of the Colonel of the Regiment, done most to enhance the name of The Royal Gurkha Rifles in the preceding year. Recipients of the Prince of Wales' Kukri are entitled to replace their regulation black lanyard, which is worn with ceremonial forms of dress, with an intertwined black and red one in recognition of their award.

THE HISTORY OF THE PRINCE OF WALES' KUKRI[231]
During his first visit to the 2nd Gurkhas in March 1979 following his appointment as Colonel-in-Chief of the Regiment, His Royal Highness The Prince of Wales expressed his wish to present a trophy to be competed for between the two battalions. It was decided that this would be a kothimora kukri (*see* Special Interest

Section 6) to be awarded annually to the warrant officer class 2, non-commissioned officer or rifleman who was considered to have contributed most to the enhancement of the Regiment's good name in the preceding year. As well as receiving the kukri, winners were given a distinctive red and black-plaited lanyard to wear on their left shoulder for the remainder of their service as a mark of their award. The kukri was kept in a display case in the Quarterguard and only removed for the presentation ceremony.

On the formation of the RGR, His Royal Highness agreed to become the new Regiment's Colonel-in-Chief. In this capacity, he asked that the award of the kukri be carried forward, suitably modified to the new Regiment. The award can be won by the same individual more than once; for example 21169783 Jiwan Prasad Gurung first won it as a sergeant in 2011 and then won it again as a colour sergeant in 2014.

His Royal Highness The Prince of Wales awarding the Prince of Wales' Kukri to Colour Sergeant Raj Rai on 14 March 2017 for his outstanding work as an Instructor at Cambridge University Officer Training Corps and the Royal Military Academy Sandhurst, as well as for his constant commitment to the 2RGR Recce Platoon.

21162366	**Colour Sergeant Krishna Prasad Gurung**	1 RGR	1994
21167350	**Lance Corporal Bishnubahadur Singh**	1 RGR	1995
21164709	**Sergeant Punendraprasad Limbu**	2 RGR	1996
21168102	**Corporal Biendrakumar Magar**	2 RGR	1997
21162986	**Warrant Officer Class 2 Rajendra Scherchan**	GDC RMAS	1998
21167359	**Sergeant Kamalprasad Rana**	1 RGR	1999
	Not Awarded		2000
	Not Awarded		2001
21167722	**Sergeant Tejbahadur Limbu**	2 RGR	2002
21168976	**Sergeant Muktiprasad Gurung**	A Coy, 1HLDRS[230]	2003
21167724	**Colour Sergeant Kulbahadur Gurung**	2 RGR	2004
21168291	**Colour Sergeant Kajiman Limbu MC**	2 RGR	2005
21169389	**Sergeant Jiwan Pun**	1RGR	2006
21168432	**Warrant Officer Class 2 Rajeshkumar Gurung**	1 RGR	2007
21169918	**Sergeant Genendra Rai**	2 RGR	2008
21169126	**Colour Sergeant Yambahadur Gurung**	1RGR	2009
21169698	**Sergeant Bikash Gurung**	1 RGR	2010
21169783	**Sergeant Jiwan Prasad Gurung**	1 RGR	2011
21170896	**Corporal Sanjib Rai**	2 RGR	2012
21170660	**Sergeant Sombahadur Chhantel**	1 RGR	2013
21169783	**Colour Sergeant Jiwan Prasad Gurung**	1 RGR	2014
21170334	**Sergeant Arjunsamyu Limbu**	2 RGR	2015
21171132	**Acting Colour Sergeant Raj Rai**	2 RGR	2016
21170743	**Colour Sergeant Phurba Tamang**	2 RGR	2017
21170307	**Colour Sergeant Mukunda Rajali**	1 RGR	2018

APPENDIX 9

Recipients of the Tuker Award

The Tuker Award is awarded on 1 January annually to the most outstanding Subaltern or Captain who has, in the opinion of the Colonel of the Regiment, done most to enhance the name of the Regiment in the preceding year.

THE HISTORY OF THE TUKER AWARD[232]

Following the death of Lady (Cynthia) Tuker on 31 October 1990, a bequest of £1,000 from the estate of her late husband, Lieutenant General Sir Francis ('Gertie') Tuker KCIE CB DSO OBE, was made available for use by 2GR in a manner to be agreed by the Committee of the Sirmoor Club. The money was invested in The Sirmoor Rifles Association Trust, and the Committee, the Colonel of the Regiment and the Commandant(s)[233] decided to use the income to provide an award for the best subaltern or acting captain in the Regiment each year. The recipient, chosen by the Commandants, had to have made a significant contribution to the Regiment either through professional or sporting achievement. The award was known as the Tuker Award.

After 1 July 1994, the Tuker Award was adopted by The Royal Gurkha Rifles and the prize is still awarded under similar rules. The cost of the annual award has been generously found by the Trustees of The Sirmoor Rifles Association (UK) Trust. Of note, Tuker Lines, the home of the Resident Infantry Battalion in Brunei, was named after General Tuker in January 1967.

Lieutenant W R Kefford	1 RGR	1997
Captain A G Alexander-Cooper	3 R IRISH	1999
Not Awarded		2000
Not Awarded		2001
Lieutenant N St J F Lea	2 RGR	2002
Lieutenant B P Gifford	1 RGR	2003
Lieutenant C R Picton	1 RGR	2004
Lieutenant P G Howgego	1 RGR	2005
Captain E D P Oldfield	2 RGR	2006
Captain A R C Mathers	2 RGR	2007
Lieutenant J A Jeffcoat	1 RGR	2008
Lieutenant A C Colquhoun	2 RGR	2009
Lieutenant A C Connolly	1 RGR	2010
Lieutenant C E F Russell	1 RGR	2011
Captain B E Norfield	Gurkha Coy, ITC Catterick	2012
Lieutenant M B Reardon	2 RGR	2013
Captain C J Schroeder	2 RGR	2014
Captain J A Armstrong	2 RGR	2015
Lieutenant M F Barney	1 RGR	2016
Lieutenant O C H Goldfinger	2 RGR	2017
Lieutenant C J R Hornby	1 RGR	2018

Opposite left: Lieutenant General Sir Francis 'Gertie' Tuker KCIE CB DSO OBE, whose generous bequest enabled the Tuker Award to be established. General Tuker was a remarkable officer. Commissioned in January 1914 and posted to India in March 1914 to join 2GR, he was wounded in the First World War but went on to become one of the Gurkhas' most distinguished and highly decorated officers. He died on 7 October 1967.

Opposite right: His Royal Highness The Prince of Wales awarding the Tuker Award to Lieutenant M F Barney of 1RGR at Buckingham Palace on 14 March 2017 (image Crown copyright 2017).

APPENDIX 10

Recipients of the Slim Trophy

Captain Babindra Gurung	1 RGR	2017
Captain Vijayprakash Subba Limbu	2 RGR	2018

The Slim Trophy is a new Regimental prize awarded on 1 January annually to the outstanding Gurkha Late Entry (LE) Captain who has, in the opinion of the Colonel of the Regiment, done most to enhance the name of the Regiment in the preceding year.

Above: General 'Bill' Slim, the legendary commander of the 14th Army, the so-called 'Forgotten Army', whose inspirational leadership led to a stunning victory against the Japanese in Burma during the Second World War.

Right: Soldiers from the 6th Gurkhas, one of the RGR's antecedent regiments, during the Gallipoli Campaign (1915 to 1916). Having served alongside Gurkhas in the campaign, the young Bill Slim was determined to transfer to the Indian Army and become an officer in a Gurkha regiment. Although he initially joined the 6th Gurkhas, he went on to command the 2/7th Gurkhas.

Field Marshal Sir William 'Bill' Slim, 1st Viscount Slim: Historical Background[234]

Born in 1891, Bill Slim had a relatively comfortable childhood until, at the age of sixteen, his father's business collapsed and he was forced to leave school and get a job. He started his working life as a primary school teacher in a tough part of Birmingham, leaving after two years to become a clerk in a local ironworks. It is there that he got to know working people,[235] developing the 'common touch' that would later characterise his leadership style. When war broke out in 1914, Slim managed to obtain a commission in The Royal Warwickshire Regiment, something that would not have been possible in peacetime given his family's modest circumstances.[236] He proved to be a natural soldier and went on to see active service at Gallipoli, where he was wounded, and in Mesopotamia where, as well as being wounded again, he was awarded a Military Cross for bravery under fire.

Slim transferred to the Indian Army at the end of the First World War, eventually joining the 6th Gurkha Rifles, a regiment he had fought alongside at Gallipoli. During the inter-war years, he established himself as one of the most capable officers of his generation, coming top of his class at the Indian Army Staff College in Quetta in 1928 and then, in 1934, being selected to be the Indian Army's representative on the instructional staff at the Army Staff College in Camberley, Surrey.[237] When the Second World War began, he pushed for a field command and soon found himself on combat operations in the Middle East, first as a brigadier and then as a major general. His rise through the ranks continued and, on 19 March 1942 and at the age of 50, he was promoted to lieutenant general and given command of the newly formed Burma Corps. That this was something of a poisoned chalice was not lost on Slim.[238] As he noted in his memoirs, "… I knew enough now to know that a command in Burma was more likely to be a test, and a tough one, than a triumph."[239]

The problem was that having already seized Malaya, then a British Colony, and taken the surrender of the 115,000 strong British garrison in Singapore,[240] an event described by Winston

Above: Soldiers from the 10th Gurkhas, one of the RGR's antecedent regiments, clearing trenches on a feature known as 'Scraggy Hill' during the Burma Campaign in the Second World War.

Gurkhas crossing the River Irrawaddy in central Burma as the 14th Army, under the command of Lieutenant General Sir William Slim, advanced south towards Rangoon.

Churchill as the 'worst disaster' and 'largest capitulation' in British military history,[241] the Japanese had advanced north from Thailand and were rampaging through the jungles of Burma, sweeping aside all opposition as they applied their own ruthless version of blitzkrieg.[242] The British, whose army in Burma comprised mainly Indian, Gurkha and Burmese troops, had tried to halt the advancing force but to no avail, sustaining thousands of casualties as they suffered defeat after defeat.[243] Things went from bad to worse when, on 9 March 1942, Rangoon fell to the Japanese. This was a huge blow. Most of the Burma Army's supplies came through the capital's

port and, with no direct road or rail access from British India and with a chronic shortage of transport aircraft, the Burma Army was effectively "cut off from the outside world".[244]

Given this situation, it is no wonder that Slim had such mixed feelings when he was appointed to command Burma Corps. Having been soundly beaten numerous times, the force he inherited was weak and demoralised. Unsure of what his exact mission was, Slim redeployed Burma Corps to try to wrest the initiative from the Japanese. He failed repeatedly, constrained by a superior who refused to accept the reality on the ground and outmanoeuvred by an enemy who appeared to have an almost superhuman ability to operate in the jungle. A little over a month after taking command of Burma Corps,[245] Slim found

Left: The Japanese surrender in Rangoon in May 1945. The picture shows Lieutenant General Namata surrendering to Major General W S Symes, the General Officer Commanding South Burma. It was General 'Bill' Slim's remarkable leadership of the Burma Campaign that led to the Japanese defeat.

Below: The painting of Field Marshal Sir William Slim, 1st Viscount Slim, which hangs in the Officers' Mess in Sir John Moore Barracks, the home of the UK based RGR battalion.

himself leading the longest and one of the most difficult retreats in British military history as his force raced north for over 900 miles to the relative safety of British India. Many generals – both then and now – would have found excuses for their failure but not Slim. Showing remarkable honesty and a high degree of self-awareness, he wrote:

"For myself, I had little to be proud of; I could not rate my generalship high. The only test of generalship is success, and I had succeeded in nothing I had attempted. Time and again, I had tried to pass to the offensive and to regain the initiative and every time I had seen my house of cards fall down as I tried to add to its crowning story."[246]

How Slim managed to turn the situation around, eventually beating the Japanese in an environment in which they were thought to be invincible, is a remarkable study in leadership. It explains why, in 2011, Slim was voted as the joint winner in a competition run by the National Army Museum to find Britain's greatest ever general. Slim's memoirs of the campaign (*Defeat into Victory*[247]) should be a 'must read' for all army officers, particularly those in the RGR given Slim was an officer in two of the

RGR's antecedent regiments. Slim finished his army service as the Chief of the Imperial General Staff, the most senior serving soldier. He was then appointed as the 13th Governor General of Australia, a post he held from May 1953 until February 1960. He died on 14 December 1970 at the age of 79, one of the most celebrated generals that Britain has ever produced.

Recipients of the Parish Memorial Trophy

The Parish Memorial Trophy, often known simply as 'The Parish Trophy', is awarded to the Rifleman who has made the greatest contribution towards upholding the name and reputation of the 1st Battalion The Royal Gurkha Rifles over the past year.

THE HISTORY OF THE PARISH MEMORIAL TROPHY[248]

Captain Julian Glynne Woodbine Parish was born on 22 July 1942, the son of Mr and Mrs P E G W Parish. He was educated at Eton College and St George's School, Newport, Rhode Island, USA. He was gazetted to 2GR from Mons Officer Cadet School on 14 April 1962, joining the 2nd Battalion in Hong Kong. On the 6 August 1966, he qualified as a Sioux Helicopter pilot and subsequently served in the 2nd Goorkhas Air Platoon in Brunei with both battalions in turn. He commanded the Air Platoon from November 1968 until he retired on 12 April 1971. After leaving the Regiment he flew helicopters from Aberdeen in support of oil and gas production in the North Sea.

Captain Parish, who was a bachelor, was killed on 3 March 1974 when returning to England from the Paris Air Show. He was a passenger in a Turkish Airlines DC10 that crashed in the Forest of Ermenonville, near Paris, shortly after take-off. All 344 people on board were killed in what was the world's worst air disaster up to that time. A bequest of £500 was made from Captain Parish's estate to be used for the benefit of soldiers in the Regiment. It was decided that the Parish Memorial Trophy would be made for annual presentation in the 2nd Battalion to the Rifleman who had made the greatest contribution to upholding the name and reputation of the Battalion during the year.

The trophy, copied from an old statuette of a khud racer belonging to the 3rd Queen Alexandra's Own Gurkha Rifles, was made by Mr Shyamlal Sunar, goldsmith of 2/2nd Gurkhas. It was presented to the first winner by Mr Parish's father, Mr Patrick Parish OBE, at Queen Elizabeth Barracks, Church Crookham on 20 September 1975.

The Parish Trophy was adopted by The Royal Gurkha Rifles following its formation in July 1994.

Opposite: Rifleman Poshraj Rai of 1RGR receives the Parish Memorial Trophy in February 2010 from the Colonel-in-Chief, His Royal Highness The Prince of Wales, during a mission rehearsal exercise before deploying to Afghanistan on Operation Herrick 12 (April 2010 to October 2010).

21169783	**Rifleman Jiwan Prasad Gurung**	2001
21169495	**Rifleman Bahadur Budha Magar**	2002
21170367	**Rifleman Prawin Malla**	2003
21170734	**Rifleman Santosh Gurung**	2005
21171045	**Rifleman Khagendra Gurung**	2006
21171247	**Rifleman Suman Ale**	2008
21171236	**Rifleman Poshraj Rai**	2009
21171688	**Rifleman Suresh Gurung**	2011
21171836	**Rifleman Roshan Gurung**	2012
30142333	**Rifleman Homendra Budha Magar**	2014
30141890	**Rifleman Surya Jirel**	2015
30142390	**Rifleman Sajendra Gurung**	2016
30141876	**Rifleman Ramesh Chemjong**	2017
30188662	**Rifleman Sanjeet Gurung**	2018

Recipients of the Warren Trophy

The Warren Trophy is awarded to the top student of each Junior Leaders Cadre in the 2nd Battalion The Royal Gurkha Rifles.[249] The Trophy was presented by Lieutenant Colonel N R StJ Warren of the 7th Duke of Edinburgh's Own Gurkha Rifles (7GR) in October 1986 and was carried forward into The Royal Gurkha Rifles on its formation in July 1994.

The Warren Trophy awarded to the top student on the Junior Leaders Cadre in 2RGR.

21168223	Rifleman Tupendra Limbu	1994
21168322	Rifleman Prembahadur Gurung	1995
21168612	Rifleman Chakrabahadur Rai	1996
21168860	Rifleman Ganesh Rai	1997
21169004	Lance Corporal Dillikumar Rai	1998
21169226	Rifleman Sanjib Rai	1998
21169352	Rifleman Nawal Kiran Yakha	1999
21169500	Rifleman Som Thulung Rai	2000
21169689	Rifleman Hemanta Tumbahangphe	2001
21169918	Rifleman Genendra Rai	2002
21169963	Rifleman Lakhbahadur Gurung	2003
21169967	Rifleman Arunhang Nembang	2004
21170528	Rifleman Naresh Gurung	2005
21170749	Rifleman Dinesh Rai	2006
21170869	Rifleman Sanjip Rai	2007
21171132	Rifleman Raj Rai	2008
21171469	Rifleman Pravin Kishor Rai	2009
21171787	Rifleman Pralon Kulung Rai	2010
21172019	Rifleman Yadesh Rai	2011
30048353	Rifleman Seemon Laksham	2012
30085748	Rifleman Subash Rai	2012
30120629	Rifleman Om Prakash Loksam	2013
30141872	Rifleman Rajesh Chemjung	2014
30142339	Rifleman Puskal Gurung	2015
30188409	Rifleman Ajay Tamrakar	2017
30207815	Rifleman Nichahang Rai	2017
30229743	Rifleman Deuman Rai	2018
30252302	Rifleman Jyotishwar Yakha	2019

Operational Deployments

The tables in this Appendix summarise the deployments on operations of RGR battalions, independent RGR sub-units and the Gurkha Reinforcement Companies (GRCs). There are three tables: the first lists deployments to the Balkans (Bosnia and Herzegovina, Kosovo and Macedonia); the second lists deployments to Afghanistan; and the third lists deployments to other operational theatres (such as Zaire/Democratic Republic of the Congo, East Timor, Sierra Leone, Iraq and the Ivory Coast). Deployments on operations in the UK, such as on Operation Pitchpole (support to those affected by flooding in February 2014) are not included, nor are deployments on Short Term Training Teams (STTTs), such as those on Operation Newcombe in Mali.

More detail about the deployments summarised in this Appendix can be found in Chapter 2 (Bosnia and Herzegovina, Kosovo and Macedonia), Chapter 3 (East Timor), Chapter 4 (Sierra Leone), Chapter 5 (Afghanistan) and Chapter 6 (Zaire/Democratic Republic of the Congo, Iraq and the Ivory Coast).

RGR Unit and Sub-Unit Operational Deployments to the Balkans

These deployments are described in detail in Chapter 2.

Operation Name	Dates	Deployment Theatre	Unit/Sub-Unit	Remarks
Operation Resolute	December 1995–July 1996	Bosnia and Herzegovina	A Company, 3RGR	The RGR's first operational deployment.
Operation Lodestar	September 1997–October 1997	Bosnia and Herzegovina	B Company, 1RGR	Surge manning during elections.
Operation Palatine	July 1998–January 1999	Bosnia and Herzegovina	B (Gallipoli) Company 1RS	The company was also known as GRC 1.
Operation Palatine	January 1999–July 1999	Bosnia and Herzegovina	C (Cassino) Company 2PARA	The company was also known as GRC 3 and, in some documents, C (Gurkha) Company 2PARA.
Operation Agricola	June 1999–August 1999	Kosovo	1RGR	Deployed as part of KFOR. In the vanguard when KFOR crossed the border from Macedonia into Kosovo.
Operation Palatine	July 1999–October 1999	Bosnia and Herzegovina	B (Gallipoli) Company 1RS	The company was also known as GRC 1.
Operation Bessemer	August 2001–October 2001	Macedonia	C (Cassino) Company 2PARA	The company recovered from Macedonia in early October 2001 and then deployed to Afghanistan on Operation Fingal (in January 2002).
Operation Palatine	September 2001–March 2002	Bosnia and Herzegovina	2RGR	
Operation Palatine	March 2003–October 2003	Bosnia and Herzegovina	A (Gallipoli) Company 1HLDRS	The company transferred from 1RS to 1HLDRS on 28 March 2000.
Operation Oculus	October 2003–April 2004	Bosnia and Herzegovina	1RGR	C Company 1RGR deployed from Bosnia and Herzegovina to Kosovo for several weeks to support the UK Spearhead Land Element (SLE) battalion.
Operation Oculus (EU name was Operation Althea)	September 2005–March 2006	Bosnia and Herzegovina	1RGR (-)	1RGR provided the first pan-Balkans BG, with a BG(-) in Bosnia and an ISR company, based on Support Company, in Kosovo.
	November 2005–April 2006	Kosovo	Support Company, 1RGR	
Operation Oculus	April 2007–September 2007	Kosovo	C Company, 2RGR	Deployed as ISR Company.

RGR Unit and Sub-Unit Operational Deployments to Afghanistan

These deployments are described in detail in Chapter 5.

Operation Name	Dates	Deployment Theatre	Unit/Sub-Unit	Remarks
Operation Fingal	January 2002–March 2002	Afghanistan	C (Cassino) Company 2PARA	Note that this GRC was also sometimes referred to as C (Gurkha) Company 2PARA.
Operations Tarrock and Fingal	October 2003–April 2004	Afghanistan	2RGR	The deployment comprised of 220 men. Deployment was Kabul-centric.
Operation Herrick 2	March 2005–October 2005	Afghanistan	2RGR	The deployment was Kabul-centric.
Operation Herrick 4	April 2006–October 2006	Afghanistan	D (Tamandu) Company RGR	This was a composite company with manpower from both 1RGR and 2RGR. The company deployed under command 16 Air Assault Brigade.
Operation Herrick 7	September 2007–April 2008	Afghanistan	1RGR	The battalion deployed from Brunei. Its role was manoeuvre strike force, not ground holding.
Operation Herrick 9	September 2008–April 2009	Afghanistan	2RGR (-)	C Company deployed on Operation Herrick 10.
Operation Herrick 10	April 2009–October 2009	Afghanistan	C Company 2RGR aka Foxtrot (Tavoleto) Company	The company was augmented by reinforcements from 1RGR and deployed under command of 19 Light Brigade.
Operation Herrick 12	April 2010–October 2010	Afghanistan	1RGR	
			G (Tobruk) Company 1MERCIAN	The company was formed with soldiers from 1RGR.
Operation Herrick 14	April 2011–October 2011	Afghanistan	2RGR	The battalion formed the core of the Police Mentoring and Advisory Group (PMAG).
Operation Herrick 15	October 2011–April 2012	Afghanistan	C Company 1YORKS (GRC 3)	The company changed its name in theatre to D (Delhi) Company when it was placed under the command of a Danish battlegroup.
Operation Herrick 17	October 2012–April 2013	Afghanistan	1RGR	Sub-units deployed under the command of other units. BG HQ incorporated into HQ 4 Mechanised Brigade.
Operation Toral 3[250]	April 2016–December 2016	Afghanistan	2RGR	Split tour construct: battalion HQ deployed for 8 months with rifle companies rotating out of theatre at the 4 month point.
Operation Toral 7	November 2018–May 2019	Afghanistan	1RGR	

RGR Unit and Sub-Unit Operational Deployments (excluding Afghanistan and the Balkans)
These deployments are described in detail in Chapters 3, 4 and 6. Note that deployments in support of the civilian authorities in UK are not included, nor are deployments to deliver training to foreign military forces (such as Operation Newcombe in Mali).

Operation Name	Dates	Deployment Theatre	Unit/Sub-Unit	Remarks
Operation Determinant	28 April 1997–22 May 1997	Zaire/Democratic Republic of the Congo	B (Sobraon) Company 1PWRR	Zaire changed its name to the Democratic Republic of the Congo in May 1997. The company deployed to Ghana as part of 1PWRR and remained on stand-by to conduct a non-combatant evacuation in Zaire which, in the event, was not required
Operation Langar	September 1999–December 1999	East Timor	A Company 2RGR, Battalion Headquarters (-)	The company group deployed as part of INTERFET, a UN mission led by an Australian 2*.
Operation Palliser	5 May 2000–25 May 2000	Sierra Leone	C (Cassino) Company 2PARA	The company deployed with 1PARA to conduct a non-combatant evacuation operation.
Operation Silkman	August 2000–October 2000	Sierra Leone	D (Gurkha) Company 1RIRISH	The company deployed as part of 1RIRISH.
Operation Silkman	December 2000–April 2001	Sierra Leone	2RGR	In total, 320 men deployed to form Short Term Training Teams (STTTs).
Operation Silkman	January 2002–March 2002	Sierra Leone	Support Company 1RGR	Deployed in early January 2002 and provided training teams to assist with basic training. 42 personnel from Support Company deployed from Brunei
	January 2002–April 2002	Sierra Leone	D Company 1RGR	Provided force protection (from 31 January 2002)
	March 2002–June 2002	Sierra Leone	A Company 1RGR	Replaced Support Company 1RGR in delivering training support.
	April 2002–July 2002	Sierra Leone	B Company 1RGR	Replaced D Company 1RGR in providing force protection.
Operation Keeling	February 2003–March 2003	Sierra Leone	2 x Companies 2RGR	Very High Readiness Spearhead Land Element (SLE) deployment to pre-empt a possible coup when the International Special Court arrested key political figures.
Operation Telic	March 2003–May 2003	Iraq	D (Gurkha) Company 1RIRISH	The company deployed as part of 1RIRISH.
Operation Phillis	11 November 2004–12 November 2004	Ivory Coast	C Company 1RGR, Battalion Headquarters (-)	Operation Phillis was a non-combatant evacuation operation.

Organisational Changes

Over the course of its 25 year history, there have been numerous changes to The Royal Gurkha Rifles' (RGR's) order of battle. These have included a reduction in the number of battalions, the formation and disbandment of Gurkha Reinforcement Companies, the Band of the Brigade of Gurkhas and the clerks exchanging their RGR cap badges for ones of their own, the transfer of the chefs to The Queen's Own Gurkha Logistic Regiment, an uplift in RGR posts within the Allied Rapid Reaction Corps (ARRC) Support Battalion and, most recently, the decision to form another RGR infantry battalion. Despite the turbulence, the overall trend is extremely positive for the RGR. With the creation of approximately 415 new posts, the RGR's total strength is set to reach 1,652 over the next few years, its highest figure for more than two decades and one that means it will account for 41% of the Gurkha manpower within the Brigade of Gurkhas' total strength of 4,030.[251]

THE RGR BATTALIONS
1RGR

1RGR was formed on 1 July 1994 when the 1st Battalion 2nd King Edward VII's Own Gurkha Rifles (2GR) and the 6th Queen Elizabeth's Own Gurkha Rifles (6GR) amalgamated.

2RGR

2RGR was formed on 1 July 1994 when the 1st Battalion 7th Duke of Edinburgh's Own Gurkha Rifles (7GR) retitled to become 2RGR. On 18 November 1996, this 2RGR then merged with 3RGR to become the current 2RGR.

3RGR

3RGR was formed on 1 July 1994 when the 10th Princess Mary's Own Gurkha Rifles (10GR) retitled to become 3RGR. 3RGR ceased to exist on 18 November 1996 when it merged with 2RGR to become the current 2RGR. However, this year (2019) the Secretary of State for Defence announced that a 'new' 3RGR would begin being formed later this year. This battalion will be the fifth of five new Specialised Infantry Battalions being formed as a result of the 2015 National Security Strategy and Strategic Defence and Security Review. The timelines for when the new 3RGR will enter operational service are still being developed.[252]

THE ORIGINAL GURKHA REINFORCEMENT COMPANIES (GRCs)

When 2RGR and 3RGR amalgamated in late 1996, some of the pain of this, in terms of making soldiers redundant, was reduced by the requirement to form three GRCs, each of about 100 men. The first three GRCs formed up in Knook Camp (on Salisbury Plain

Training Area (SPTA)) in November 1996 before joining their new units in December 1996.

GRC 1

GRC 1 joined the 1st Battalion The Royal Scots (1RS) as B (Gallipoli) Company 1RS in December 1996. It deployed twice to Bosnia and Herzegovina on Operation Palatine: the first deployment took place from July 1998 to January 1999 and was as the Banja Luka based Divisional Defence Company; the second deployment took place only six months later from July 1999 to October 1999. The role on the second deployment was the same as the role on the first but the name had changed to the Banja Luka Operations Company (BLOC).

The company transferred to the 1st Battalion The Highlanders (Seaforth, Gordons and Camerons) (1HLDRS) on 28 March 2000 and changed its name from B (Gallipoli) Company 1RS to A (Gallipoli)

Company 1HLDRS. Following a tour in the Falkland Islands (July 2000 to November 2000), it deployed with 1HLDRS to the Balkans on Operation Palatine from March 2003 to October 2003.

Throughout its tour with 1HLDRS on Operation Palatine, the company had its own area of responsibility centred on Mrkonjic Grad Bus Depot (MGBD), with platoons located in the outlying areas of Knesevo and Kotor Varos. The company's mission was to: "conduct operations to maintain and extend the safe and secure environment (SSE) and, selectively, to support civil implementation within boundaries and consolidate stability in Bosnia Herzegovina".[253] The company disbanded in March 2004.

GRC 2

GRC 2 joined the 1st Battalion The Princess of Wales's Royal Regiment (1PWRR) as B (Sobraon) Company 1PWRR in December 1996. Whilst with 1PWRR, it deployed to Zaire (later the Democratic Republic of the Congo) on Operation Determinant from 28 April 1997 to 22 May 1997. It remained with 1PWRR until December 1999, when it transferred to the 1st Battalion The Royal Irish Regiment (1RIRISH), becoming D (Gurkha) Company 1RIRISH. It deployed to Sierra Leone from August 2000 until October 2000 on Operation Silkman and to Iraq from March 2003 until May 2003 on Operation Telic. The company disbanded in May 2003 on return from Iraq.

Above left: Members of the command team of B (Sobraon) Company 1PWRR in the Republic of the Congo waiting to deploy forward to evacuate entitled personnel from Zaire/the Democratic Republic of the Congo during Operation Determinant (28 April to 22 May 1997).

Left: Members of A (Gallipoli) Company 1HLDRS proudly displaying some of the weapons and munitions they recovered in Bosnia and Herzegovina during their deployment with 1HLDRS on Operation Palatine (from March 2003 to October 2003).

Left: Members of C (Cassino) Company 2PARA in Afghanistan during Operation Fingal (January to March 2002).

Above: D (Tamandu) Company in Afghanistan on Operation Herrick 4 (April to October 2006). The photograph was taken towards the end of the company's tour on 1 October 2006.

GRC 3

GRC 3 joined the 2nd Battalion The Parachute Regiment (2PARA) as C (Cassino) Company 2PARA in December 1996. The company deployed to Bosnia on Operation Palatine from January 1999 to July 1999 and was based in the Banja Luka Metal Factory as the Banja Luka Operations Company (BLOC). It deployed to Sierra Leone on Operation Palliser from 5–25 May 2000 and then to Macedonia on Operation Bessemer from August 2001 until October 2001. Within a few months of its return, it deployed to Afghanistan on Operation Fingal from January 2002 to March 2002.

The company, which was sometimes referred to as C (Gurkha) Company by non-Brigade of Gurkhas units/organisations, was disbanded in May 2002.

SUBSEQUENT GRCs AND ADDITIONAL COMPANIES

D (Tamandu) Company RGR

In early 2006, both 1RGR, which was in Bosnia and Herzegovina at the time, and 2RGR contributed manpower to form D (Tamandu) Company RGR. The company formed up in Risborough Barracks in Shorncliffe in January 2006 and deployed on Operation Herrick 4 with 16 Air Assault Brigade in April 2006.

The company returned from Afghanistan in October 2006, disbanding in January 2007 with soldiers returning to their parent battalions. This company is sometimes referred to as another GRC 1.

Foxtrot (Tavoleto) Company

When 2RGR deployed on Operation Herrick 9, much of the manpower from C Company 2RGR was taken to reinforce the other companies. However, reinforcements arrived from 1RGR to bring the company up to strength before it deployed on Operation Herrick 10 under the direct command of 19 Light Brigade. In recognition of its composite nature, the company was given the title 'Foxtrot (Tavoleto) Company', supposedly after 'Ferret Force', a composite company that saw service during the Malayan Emergency. The company deployed to Afghanistan in April 2009 and returned to UK in October 2009, shedding its additional manpower back to 1RGR and disbanding as Foxtrot (Tavoleto) Company. Perhaps unhelpfully, this company is occasionally also referred to as another GRC 1.

G (Tobruk) Company/D (Kandahar) Company

In December 2008, the RGR was tasked to form a GRC to support the 1st Battalion The Mercian Regiment (Cheshire) (1MERCIAN) on Operation Herrick 12. The company was formed with soldiers from 1RGR and was known as G (Tobruk) Company 1MERCIAN. It deployed with 1MERCIAN to Afghanistan from April until October 2010 on Herrick 12. Following its return from Afghanistan, it was reattributed to 1RGR on 31 March 2011 to become D (Kandahar) Company 1RGR, deploying on Operation Herrick 17 with 1RGR in October 2012.

The company's formal disbandment took place on 28 June 2013 at a medals parade held in Sir John Moore Barracks during which operational service medals for Afghanistan were awarded by Brigadier Robert 'Bob' Bruce, the Commander of 4 Mechanised Brigade during Operation Herrick 17. The company is sometimes referred to as another GRC 2.

C Company 1YORKS/D (Delhi) Company

In July/August 2009, a GRC was formed from 2RGR personnel to serve with the 1st Battalion The Yorkshire Regiment (1YORKS) as its C Company. Initially, the aim was that the company would serve for six years but this was subsequently reduced to three years, culminating in a deployment to

Afghanistan with 1YORKS in October 2011 on Operation Herrick 15.[254] The company changed its name to D (Delhi) Company in theatre when it was placed under the operational command of a Danish battlegroup.

The company returned from Afghanistan in April 2012 and was disbanded in September 2012.

PERMANENT COMPANIES

Gurkha Company Sittang – Royal Military Academy Sandhurst

Gurkha Company Sittang (GCS) provides support to the Royal Military Academy Sandhurst (RMAS). The majority of its soldiers and officers come from 1RGR and 2RGR but it also includes officers and soldiers from The Queen's Gurkha Engineers, The Queen's Own Gurkha Logistic Regiment, Queen's Gurkha Signals and the Gurkha Staff and Personnel Support Company.

Gurkha Company Mandalay – Infantry Battle School, Brecon

Gurkha Company Mandalay (GCM) provides general training and duties support to Headquarters Infantry Battle School (IBS) and the Training Divisions in Brecon, Wales. Like Gurkha Company Sittang, the majority of its soldiers and officers come from 1RGR and 2RGR, though it also includes a small number of personnel from The Queen's Gurkha Engineers, The Queen's Own Gurkha Logistic Regiment, Queen's Gurkha Signals and the Gurkha Staff and Personnel Support Company.

G (Tobruk) Company on parade with 1MERCIAN, which, on 3 June 2009, exercised its Freedom of the City of Chester by marching through the city's streets (image Crown copyright 2009).

Gurkha Company Tavoleto – Specialist Weapons School, Land Warfare Centre, Warminster

Gurkha Company Tavoleto (GCT) provides manpower and equipment support to the Specialist Weapons School (SWS) and the Reconnaissance and Armoured Tactics Division within the Land Warfare Centre (LWC) in Warminster. The transition of the old Training Support Company (TSC) to an all-Gurkha structure started in 2017 but it was not until 30 August 2018 that the company was officially renamed as GCT.

Like GCS and GCM, the majority of GCT's soldiers and officers come from 1RGR and 2RGR, though it also includes a small number of personnel from The Queen's Gurkha Engineers, The Queen's Own Gurkha Logistic Regiment, Queen's Gurkha Signals and the Gurkha Staff and Personnel Support Company.

Gurkha Company Catterick

Gurkha Company Catterick is part of the 2nd Infantry Training Battalion (2ITB) at the Infantry Training Centre (ITC) in Catterick. It is responsible for delivering basic infantry training to all Gurkha recruits, not just those destined for the RGR. It was set up in December 1999 when the previous recruit training organisation, known as the Gurkha

Training Wing, relocated from Queen Elizabeth Barracks, Church Crookham. Gurkha Company now delivers a 39 week Combat Infantryman's Course (Gurkha) (CIC(G)). Its mission is to "…deliver trained Gurkha soldiers in order to meet the operational

Above: Lieutenant General Sir David Bill presenting a prize to one of the instructional staff of Gurkha Company Catterick during the end of course parade for Gurkha Recruits in 2010. A senior Gurkha officer from the RGR looks on, demonstrating the multi-cap badge nature of the company (image Crown copyright 2009).

Left: The General Officer Commanding the Army Recruiting and Individual Training Command (ARITC), Major General P A E Nanson CBE, was the Reviewing Officer at Gurkha Company Tavoleto's Formation Parade held on 30 August 2018 (image Crown copyright 2018).

Left: Drums of the Band of the Brigade of Gurkhas showing the cap badge adopted by the band in 2002. Until then, band members wore the RGR cap badge (shown to the left of the band's cap badge on the left hand drum).

Above and top: A bugler from the RGR and a trumpet player from the Band of the Brigade of Gurkhas taking part in a parade in February 2009. The differences in the cap badges and uniforms are readily apparent (images Crown copyright 2009).

requirements of the Brigade of Gurkhas".[255] The company's composition broadly reflects the composition of the serving Brigade of Gurkhas. As a result, there is a mix of Gurkha cap badges, though the majority of personnel are from 1RGR and 2RGR.

Other Organisations

The Band of the Brigade of Gurkhas

From 1 July 1994 when the RGR was formed, the Band of the Brigade of Gurkhas, which had previously worn the cap badge of the 2nd King Edward VII's Own Gurkha Rifles (2GR), adopted the cap badge of the RGR. It retained this cap badge until 2002 when it was given permission to wear its own cap badge. The band is based in Sir John Moore Barracks with the resident UK Gurkha Battalion (UKGB). In early 2019 following a formal review of Army Bands, an uplift of a 13 posts to the strength of the Band of the Brigade of Gurkhas was announced, making it a Type 54 Band and bringing it into line with other Army Bands.

The Band of the Brigade of Gurkhas and the Pipes and Drums of the two RGR battalions frequently perform together as in this photograph taken during a Brigade Reunion in July 2011.

Above: Members of the Band of the Brigade of Gurkhas in conversation with the Colonel-in-Chief of the RGR, His Royal Highness The Prince of Wales, during a medal parade for 1RGR in 2011 (image Crown copyright 2011).

Left: The Band of the Brigade of Gurkhas giving a concert in Cyprus. The band works hard to make its concerts interesting by including traditional Nepali dances, including the kukri dance, in its programme.

The Gurkha Staff and Personnel Support Company (GSPS Company)

On 1 July 1994 when the RGR was formed, clerks within the Brigade of Gurkhas' infantry battalions replaced the cap badges of their antecedent regiments with that of the RGR. They retained this cap badge until, on 30 June 2011, a Formation Parade was held at Sir John Moore Barracks in Shorncliffe at which the clerks of the Brigade of Gurkhas exchanged their RGR cap badges for the badge of the newly formed Gurkha Staff and Personnel Support Company (GSPS Company).

Chefs of The Queen's Own Gurkha Logistic Regiment

On 5 April 2002, the chefs of the RGR exchanged their RGR cap badges for those of The Queen's Own Gurkha Logistic Regiment. Although it was sad to see many old friends cease to be members of the RGR, the move made sense in terms of improving the career management of these vital professionals.

Above: The Reviewing Officer for the Formation Parade was General Sir David (later Lord) Richards, the Chief of Defence Staff (CDS). Despite the inclement weather, the parade was a success and provided a fitting launch for the GSPS.

The weather continued to deteriorate during the course of the GSPS Formation Parade on 30 June 2011. Notwithstanding this, the stalwart members of the GSPS delivered an excellent performance, thanking the Chief of Defence Staff (CDS) with a rousing cheer at the conclusion of the parade.

Battle Honours of The Royal Gurkha Rifles

CAP BADGE

The cap badge of The Royal Gurkha Rifles incorporates crossed kukris with Sovereign's (St Edward's) Crown on top, blades crossed left over right, cutting edges outwards, all in silver.

ANTECEDENT REGIMENTS

2nd King Edward VII's Own Gurkha Rifles (The Sirmoor Rifles)
6th Queen Elizabeth's Own Gurkha Rifles
7th Duke of Edinburgh's Own Gurkha Rifles
10th Princess Mary's Own Gurkha Rifles

REGIMENTAL BATTLE HONOURS

Note that battle honours in bold are authorised for emblazonment on the Regimental drums.

Amboor, Carnatic, Mysore, Assaye, Ava, Bhurtpore, Aliwal, Sobroan. Delhi 1857, Kandahar 1880, Afghanistsan 1878–80, Burma 1885–87, Tirah, Punjab Frontier.

The First World War: La Bassée 1914, **Festubert 1914, 1915, Givenchy 1914, Neuve Chapelle, Aubers, Loos,** France and Flanders 1914–15, **Helles, Krithia, Suvla, Sari Bair, Gallipoli 1915,** Suez Canal, **Megiddo,** Egypt 1915–16, **Sharon,** Palestine 1918, Shaiba, **Kut al Amara 1915, 1917, Ctesiphon, Defence of Kut al Amara, Tigris 1916,** Baghdad,

Khan Baghdadi, **Sharqat, Mesopotamia 1915–18, Persia 1918, North West Frontier India 1915,** Baluchistan 1918

Afghanistan 1919

The Second World War: Iraq 1941, Deir ez Zor, Syria 1941, **Tobruk 1942, El Alamein, Mareth,** Akarit, Djebel el Meida, Enfidaville, **Tunis,** North Africa 1942-43, **Cassino I,** Monastery Hill, Pian di Maggio, Campriano, **Poggio Del Grillo, Gothic Line, Tavoleto, Coriano,** Poggio San Giovanni, Montebello-Scorticata Ridge, **Santarcangelo,** Monte Reggiano, **Monte Chicco,** Lamone Crossing, Senio Floodbank, **Bologna,** Sillaro Crossing, **Medicina,** Gaiana Crossing, **Italy 1944–45,** Greece 1944–45, North Malaya, **Jitra,** Central Malaya, Kampar, **Slim River,** Johore, Singapore Island, Malaya 1941-42, **Sittang 1942, 1945,** Pegu 1942, 1945, **Kyaukse 1942,** 1945, Monywa 1942, Shwegyin, **North Arakan, Imphal, Tuitum,** Tamu Road, Shenam Pass, Litan, **Bishenpur, Tengnoupal,** Shwebo, **Kyaukmyaung Bridgehead, Mandalay, Myinmu Bridgehead, Fort Dufferin,** Maymo, **Meiktila,** Capture of Meiktila, Defence of Meiktila, **Irrawaddy,** Magwe, **Rangoon Road,** Pyawbwe, Toungoo, Point 1433, Arakan Beaches, Myebon, **Tamandu, Chindits 1943, 1945, Burma 1942–45**

Falkland Islands 1982

A painting by Terence Cuneo showing the battle for Medicina in April 1945. 2/6th Gurkhas fought alongside 14th/20th King's Hussars, forging a friendship which continues to this day between The Royal Gurkha Rifles and The King's Royal Hussars. To commemorate this battle, Support Company 1RGR has Medicina in its full title and observes Medicina Day on 16 April every year.

REGIMENTAL MARCHES

Quick March: Bravest of the Brave
Double March: The Keel Row
Slow March (Band): God Bless the Prince of Wales
Slow March (Pipes): The Garb of Old Gaul

REGIMENTAL HOLIDAYS

Meiktila Day (7GR): 1 March (1945)
Medicina Day (6GR): 16 April (1945)
The Royal Gurkha Rifles' Regimental Birthday:
    1 July (1994)
Gallipoli Day (10GR): 7 August (1915)
Delhi Day (2GR): 14 September (1857)

AFFILIATED REGIMENTS

The King's Royal Hussars
The Royal Regiment of Scotland
The Rifles

COLONEL-IN-CHIEF

His Royal Highness The Prince of Wales KG KT GCB OM AK QSO NPC ADC

REGIMENTAL COLONEL

Major General G M Strickland DSO MBE

REGIMENTAL SECRETARY

Major (Retd) B McKay MBE

COMPANY BATTLE HONOUR DAYS

Every company in The Royal Gurkha Rifles (RGR) has the name of a famous battle in which one of the antecedent regiments fought incorporated into its name. For example, in 1RGR, A Company's full name is A (Delhi) Company and in 2RGR, A Company's full name is A (Amboor) Company. Each company celebrates its battle honour on a particular date depending on when the battle took place. Again, taking A Company as an example, in 1RGR, A (Delhi) Company celebrates Delhi Day on 14 September and in 2RGR, A (Amboor) Company celebrates Amboor Day on 16 December. The notes that follow were researched and drafted by Captain Michael Barney RGR and give the background to each company's Battle Honour Day.

FIRST BATTALION THE ROYAL GURKHA RIFLES

A COMPANY

Battle Honour: DELHI
Date: 14 September (1857)
Campaign: The Indian Mutiny (1857–59)

Antecedent Unit: The Sirmoor Battalion (later 2nd King Edward VII's Own Gurkha Rifles (The Sirmoor Rifles)).

Background: During the Indian Mutiny, Delhi became a base for over 40,000 mutineers. On 8 June 1857, The Sirmoor Battalion, under Major Charles Reid, was ordered to hold Hindu Rao's House on the ridge overlooking the city. This was the southernmost British position and within 1,200 metres of the City Walls. Elements of the Corps of Guides and the 60th Rifles were also stationed in this main piquet and a close relationship developed with both regiments. When reinforcements finally arrived the final attack on Delhi was ordered for 14 September 1857. The Sirmoor Battalion joined the Fourth Assault Column for the attack and on 21 September the city was declared captured. For three months and eight days Hindu Rao's House had been under daily artillery fire and attack from up to 10,000 mutineers. The Sirmoor Battalion suffered 327 casualties of the 490 who had entered the siege, including 8 of 9 British Officers killed or wounded.

In 1858, the Sirmoor Battalion was awarded a third honorary colour for its part in the siege. Later that year it was renamed the Sirmoor Rifle Regiment, allowed to wear the rifle green uniforms and scarlet (known as 'lali' in Nepali) of the 60th Rifles and ordered that their private soldiers should be known as riflemen rather than sepoys. In 1863, the Regiment was presented with the Queen's Truncheon to replace the old colours no longer allowed to be carried by a regular rifle regiment. For more details of the Queen's Truncheon see Special Interest Section 1.

B COMPANY

Battle Honour: SARI BAIR
Date: 9 August (1915)
Campaign: Gallipoli, First World War (1914–18)

Antecedent Unit: 1/6th Gurkha Rifles (later 6th Queen Elizabeth's Own Gurkha Rifles)

Background: During the First World War, the Allies landed troops on the Gallipoli Peninsula in an attempt to capture Constantinople and knock Turkey out of the War, which would force Germany to fight a war on two fronts. 1/6GR arrived in Gallipoli in April 1915 and fought a number of hard battles, including the capture of a prominent enemy position that subsequently became known as Gurkha Bluff. By August a stalemate had developed and a new offensive was planned. An attack was ordered on the Sari Bair ridge and 1/6GR were tasked with capturing an objective known as Hill Q. During the afternoon of 7 August the battalion conducted recces and early on the morning of 8 August the battalion began its move up the hill. 200 yards from the crest, the battalion came under heavy fire and by the night of the 8 August had only managed to gain 50 yards. A final assault was ordered for dawn on the 9 August and after 30 minutes of accurate artillery fire the battalion advanced under Major Cecil Allanson. Hand-to-hand fighting then ensured, with the Turks eventually retreating down the far side of the hill pursued by the Gurkhas until they were hit by friendly artillery fire.

The men of the 6th Gurkhas held the top of the ridge for 15 minutes until, realising that they were isolated and in the face of Turks advancing back up the hill, they were forced to return to their positions of the night before. By the morning of 10 August the battalion had lost all of its British Officers killed or wounded, and command had devolved to Captain E S Phipson, the Regimental Medical Officer, who by virtue of being a British Officer outranked the remaining Gurkha officers, including Subedar Major Gambirsingh Pun. Receiving the order to withdraw, Phipson sent his *salaams* to Gambirsingh who, although unable to speak, read or write English, had the experience required to withdraw the battalion in good order. Gambirsingh organised the men whilst Phipson liaised with the British units to their rear and by late afternoon on 10 August the battalion had withdrawn from the Hill with all its wounded, having destroyed any materiel that could not be carried. 1/6GR were the only unit to capture their objective during the attack on the Sari Bair feature.

C COMPANY

Battle Honour: MOGAUNG
Date: 23 June (1944)
Campaign: Burma, Second World War (1939–45)

Antecedent Unit: 3/6th Gurkha Rifles (later 6th Queen Elizabeth's Own Gurkha Rifles)

Background: The Chindits, named after the Chinthe, the mythical half-lion, half-griffin that guards Burmese monasteries and temples, were a special force created to conduct guerrilla warfare and long-range penetration behind the Japanese lines in Burma during the Second World War. Although the first Chindit expedition, which was launched in February 1943, might have achieved little militarily, it was beyond price as propaganda; the Chindits were portrayed as having run rings round the Japanese, helping to destroy the myth that they could not be beaten in the jungle. A second Chindit expedition was ordered for March 1944. This time, the aim was to establish strongholds deep behind enemy lines from which to launch attacks against the enemy's lines of communication. From March 1944, 3/6GR, as part of 77 Brigade, defended their stronghold known as *White City* until May when they were ordered to capture Mogaung where 4,000 Japanese

were opposing Chinese forces. The 160 mile approach march to Mogaung was marked by a series of bloody encounters. In addition, the monsoon had broken and conditions were appalling; malaria and typhus were rife. By the time the brigade reached Mogaung less than 550 fighting men remained of the original 3,500; 230 of these were the Gurkhas of 3/6GR.

During the advance, on 11 June Captain Michael Allmand carried out the first act of gallantry for which he would subsequently be awarded the Victoria Cross (VC). The second act was on 13 June on a ridge closer to the town whilst he was commanding B Company. On 23 June, Allmand's leadership and example led to the capture of the Railway Bridge at Mogaung, though he was mortally wounded in the assault. On the same day, Rifleman Tulbahadur Pun's assault on a position known as Red House led to him also being awarded the VC. That night the Japanese abandoned the town. Mogaung was the first main town in Burma to be re-captured and, while technically not a Battle Honour, is commemorated by the RGR in recognition of the VCs awarded during the action.

SUPPORT COMPANY

Battle Honour: MEDICINA
Date: 16 April (1945)
Campaign: Italy, Second World War (1939–45)

Antecedent Unit: 2/6th Gurkha Rifles (later 6th Queen Elizabeth's Own Gurkha Rifles)

Background: The Battle of Medicina took place in the closing weeks of the Second World War. Although the war in Europe was almost over the German troops in northern Italy offered staunch resistance in ground that was easy to defend. 2/6GR had been motorised in 1940 and arrived with their 'Kangaroos' in Italy in August 1944. Kangaroos were rudimentary armoured personnel carriers made from Sherman tanks with the turrets removed. Each carrier could carry ten infantry soldiers, and men of the 14th/20th King's Hussars drove 2/6GR's Kangaroos. Protecting the Corps' right flank, 2/6GR were ordered to capture Medicina. The town was not of particular importance but for its garrison of German paratroopers, well-armed and well-led, who were dug-in and prepared to hold the town for as long as possible. The town's streets were narrow and the houses had cellars and attics which gave the defenders an advantage.

By 1800 hours on 16 April 1945, 2/6GR were dismounted and, following dive-bombing by Allied aircraft, entered the town. In one case Subedar Raghu Gurung rushed forward and killed a German gun crew with his kukri in order to prevent an Allied tank from being destroyed. Similarly, throughout the battle, the tanks of the 14th/20th were extremely close, destroying German strong points, creating entry points to buildings and providing fire support for the Gurkha troops as they cleared cellars and rooftops.

By 2100 hours, the key points had been captured but flushing the defenders from the buildings continued until daybreak the following morning when the remaining Germans surrendered. 70 Germans were captured, as well as a number of artillery pieces and one Tiger tank. The number of German dead is unknown but the number cannot have been less than 100. Between them, 2/6GR and 14th/20th King's Hussars suffered fewer than 30 casualties. 2/6GR and the 14th/20th King's Hussars were the only regiments in the British Army to receive the Battle Honour 'Medicina'. The battle resulted in the two regiments forming a relationship that still exists today in that the King's Royal Hussars (the successor regiment to the 14th/20th King's Hussars) is formally affiliated to The Royal Gurkha Rifles (the successor regiment to the 6th Gurkha Rifles).

HEADQUARTER COMPANY

Battle Honour: BURMA

Date: 1 March (1945)

Campaign: Burma, Second World War (1939–45)

Antecedent Unit: 2nd King Edward VII's Own Gurkha Rifles (The Sirmoor Rifles); 6th Gurkha Rifles (later 6th Queen Elizabeth's Own Gurkha Rifles); 7th Gurkha Rifles (later 7th Duke of Edinburgh's Own Gurkha Rifles); 10th Gurkha Rifles (later 10th Princess Mary's Own Gurkha Rifles)

Background: The Burma Campaign was fought by Allied forces against the invading forces of Imperial Japan. Gurkha regiments were involved throughout, each at different stages of the campaign, as part of XIVth Army. The Burma Campaign was characterised by the fanatical Japanese enemy, unforgiving terrain and climate, and Churchill's policy of defeating 'Germany first' which meant that Burma was simply not a priority for Allied resources, a situation that led to the XIVth Army being nicknamed: "The Forgotten Army". Allied forces were unprepared for the tenacity and relentlessness of the Japanese and initially suffered catastrophic losses, which forced them back into northern India. Under the leadership of Lieutenant General William 'Bill' Slim, a former British Officer of 6GR and 7GR, the Allies were able to reverse the situation and, fighting a long campaign down through Burma, force the Japanese out in 1945. For more details about General 'Bill' Slim, one of the British Army's greatest ever generals, see Appendix 10.

The 1 March was the first day of the battle for Meiktila. This marked the defeat of most of the Japanese forces in Burma and allowed the relatively swift recapture of Rangoon and the rest of the country. During the Burma campaign, Gurkha infantry regiments won 9 VCs, a quite remarkable achievement.

SECOND BATTALION THE ROYAL GURKHA RIFLES

A COMPANY

Battle Honour: AMBOOR

Date: 16 December (1767)

Campaign: First Anglo–Mysore War (1766–1769)

Antecedent Unit: 10th Regiment of Madras Native Infantry (later 10th Princess Mary's Own Gurkha Rifles)

Background: The 16 December 1767 commemorates the 10th Madras Native Infantry's (antecedent regiment of 10th Princess Mary's Own Gurkha Rifles) defence of Amboor against the huge armies of Hyder Ali Khan of Mysore and the Nizam of Hyderabad during the first Mysore War of 1767 – 1769. The Regiment successfully held Amboor from 10 November to 7 December 1767, despite a bombardment lasting thirteen days and nights, several attacks and repeated attempts at intrigue and bribery. By holding Amboor, the Regiment bought time for the main field army to reassemble and drive the enemy out of British territory. The 16 December was chosen by 10GR to mark Amboor Day as it was the date the Regiment was granted new colours bearing the word 'Amboor' and the badge of a Rock Fort. It was the first time that any unit of the British Indian Armies had been granted an 'Honorary Distinction' or 'Battle Honour' as a reward for success in action; The Royal Gurkha Rifles is the only regiment in the British Army to bear the Battle Honour Amboor.

B COMPANY

Battle Honour: GALLIPOLI

Date: 07 August (1915)

Campaign: Gallipoli, First World War (1914–18)

Antecedent Unit: 2/10th Gurkha Rifles (later 10th Princess Mary's Own Gurkha Rifles)

Background: During the First World War the Allies landed troops on the Gallipoli Peninsula in an attempt to capture Constantinople and knock Turkey out of the War, which would force Germany to fight a war on two fronts. 2/10GR arrived in Gallipoli on 3 June 1915 and fought a number of hard battles before being given a role in the August Offensive, which was designed to end the stalemate that had developed on the peninsula.

The 10th Gurkhas, as part of 29th Indian Brigade along with the 1/5th and 1/6th Gurkha Rifles, began its attack on 7 August. Despite the confusion caused by the inhospitable terrain and difficulties in communication between a plethora of units and sub-units, 2/10GR, along with 1/5GR, managed to push further towards its objective, Hill Q, than any other unit on the first day of the battle until it was pinned down by Turkish machine gun fire and forced to retire. 2/10GR continued its attacks over the course of 8 August but, on the 9 August and within view of their objective, suffered 20% casualties to a Turkish counter-attack and was forced to withdraw. 2/10GR was in the forefront of this bitter battle and lost nearly half of its effective strength in four days. While the August Offensive was ultimately a defeat, the role of 2/10GR in the battle was highly regarded and the Regiment chose 7 August, the day the offensive started, to mark the Battle Honour.

C COMPANY

Battle Honour: TAMANDU

Date: 5 March (1945)

Campaign: Burma, Second World War (1939–45)

Antecedent Unit: 3rd Battalion 2nd King Edward VII's Own Gurkha Rifles (The Sirmoor Rifles).

Background: The Battle of Tamandu was 3/2GR's last battle of the Second World War. 3/2GR had been in the Arakan, an unforgiving area of coastal jungle and mangrove swamps on the border between Burma and India, since March 1944 and after a year were in sight of closing the final escape route for Japanese troops in the east of Burma.

3/2GR were ordered to capture a ridge known as Snowdon, which it did almost without a shot being fired on 4 March. However, that evening as the battalion was digging in, the Japanese counter-attacked and fighting continued through the night until, despite great bravery and loss, Snowdon East was back in the enemy's hands. Heavy mist delayed operations but on the afternoon of 5 March 3/2GR attacked again. The Japanese put up fierce resistance and the Commanding Officer was in the middle of sending a radio message to Brigade Headquarters asking to postpone the attack until the next day when news reached him that the leading platoons had reached the objective. It then emerged that Rifleman Bhangbaghta Gurung had carried the assault almost single-handedly. On no fewer than five individual occasions, Bhangbaghta had advanced ahead of his platoon and captured machine gun, tree sniper and bunker positions alone. This gallantry had inspired the other men of his platoon to advance, and eventually reach their objective. Rifleman Bhangbhagta received the VC.

SUPPORT COMPANY

Battle Honour: IMPHAL

Date: 21 June (1944)

Campaign: Burma, Second World War (1939–45)

Antecedent Unit: 10th Gurkha Rifles (later 10th Princess Mary's Own Gurkha Rifles)

Background: From 12 March to 21 June of 1944, 1/10GR, 3/10GR and 4/10GR were involved in the heaviest fighting of the entire Burma campaign in the defence of Imphal. A major Japanese offensive was conducted in the Imphal-Kohima area of Burma and India; this failed attempt by the Japanese to sever lines of communication between the British and the Chinese paved the way for an Allied counterattack, which eventually led to the defeat of the Japanese in Burma. 1/10GR and 3/10GR distinguished themselves in actions around the Tiddim Road and 1/10GR repulsed repeated Japanese attacks between 13 and 25 March, killing over 250 Japanese and themselves suffering 21 killed and over 100 wounded. In recognition of this achievement, the Divisional Commander conferred upon the Battalion the unique privilege of flying his divisional banner (the Black Cat) with the Regimental crest superimposed upon it at the Quarter Guard. 4/10GR defended the Shenam Pass and fought at Ukhral over the same period. 10GR marked Imphal Day on 21 June, the date on which the Battle of Imphal officially ended and the last of the Japanese road blocks were cleared from the Imphal-Kohima Road. The 3 battalions of 10GR, to whom the Battle Honour was awarded, suffered over 1,000 casualties.

The battle for the high ground at Monte Cassino in February 1944 involved three Gurkha units, 1/2nd, 2/7th and 1/9th Gurkha Rifles. However, despite a number of spirited assaults, they were unable to take the position, which was defended by some of the German army's most capable units. The picture shows some of the position's key features. Combat Service Support Company 2RGR has 'Cassino' in its full title and commemorates the battle on 18 February every year.

COMBAT SERVICE SUPPORT COMPANY

Battle Honour: CASSINO

Date: 18 February (1944)

Campaign: Italy, Second World War (1939–45)

Antecedent Unit: 2/7th Gurkha Rifles (later 7th Duke of Edinburgh's Own Gurkha Rifles)

Background: Monte Cassino, and the Benedictine monastery that sat atop it, was a key component of the German Army's Gustav Line, a series of immensely strong fortified positions on the western side of the Italian peninsula and one of the major barriers to an advance by the Allied Forces. The monastery had been reinforced in the face of the Allied advance and was defended by two elite German units. Three Gurkha units, 1/9GR, 1/2GR and 2/7GR, took part in the first battle to capture Cassino which began in Spring 1944. Under 4th Division, commanded by Major General Francis Tuker (himself a Gurkha officer – see Appendix 9), 2/7GR were detailed as porters to 1/2GR's assault, which began on 18 February 1944. Two companies of the battalion advanced towards the monastery. Within 800 yards of the objective, the

Gurkhas came under heavy machine gun fire and became trapped in scrub laced with booby traps and mines. 1/2GR engaged in fierce fighting, supported by 2/7GR, but eventually the units were forced to withdraw. The men of 2/7GR – who had been behind the front line as 1/2GR bore the brunt of the defence – complained that they had had to suffer punishment without having been given the opportunity to respond. Within a month of the 1/2GR and 2/7GR assault, Allied attacks on the monastery were halted due to the high casualty rates and lack of territorial gain. A plan was devised to outflank Monte Cassino and the Germans there were finally defeated on 18 May by a Polish Division.

MINOR UNIT BATTLE HONOUR DAYS

Although not entirely made up of soldiers from the RGR, the Gurkha companies based at the Royal Military Academy Sandhurst, the Infantry Battle School in Brecon and the Specialist Weapons School at the Land Warfare Centre in Warminster have incorporated battle honours from the RGR's antecedent regiments into their titles. They are therefore included in this appendix for completeness.

ROYAL MILITARY ACADEMY SANDHURST

Battle Honour: SITTANG

Date: 23 February (1942)

Campaign: Burma, Second World War (1939– 45)

Antecedent Unit: 1/7th and 3/7th Gurkha Rifles (later 7th Duke of Edinburgh's Own Gurkha Rifles)

Background: 7GR were the only antecedent regiment of The Royal Gurkha Rifles to be awarded the battle honour 'Sittang 1942', although they, 2GR and 10GR were all awarded 'Sittang 1945' for their parts in the Battle of the Sittang Bend. Having crossed the Thai border into Burma, the Japanese were advancing on Rangoon and had reached the Sittang River. The only means of crossing the river without using boats was a single-track railway bridge and 17th Indian Infantry Division were ordered to hold this at all costs.

1/3rd, 1/4th, 1/7th, 3/7th and 2/5th Gurkhas were all involved in defending the bridge and its eastern approaches against relentless Japanese attacks and in the face of friendly fire and poor communication. At 0530 hours on 23 February 1942, Major General J G 'Jackie' Smyth VC gave the order to blow the bridge. Whilst this delayed the Japanese for a few days, it also saw nearly 6,000 men of the division trapped on the Eastern bank. Amongst these were 1/3rd, 1/7th, 3/7th and 2/5th Gurkha Rifles, now faced with no means of crossing the half-mile of fast flowing water. The order was given for the defending force to exfiltrate back across the river and many troops subsequently drowned. Of the 2,500 troops lost by the 17th Division in its attempts to stop the Japanese advance, about two-thirds were Gurkhas. Following the battle, the two battalions of 7GR could only muster about 470 men between them.

This painting by David Rowlands shows men of the 3rd Gurkhas and the Duke of Wellington's Regiment assaulting a Japanese position at the eastern end of the Sittang Bridge. The Japanese were determined to capture the bridge as they advanced towards Rangoon. In the event, it was blown prematurely, leaving some 6,000 soldiers from 17th Division, including 1/3rd, 1/7th, 3/7th and 2/5th Gurkha Rifles, trapped between the river and the advancing Japanese. The Gurkha company at the Royal Military Academy Sandhurst, known as Gurkha Company Sittang, commemorates the battle for the bridge on 23 February every year.

INFANTRY BATTLE SCHOOL, BRECON

Battle Honour: MANDALAY

Date: 20 March (1945)

Campaign: Burma, Second World War (1939–45)

Antecedent Unit: 2/6th Gurkha Rifles (later 6th Queen Elizabeth's Own Gurkha Rifles)

Background: The 20 March marks the fall of Mandalay, the culmination of 19 Indian Division's 400 mile advance against ever increasing opposition. The city of Mandalay was dominated by Mandalay Hill, and the monastery atop it which overlooked the entire city, and by Fort Dufferin, a 2km square fortress with moats and walls which were 30 feet high and 4 feet thick. By the time 2/6GR arrived in the city on 10 March 1945, Mandalay Hill had already been captured by 4/4GR but bitter fighting continued in the streets of the city against the Japanese garrison. On 12 March, 2/6GR moved into the city and, on 13 March, began house-to-house fighting. By the night of 16 March, the battalion was involved in various attempts to capture Fort Dufferin. All of these failed, including the Napoleonic tactic of trying to create a breech in the walls by firing artillery at point blank range. A silent attack using scaling ladders and assault boats also failed. However, during the night of 19 March, the Japanese reneged on their order to hold Mandalay at all costs and withdrew, allowing the recapture of the fort the next morning. 2/6GR received one Military Cross (MC), one Military Medal (MM) and one MBE (Member of the Most Excellent Order of the British Empire) for their actions in Mandalay.

SPECIALIST WEAPONS SCHOOL, LAND WARFARE CENTRE, WARMINSTER

Battle Honour: TAVOLETO

Date: 3 September (1944)

Campaign: Italy, Second World War (1939–45)

Antecedent Unit: 2/7th Gurkha Rifles (later 7th Duke of Edinburgh's Own Gurkha Rifles)

Background: The Battle of Tavoleto formed part of the 8th Army's assault on the Gothic Line, the German's last major line of defence in northern Italy which ran along the top of the northern Apennine Mountains and stretched from the west to east coasts. The village of Tavoleto was a small place, remarkable only because of its situation on a ridge giving a tactical advantage over the low ground and steep approaches around it. Two companies of 2/7GR were ordered to attack uphill towards the village and to clear it of enemy at any cost. A Company repulsed an attack by German troops, supported by tanks, and then set off to a flanking position to support C Company's assault on the village. In the early hours of 3 September 1944, C Company stepped off and ran into withering fire before they reached the outskirts of the village where they were pinned down. Under the cool leadership of E D Smith, the Coy regrouped and began clearing house to house, the Germans giving no quarter and taking until 0500 hours to be ousted. The two Companies, burdened by casualties and over 100 German prisoners, were shelled and mortared for several hours before they were reinforced by B Company. Tavoleto was a success in the face of great difficulty and heavy casualties. The defeat of the Germans in the village allowed the advance of the Allies to the east and Tavoleto remains one of the few battle honours earned by a single battalion of the British Army.

APPENDIX 16

Battle Honours of The Royal Gurkha Rifles' Antecedent Regiments

The Battle Honours of those Regiments that remained in the Indian Army after 1947 are only shown up until that date.

1st King George V's Own Gurkha Rifles (The Malaun Regiment)

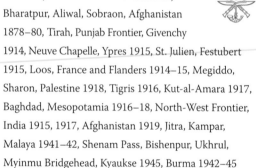

Bharatpur, Aliwal, Sobraon, Afghanistan 1878–80, Tirah, Punjab Frontier, Givenchy 1914, Neuve Chapelle, Ypres 1915, St. Julien, Festubert 1915, Loos, France and Flanders 1914–15, Megiddo, Sharon, Palestine 1918, Tigris 1916, Kut-al-Amara 1917, Baghdad, Mesopotamia 1916–18, North-West Frontier, India 1915, 1917, Afghanistan 1919, Jitra, Kampar, Malaya 1941–42, Shenam Pass, Bishenpur, Ukhrul, Myinmu Bridgehead, Kyaukse 1945, Burma 1942–45

2nd King Edward VII's Own Gurkhas (The Sirmoor Rifles)

Bhurtpore, Aliwal, Sobraon, Delhi 1857, Kabul 1879, Kandahar 1880, Afghanistan 1878–80, Tirah, Punjab Frontier, La Bassée 1914, Festubert 1914–15, Givenchy 1914, Neuve Chapelle, Aubers, Loos, France and Flanders 1914–15, Egypt 1915, Tigris 1916, Kut-al-Amara 1917, Baghdad, Mesopotamia 1916, 1918, Persia 1918, Baluchistan 1918, Afghanistan 1919, El Alamein, Mareth, Akarit, Djebel el Meida, Enfidaville, Tunis, North Africa 1942–43, Cassino I, Monastery Hill, Pian di Maggio, Gothic Line, Coriano, Poggio San Giovanni, Monte Reggiano, Italy 1944–45, Greece 1944–45, North Malaya, Jitra, Central Malaya, Kampar, Slim River, Johore, Singapore Island,

Malaya 1941–42, North Arakan, Irrawaddy, Magwe, Sittang 1945, Point 1433, Arakan Beaches, Myebon, Tamandu, Chindits 1943, Burma 1943–45

3rd Queen Alexandra's Own Gurkha Rifles

Delhi 1857, Ahmed Khel, Afghanistan 1878–80, Burma 1885–87, Chitral, Tirah, Punjab Frontier, La Bassée 1914, Armentieres 1914, Festubert 1914, 1915, Givenchy 1914, Neuve Chapelle, Aubers, Loos, France and Flanders 1914–15, Egypt 1915–1916, Gaza, El Mughar, Nebi Samwil, Jerusalem, Tell, Asur, Megiddo, Sharon, Palestine 1917–18, Sharqat, Mesopotamia 1917–18, Afghanistan 1919, Deir el Shein, North Africa 1940–43, Monte della Gorgace, Il Castello, Monte Farneto, Monte Cavallo, Italy 1943–45, Sittang 1942, Kyaukse 1942, Imphal, Tuitum, Sakawng, Shenam Pass, Bishenpur, Tengnoupal, Meiktila, Defence of Meiktila, Rangoon Road, Pyawbwe, Pegu 1945, Burma 1942–45

4th Prince of Wales's Own Gurkha Rifles

Ali Masjid, Kabul 1879, Kandahar 1880, Afghanistan 1878–80, Waziristan 1895, Chitral, Tirah, Punjab Frontier, China 1900, Givenchy 1914, Neuve Chapelle, Ypres 1915, St. Julien, Aubers, Festubert 1915, France and Flanders 1914–15, Gallipoli 1915, Egypt 1916, Tigris 1916, Ku-al-Amara 1917, Baghdad, Mesopotamia 1916–18, North-West Frontier, India 1917,

Baluchistan 1918, Afghanistan 1919, Iraq 1941, Syria 1941, The Cauldron, North Africa 1940–43, Trestina, Monte Cedrone, Italy 1943–45, Pegu 1942, Chindits 1944, Mandalay, Burma 1942–45, Bishenpur, Shwebo

5TH ROYAL GURKHA RIFLES (FRONTIER FORCE)

Peiwar Kotal, Charasiah, Kabul 1879, Kandahar 1880, Afghanistan 1878–80, Punjab Frontier, Helles, Krithia, Suvla, Sari Bair, Gallipoli 1915, Suez Canal, Egypt 1915–16, Khan Baghdadi, Mesopotamia 1916–18, North-West Frontier, India 1917, Afghanistan 1919, The Sangro, Caldari, Cassino II, Sant'Angelo in Teodice, Rocca d'Arce, Ripa Ridge, Femmina Morte, Monte San Bartolo, The Senio, Italy 1943–45, Sittang 1942, 1945, Kyaukse 1942, Yenangyaung 1942, Stockades, Buthidaung, Imphal, Sakawng, Bishenpur, Shenam Pass, The Irrawaddy, Burma 1942–45

6TH QUEEN ELIZABETH'S OWN GURKHA RIFLES

Burma 1885–87, Helles, Krithia, Suvla, Sari Bair, Gallipoli 1915, Suez Canal, Egypt 1915–16, Khan Baghdadi, Mesopotamia 1916–18, Persia 1918, North-West Frontier, India 1915, Afghanistan 1919, Coriano, Santarcangelo, Monte Chicco, Lamone Crossing, Senio Floodbank, Medicina, Gaiana Crossing, Italy 1944–45, Shwebo, Kyaukmyaung Bridgehead, Mandalay, Fort Dufferin, Maymyo, Rangoon Road, Toungoo, Sittang 1945, Chindits 1944, Burma 1942–45

7TH DUKE OF EDINBURGH'S OWN GURKHA RIFLES

Suez Canal, Egypt 1915–16, Megiddo, Sharon, Palestine 1918, Shaiba, Kut-al-Amara 1915, 1917, Ctesiphon, Defence of Kut-al-Amara, Baghdad, Sharqat, Mesopotamia 1915–1918, Afghanistan 1919, Tobruk 1942, North Africa 1942, Cassino I, Campriano, Poggio del Grillo, Tavoleto, Montebello Scorticata Ridge, Italy 1944, Sittang 1942, 1945, Pegu 1942, Kyaukse 1942, Shwegyin, Imphal, Bishenpur, Meiktila, Capture of Meiktila, Defence of Meiktila, Rangoon Road, Pyawbwe, Burma 1942–45, Falkland Islands 1982

8TH GURKHA RIFLES

Burma 1885–87, La Bassée 1914, Festubert 1914, 1915, Givenchy 1914, Neuve Chapelle, Aubers, France and Flanders 1914–15, Egypt 1915–16, Megiddo, Sharon, Palestine 1918, Tigris 1916, Kut-al-Amara 1917, Baghdad, Mesopotamia 1916–17, Afghanistan 1919, Iraq 1941, North Africa 1940–43, Gothic Line, Italy 1943–45, Coriano, Santarcangelo, Gaiana Crossing, Point 551, Imphal, Tamu Road, Bishenpur, Kanglatongbi, Mandalay, Myinmu Bridgehead, Singhu, Shandatgyi, Sittang 1945, Burma 1942–45

9TH GURKHA RIFLES

Bhurtpore, Sobraon, Afghanistan 1879–80, Punjab Frontier, La Bassée 1914, Armentieres 1914, Festubert 1914, 1915, Givenchy 1914, Neuve Chapelle, Aubers, Loos, France and Flanders 1914–15, Tigris 1916, Kut-al-Amara 1917, Baghdad, Mesopotamia 1916–18, Afghanistan 1919, Djebel el Meida, Djebel Garci, Ragoubet Souissi, North Africa 1940–43, Cassino I, Hangman's Hill, Tavoleto, San Marino, Italy 1943–45, Greece 1944–45, Malaya 1941–42, Chindits 1944, Burma 1942–45

10TH PRINCESS MARY'S OWN GURKHA RIFLES

Amboor, Carnatic, Mysore, Assaye, Ava, Burma 1885–87, Helles, Krithia, Suvla, Sari Bair, Gallipoli 1915, Suez Canal, Egypt 1915, Sharqat, Mesopotamia 1916–18, Afghanistan 1919, Iraq 1941, Deir es Zor, Syria 1941, Coriano, Santarcangelo, Senio Floodbank, Bologna, Sillaro Crossing, Gaiana Crossing, Italy 1944–45, Monywa 1942, Imphal, Tuitum, Tamu Road, Shenam Pass, Litan, Bishenpur, Tengnoupal, Mandalay, Myinmu Bridgehead, Kyaukse 1945, Meiktila, Capture of Meiktila, Defence of Meiktila, Irrawaddy, Rangoon Road, Pegu 1945, Sittang 1945, Burma 1942–45

11TH GURKHA RIFLES

Afghanistan 1919

257

Before The Royal Gurkha Rifles: A Brief History of Britain's Gurkhas

1815 was a defining year in British military history. Not only did Wellington finally defeat Napoleon at the Battle of Waterloo, but Britain's Honourable East India Company also began recruiting Gurkha soldiers for the first time, a tradition that has now continued uninterrupted for over 200 years. This Appendix aims to provide a brief history of the Gurkhas up until the formation of The Royal Gurkha Rifles (RGR) on 1 July 1994 in order to explain the rich history that underpins this relatively new regiment.

WAR AGAINST NEPAL – BRITAIN MEETS THE GURKHAS
It all started in October 1814 on a lonely hilltop in a place called Kalunga (now known as Nalapani). The Honourable East India Company had despatched an army of some 30,000 troops to bring the 'aggressive little state of Nepal' to heel for expanding its empire into parts of northern India that 'John Company' wanted for itself. Kalunga was the location of the first battle between one of the army's four columns and the expansionist Nepalese. What was significant about the engagement was that a relatively small force of

Above: Eight Gurkhas circa 1815. The first Gurkha battalion was raised by the Honourable East India Company in 1815 during the Anglo-Nepal Wars of 1814–16. Note the kukris, the famous Gurkha fighting knives, in their belts.

Above right: A painting by Jason Askew of the Battle of Kalunga which took place in October 1814. A force of 650 Gurkhas defended a hill fort against a superior force of some 4,000 troops of the East India Company for nearly a month. That such a small force of 'native' troops was able to hold out against the might of the British Empire for so long sent shock waves across British India.

After the Battle of Kalunga, the British erected two monuments, one to their own fallen and one to the brave Gurkha defenders of the hill fort.

Bottom: The inscription on the monument to the Gurkhas at Kalunga.

'native' troops was able to hold out against the might of the East India Company for nearly a month. It sent shockwaves throughout British India. The 'natives' at Kalunga were Gurkhas, well trained soldiers belonging to the army of Nepal. They took their name from the ruling House of Gurkha which, under the leadership of Prithvi Narayan Shah, had, by 1768, succeeded in unifying Nepal's many petty principalities.

In May 1815 and after several months of fierce fighting, General Amar Singh Thapa, the Gurkhas' senior commander, accepted defeat when, outmanoeuvred by the East India Company's Major General David Ochterlony, his position in the mountain fortress of Malaun became untenable. A treaty, known as the Treaty of Segauli, was drafted which required the Nepalese to relinquish the land they had seized in the west and east. As a punishment, it also required Nepal to give up large tracts of its own most fertile territory on the border with India. However, much of this was owned by the Nepalese ruling elite and they had no intention

of signing the treaty. In January 1816, the East India Company despatched a second Army of some 17,000 under the command of General Ochterlony to force compliance. The Gurkhas resisted and fought with remarkable courage and skill but, outnumbered and outgunned, they were eventually defeated at the Battle of Makwanpur in February 1816. A few days later on 4 March, the Treaty of Segauli was eventually ratified, bringing the East India Company's two wars with Nepal and its Gurkhas to an end.

THIS IS INSCRIBED
AS A TRIBUTE OF RESPECT
FOR OUR GALLANT ADVERSARY
BULBUDDER
COMMANDER OF THE FORT
AND HIS BRAVE GOORKAS
WHO WERE AFTERWARDS
WHILE IN THE SERVICE
OF RUNJEET SING
SHOT DOWN IN THEIR RANKS
TO THE LAST MAN
BY AFGHAN ARTILLERY.

Bhim Sen Thapa, the Prime Minister of Nepal at the time of the wars with Britain and the Honourable East India Company. A remarkable man, he was Prime Minister for over 30 years from 1806 to 1837.

THE BRITISH RECRUIT THEIR FIRST GURKHAS

The British were so impressed by the martial qualities of their Gurkha enemy that, even before the end of the first war, they had started recruiting Gurkhas into the ranks of the East India Company. The first three battalions of Gurkhas were known as the 1st Nusseree Battalion (later to become the 1st Gurkha Rifles), the Sirmoor Battalion (later 2nd Gurkha Rifles) and the Kumaon Battalion (later 3rd Gurkha Rifles). Formally raised on 24 April 1815, they began the two centuries of Gurkha martial service to the British Crown that were celebrated in 2015. The locations of Sirmoor and Kumaon were in the then western part of Nepal, which was given up by the Nepalese as one of the conditions contained in the Treaty of Segauli.

Gurkha steadfastness during the Indian Mutiny

The Gurkhas achieved real prominence during the Indian Mutiny of 1857 by remaining loyal to the East India Company when many other 'native' regiments rebelled. Their courageous and spirited performance during the Siege of Delhi, where they fought alongside the British Army's 60th Rifles in conditions of real privation, resulted in them being

Above: Major General Sir David Ochterlony, the talented field commander who eventually defeated the Gurkhas of Prime Minister Bhim Sen Thapa at the Battle of Makwanpur in February 1816. On 4 March 1816, the Gurkhas ratified the Treaty of Segauli, bringing Britain's wars with Nepal to an end. Ochterlony was a fascinating and colourful character. Born in Boston Massachusetts on 12 February 1758, he arrived in India as an officer cadet in 1778 and remained there until his death on 15 July 1825. He reputedly had 13 Indian 'wives' and was awarded the Knight Grand Cross of the Order of the Bath for his success against the Nepalese, the first of the Honourable East India Company's own Army officers to receive the award. This painting of Ochterlony was done by Arthur William Devis in about 1816 and now hangs in the Scottish National Portrait Gallery in Edinburgh.

Right: Major General Sir Rollo Gillespie who was killed at the Battle of Kalunga on 31 October 1814 leading British and East India Company troops against the Gurkha defenders. Born in County Down in Ireland in 1766, Gillespie was another colourful character. He killed a man in a duel in 1788, was shipwrecked off Madeira in 1792, killed six men who tried to burgle his home in St Domingo and used a spear to kill an escaped tiger on Bangalore racecourse. He was knighted posthumously on 1 January 1815.

Soldiers of the Sirmoor Battalion (later the 2nd Gurkhas) in front of Hindu Rao's House on Delhi Ridge. The ridge dominated the city of Delhi which, in 1857, became the focus of the Indian Mutiny. Despite suffering tremendous losses, the Sirmoor Battalion, along with the 60th Rifles and the Corps of Guides, succeeded in holding the ridge until reinforcements arrived.

allowed to call their soldiers 'riflemen', rather than 'sepoys', and adopt many of the 60th's regimental accoutrements. The Gurkhas were also awarded a commemorative Truncheon by Queen Victoria. This has the status of a regimental 'colour' and, as the only one of its kind, is still carried with immense pride by today's RGR. A fuller description of the Queen's Truncheon is contained in Special Interest Section 1. The Gurkhas also earned the first of their twenty six Victoria Crosses during the Mutiny when Lieutenant John Tytler, an officer serving with the 66th or Goorkha Regiment (later to become the 1st Gurkha Rifles), succeeded in storming a rebel gun position despite being shot in the arm and having a spear through his chest!

The First World War and the first Gurkha Victoria Cross

The First World War saw the Gurkhas transition from operations against the wily tribesmen of the North West Frontier (the border territory between modern-day Pakistan and Afghanistan) to the 'modern' warfare of the trenches. On the Western Front, in Mesopotamia and on the Gallipoli Peninsula, some 90,780 Gurkhas served the British Crown during the First World War. Of these, over 20,000 became casualties. Their bravery earned accolades from all quarters and resulted in the award of three Victoria Crosses. The first of these was won by Rifleman Kulbir Thapa at the Battle of Loos in September 1915, the same battle in which Rudyard Kipling's son was killed. It was particularly significant because it was the first ever Victoria Cross won by a Gurkha soldier, rather than a British officer from a Gurkha regiment. Although British officers serving with Gurkha regiments were eligible for the award from its introduction in 1856, 'native' soldiers only became eligible in 1911.

Below: Rifleman Kulbir Thapa of 2/3rd Gurkhas who earned a Victoria Cross for his actions at the Battle of Loos in September 1915, becoming the first Gurkha soldier to receive the award. Although the Victoria Cross was brought into being by Royal Warrant on 29 January 1856, it was not until 1911, on the occasion of the visit of King George V to India, that Gurkhas became eligible for the award. To date, officers and soldiers of the Gurkha infantry have been awarded a total of 26 Victoria Crosses.

Gurkhas in the Second World War

The number of Gurkhas serving the British Crown increased during the Second World War to some 138,000. Again, they distinguished themselves, earning 2,760 awards for bravery or distinguished service. These awards included 12 Victoria Crosses and a remarkable 333 Military Crosses. Both medals are awarded for acts of valour in the face of the enemy and it is therefore no surprise that the casualties amongst Gurkha officers and soldiers were high: 7,539 Gurkhas were either killed or died of wounds; 1,441 Gurkhas were posted as missing, presumed dead; and a further 14,082 Gurkhas were wounded.

A painting by the artist Terence Cuneo showing 1/6th Gurkhas assaulting well, prepared Turkish positions on the highest feature of the Sari Bair Massif on the Gallipoli Peninsula. The painting shows Major Cecil Allanson leading his men from the front on 9 August 1915. A remarkable officer and superb athlete, Allanson held the Army record for the 2 miler for a number of years. He was written up for a Victoria Cross for his actions on Sari Bair but this was downgraded to the Distinguished Service Order (DSO). Prior to the assault and having been briefed on the plan which he thought was hazardous in the extreme, Allanson wrote in his diary: "what would one have done to a subaltern at a promotion examination who made any such proposition?"

Burma and the Chindits

Although there are numerous instances of Gurkhas turning the tide of particular battles in Italy and North Africa during the Second World War, they are probably best known for their role in the Burma Campaign as part of General Bill Slim's 'forgotten' 14th Army. Large numbers of Gurkhas died defending Sittang Bridge in February 1942, many drowning when the bridge was blown and 6,000 men of the 17th Division found themselves unexpectedly trapped between the fast flowing river and the advancing Japanese. Gurkhas also made a significant contribution to Brigadier (later Major General) Orde Wingate's two Chindit operations of 1943 and 1944 and they fought with distinction during the defence of Imphal in June 1944. In June of 2015, the Second Battalion of the RGR joined the UK's elite 16 Air Assault Brigade,

Opposite: Gurkhas of the 4th Indian Division meet American GIs. US forces arrived in North Africa as part of Operation Torch which saw some 650 ships put ashore four US and British Divisions on 8 November 1942. The Germans eventually surrendered in North Africa on 12 May 1943 after a three year campaign. The total German and Italian prisoners amounted to some 250,000.

Right: Brigadier (later Major General) Orde Wingate who commanded the Chindits. He was killed when his aircraft crashed during a visit to one of the strongholds established behind enemy lines during the second Chindit operation. Large numbers of Gurkhas took part in both Chindit operations.

Left: Rifleman Asman Gurung of the 6th Gurkhas crossing the Irrawaddy River during the Burma Campaign.

Below: Brigadier Mike Calvert (left) who commanded one of the columns during the second Chindit operation and Major James Lumley (right), the father of Joanna Lumley, in the ruins of Mogaung, Burma after its capture in June 1944.

a return to the airborne role that Gurkhas first embraced in Burma when 153 and 154 (Gurkha) Parachute Battalions were formed for operations against the Japanese. Lieutenant Colonel (later Major General) F J Loftus-Tottenham, who raised the first Gurkha parachute battalion in 1941, described Gurkhas as "... probably the best natural parachutist in the world," something they would demonstrate when they parachuted in to capture key gun positions at the start of Operation Dracula, General Slim's air, sea and land offensive to secure Rangoon, the capital of Burma, in May 1945.

Naik Agansing Rai of 2/5th Gurkhas was awarded a Victoria Cross for his bravery on the 26 June 1944 during assaults to capture the key positions of Mortar Bluff and Water Piquet in Mogaung.

Nine Gurkha Victoria Crosses in Burma

During the course of the Burma Campaign, officers and soldiers of Gurkha units were awarded no less than nine Victoria Crosses. An extract from the citation of one of these gives an idea of the sort of fighting they were involved in:

"In the subsequent advance heavy machine-gun fire and showers of grenades from an isolated bunker position caused further casualties. Once more, with indomitable courage, Naik Agansing Rai, covered by his Bren gunner, advanced alone with a grenade in one hand and his Thompson Sub-Machinegun in the other. Through devastating fire he reached the enemy position and with his grenade and bursts from his Thompson Sub-Machinegun killed all four occupants of the bunker."

INDEPENDENCE OF INDIA, THE MALAYAN EMERGENCY AND THE BORNEO CONFRONTATION

In 1947, India achieved its independence. This was a difficult period for the ten Gurkha regiments that had fought for the British Crown during the Second World War as only four of them (the 2nd Gurkhas, 6th Gurkhas, 7th Gurkhas and 10th Gurkhas) transferred to the British Army, moving to new 'home' locations in and around Malaya. The other six regiments (the 1st Gurkhas, 3rd Gurkhas, 4th Gurkhas, 5th Gurkhas, 8th Gurkhas and 9th Gurkhas) remained in the Indian Army. But there was little time for reflection as, in June 1948, a state of emergency was declared in Malaya. Britain's Gurkha infantry, along with newly formed units of Gurkha Signals, Gurkha Engineers, Gurkha Military Police and later Gurkha Transport, played a key role in the twelve year campaign against the communist terrorists of Chin Peng and the Malayan Races Liberation Army (MRLA). The Brunei Revolt and the Borneo Confrontation followed in quick succession. Although the Revolt was short-lived, the Borneo Confrontation lasted from April 1963 until August 1966 with the Gurkha infantry bearing the lion's share of the operational burden. Conducting secret 'Claret' operations deep behind enemy lines, they took the fight to the Indonesian troops of President Sukarno, firmly establishing themselves

as the masters of jungle warfare. It was during one such 'Claret' operation in November 1965 that Lance Corporal Rambahadur Limbu of the 10th Gurkhas became the last Gurkha to be awarded a Victoria Cross for his courageous actions in the face of the enemy.

Reduction in the strength of the Brigade of Gurkhas and the founding of the Gurkha Welfare Trust
Perhaps surprisingly, barely six months after the end of the Borneo Confrontation, Britain's Gurkha strength was reduced from 15,000 to 7,000. This entailed many fine Gurkha soldiers leaving the Army with no pensions and very small gratuities. Realising that this would add to the number of ex-British Gurkhas living in conditions of privation in Nepal, the Gurkha Welfare Trust was formed from generous donations in the UK and Far East. This original aspect of the Trust's work continues to this day with over 4,500 ex-soldiers or widows receiving welfare pensions of 11,000 rupees per month (about £75.00), enabling them to live the remainder of their lives with dignity.[256]

The rivers in Borneo are used as arterial transport routes. During the Borneo Confrontation, both British and Indonesian forces used them to move troops and supplies. In August 1965, Support Company of 2/2nd Gurkhas carried out a highly successful boat ambush on the River Sentimo, killing 12 Indonesians who were travelling in an assault boat. Rivers remain important arterial routes in Brunei and the RGR battalion based there works hard to maintain a high level of competence in jungle riverine operations.

Gurkhas in the Falkland Islands and other deployments

The Gurkhas hit the headlines in 1982 when the First Battalion of the 7th Duke of Edinburgh's Own Gurkha Rifles deployed as part of the Task Force to retake the Falkland Islands. Although the majority of the fighting was done by the Parachute Regiment and The Royal Marines, the Gurkhas consolidated their position as highly capable light infantry. Numerous other deployments followed with the Gurkha infantry deploying on operations in Kosovo, Bosnia, East Timor, Sierra Leone and Afghanistan. These were undertaken by the RGR and they are therefore described in the main body of the book.

Conclusion

As explained at the beginning of this abridged history, the purpose of this Appendix is to ensure that the exploits of the 25 year old RGR described in this book are seen in the context of nearly two centuries of loyal and courageous service by the Regiment's forebears. To put it bluntly, the youthful RGR very much stands on the shoulders of the giants that were its antecedent regiments and whose battle honours are so impressively listed in Appendix 16.

Soldiers from 1/7th Gurkhas with a captured Argentinean anti-aircraft gun during the Falklands War of 1982. The Battalion deployed as part of 5 Infantry Brigade and took part in the final battle for Port Stanley.

The Royal Gurkha Rifles Regimental Association

'ONCE A GURKHA ALWAYS A GURKHA!'

The Royal Gurkha Rifles has a strong family spirit and membership of this Regimental family does not cease on retirement from the Army. The Royal Gurkha Rifles Regimental Association is a thriving organisation of serving and retired Gurkhas that seeks to foster this family spirit by bringing young and old together across the globe.

A growing network of Regimental veterans, which extends across Nepal and the United Kingdom, actively supports the Association by coordinating gatherings for serving and retired members of the Regiment and their families. Sometimes these are nothing more than simple social occasions for old friends to catch up but often they are more formal occasions to mark important Regimental events or to remember those who have paid the ultimate sacrifice whilst serving with the Regiment.

The objectives of The RGRRA are:

- **Camaraderie:** To foster a strong sense of camaraderie and élan amongst RGR veterans and the Regiment.

- **Reputation:** To preserve, protect and promote the good name and reputation of the Regiment and of its Members and of Gurkhas generally.

- **Welfare and Benevolence:** To act as a line of communication between Members in need and the many sources of welfare support and benevolence.

- **Antecedent Regiments:** Maintain the legacy of the antecedent Regiments through close cooperation with all Regimental Associations.

To find out more about the Association, or to become a member, contact the Regimental Secretary:

Major (Retired) Bruce McKay MBE
Tel: 07956 080378
E-Mail: GurkhasBde-RegtSec@mod.gov.uk

You can also find out more about the Association at: https://www.gurkhabde.com/royal-gurkha-rifles-regimental-association/

The Colonel of the Regiment and President of The Royal Gurkha Rifles Regimental Association, Major General Gez Strickland DSO MBE, in Nepal in February 2019 meeting members of the Nepal Branch of the Association.

The Nepal Branch of The Royal Gurkha Rifles Regimental Association met in Pokhara to celebrate the Regiment's 24th Birthday on 1 July 2018.

A meeting of the 'Gurkhas in the City' held on 2 April 2019. All past and serving members of The Royal Gurkha Rifles are welcome to attend these informal meetings, which are held approximately every quarter.

The Royal Gurkha Rifles Regimental Association provides an effective way of maintaining the social networks that members of the RGR establish whilst they are serving.

The Gurkha Museum

The first Gurkha Museum was inaugurated by Field Marshal The Lord Harding of Petherton at Queen Elizabeth Barracks in Church Crookham, Hampshire on 21 June 1974. Church Crookham had been the home of the UK based battalion of Gurkha Rifles since the end of 1971 and remained so until 2000 when their home moved to Shorncliffe in Kent. A small barrack block contained many items donated by Gurkha regiments and individuals to record Gurkha service over the years. Twenty five years later and with a much larger collection, the Museum moved to its current site at Peninsula Barracks, Winchester in Hampshire and was officially opened by Field Marshal The Lord Bramall of Bushfield on 16 July 1990. The collection and archive are housed in the now converted Short Block at Peninsula Barracks, the former home of the Rifle Depot and The Royal Green Jackets who have their own Museum with The Rifles museum located nearby.

Peninsula Barracks in Winchester. The former Rifle Depot and home of the Gurkha Museum since 16 July 1990.

The Museum houses an exceptional collection of artefacts relating to the history of the brigade of Gurkhas stretching back over 200 years. Starting with the Nepal Wars in 1814–16 the story is told of service, loyalty and valour in campaigns and wars across the world; from North Africa to Borneo and from Iraq to Afghanistan. The collection contains not just historic items from former wars on the distant frontiers of empire but also poignant artefacts from more recent conflicts and deployments around the globe. Among these are the combat helmet and Kukri of Lance Corporal Tuljung Gurung 1RGR who was awarded the Military Cross for gallantry for an action in Afghanistan in March 2013 (see Chapter 5).

The Museum graphically tells the story of The Royal Gurkha Rifles and its antecedent regiments with many displays, tableaux, uniforms, weapons, objects and medals, including ten of the twenty six Victoria Crosses awarded to Gurkha Regiments. In addition to the military exploits of the Gurkha soldier, an important part of the Museum's work is the provision of displays and archives recording the diverse language, culture and religion of Nepal.

The interior of the first Gurkha Museum opened at Queen Elizabeth Barracks, Church Crookham on 21 June 1974.

Lance Corporal Tuljung Gurung at the Gurkha Museum in June 2014 donating his combat helmet and the kukri he used to beat off an attack by Taliban fighters on 22 March 2013 in Lashkar Gah, Afghanistan during Operation Herrick 17. Lance Corporal Tuljung was awarded the Military Cross (MC) for his actions (see Chapter 5).

A display at the current Gurkha Museum showing the circumstances that led to Lance Corporal Rambahadur Limbu of 2/10th Gurkhas being awarded the Victoria Cross during the Borneo Confrontation (see Chapter 7).

One of the many life-sized displays that chronicle the Gurkhas' involvement in Britain's wars. This one shows machine-gunners from one of the Gurkha infantry regiments in Africa during the Second World War.

A life-sized display in the Museum of a soldier from the 2nd Gurkhas in the jungle during the Malayan Emergency (see Chapter 7).

To complement this collection there is a fine archive of documents, images, books and film recording that detail the history of the regiments, corps and other units of the Brigade. The regimental records of all The Royal Gurkha Rifles' antecedent regiments are held in the archives, together with many other historically important collections. Modern technological advances have now enabled the Museum to reach and engage with much wider audiences in the UK and around the world through the internet via its website and social media.

The Gurkha Museum is a registered Charitable Trust and welcomes donations to help grow and develop its charitable aims and objectives in commemorating the service of Gurkhas to the British Crown since 1815, and in safeguarding the heritage of the Brigade of Gurkhas. If you would like to find out more about the work of the Museum, please do not hesitate to get in touch via the website at: https://thegurkhamuseum.co.uk/.

A display describing the Battle of Dargai of October 1897. The painting in the background shows Piper George Frederick Findlater of the Gordon Highlanders who, despite being shot in the feet and exposed to enemy fire, continued to play his bagpipes to encourage the assaulting force, which consisted of the 2nd Gurkhas, the Gordon Highlanders, the Dorsets, the Derbyshires and the 3rd Sikhs. Piper Findlater was awarded the Victoria Cross for his actions.

Endnotes

1   Ministry of Defence, General Staff Order: Authority for Amalgamation of 2 and 6 GR and Retitling of 7 and 10 GR, D INF 54/1 dated 3 May 1994 (Gurkha Museum Folio Reference 'RGR 007').

2   Interestingly, notwithstanding the orders published by the MOD, the 1RGR newsletter published in the 1996 edition of 'The Kukri' notes that 1RGR '…became operational on 1 October 1994'.

3   Lieutenant Colonel G C J L Pearson, 'Regimental Headquarters News', The Royal Gurkha Rifles Regimental Newsletter: July – December 1996 (Headquarters Brigade of Gurkhas, 1996), 6.

4   The three GRCs formed up in Knook Camp on Salisbury Plain in November 1996 and deployed to their 'new' units in December 1996. GRC 1 (Gallipoli Company) went to the 1st Battalion The Royal Scots in Colchester, GRC 2 (Sobraon Company) went to the 1st Battalion The Princess of Wales's Royal Regiment in Canterbury and GRC 3 (Cassino Company) went to the 2nd Battalion The Parachute Regiment in Aldershot.

5   Defence Options for Change https://api.parliament.uk/historic-hansard/commons/1990/jul/25/defence-options-for-change accessed on 2 January 2019.

6   Defence Options for Change https://api.parliament.uk/historic-hansard/commons/1990/jul/25/defence-options-for-change accessed on 2 January 2019.

7   Lieutenant General Sir Peter Duffell, A Gurkha Odyssey (due for publication in October 2019).

8   Lieutenant General Sir Peter Duffell e-mail to the author dated 18 March 2019 @17:16hrs.

9   Lieutenant General Sir Peter Duffell, A Gurkha Odyssey (due for publication in October 2019).

10 Christopher Bullock, Britain's Gurkhas (Third Millennium Publishing, 2009), 226.

11 Lieutenant General Sir Peter Duffell, A Gurkha Odyssey (unpublished draft), 31.

12 Traditionally, 2GR and 6GR recruited soldiers from the west of Nepal whereas 7GR and 10GR recruited from the east.

13 Lieutenant General Sir Peter Duffell, A Gurkha Odyssey (unpublished draft), 31.

14 Tony Gould, Imperial Warriors: Britain and the Gurkhas (Granta Books, 1999), 384.

15 Gordon Corrigan, 'The Formation of The Royal Gurkha Rifles', 6GR Newsletter, Volume 74, 1994, 46 (Gurkha Museum Folio Reference 'RGR/006').

16 Gordon Corrigan, 'The Formation of The Royal Gurkha Rifles', 6GR Newsletter, Volume 74, 1994, 47 (Gurkha Museum Folio Reference 'RGR/006').

17 '1RGR (2GR) Newsletter', The Kukri, No. 47 (Headquarters Brigade of Gurkhas, 1995), 32.

18 Tony Gould, Imperial Warriors: Britain and the Gurkhas (Granta Books, 1999), 380.

19 '3RGR (10GR) Newsletter', The Kukri, Number. 47 (Headquarters Brigade of Gurkhas, 1995), 41. The CO at the time was Lieutenant Colonel P T C Pearson. He remained in command of the 'new' 3RGR until December 1995 but returned to the RGR as its Regimental Colonel from 1 July 1999 to 1 July 2009.

20 Speaking Notes for HRH's Address to The Royal Gurkha Rifle Formation Parade at Church Crookham, Saturday 10th September 1994. Reproduced by kind permission of His Royal Highness The Prince of Wales.

21 A Company 3RGR deployed to Bosnia in December 1995.

22 John Parker, The Gurkhas (Headline Book Publishing, 2000), 56.

23 Christopher Bullock, Britain's Gurkhas (Third Millennium Publishing Ltd, 2009), 35.

24 Christopher Bullock, Britain's Gurkhas (Third Millennium Publishing Ltd, 2009), 36.

25 John Parker, The Gurkhas (Headline Book Publishing, 2000), 58.

26 John Parker, The Gurkhas (Headline Book Publishing, 2000), 59.

27 Christopher Bullock, Britain's Gurkhas (Third Millennium Puxblishing Limited, 2009), 39.

28 John Parker, The Gurkhas (Headline Book Publishing, 2000), 38.

29 Christopher Bullock, Britain's Gurkhas (Third Millennium Publishing Ltd, 2009), 38.

30 John Parker, The Gurkhas (Headline Book Publishing, 2000), 59.

31 Christopher Bullock, Britain's Gurkhas (Third Millennium Publishing Ltd, 2009), 39.

32 Anthony Read and David Fisher, The Proudest Day: India's Long Road to Independence (Random House, 1998), 57.

33 John Parker, The Gurkhas (Headline Book Publishing, 2000), 61.

34 Maurice Biggs, The Story of Gurkha VCs (FireStep, 2012), 21.

35 This list is an extract from research conducted by Captain Michael Barney RGR during the production of a Regimental Pamphlet relating to the Queen's Truncheon.

36 Captain Michael Barney draft Pamphlet The Queen's Truncheon (Nishani Mai) (undated) citing 'Adjutant General Letter to the Secretary of State for India, No. 46 of 1859'.

37 The Honourable East India Company was effectively abolished through the Government of India Act which was passed by Parliament on 2 August 1858. This transferred all property and other assets of the Company to the British Crown.

38 Captain Michael Barney draft Pamphlet The Queen's Truncheon (Nishani Mai) (undated) citing 'Military General Letter from the Secretary of State for India, 31 August 1859'.

39 Captain Michael Barney draft Pamphlet The Queen's Truncheon (Nishani Mai) (undated) citing 'Military General Letter from the Secretary of State for India, 28 February 1860'.

40 Captain Michael Barney draft Pamphlet The Queen's Truncheon (Nishani Mai) (undated) citing 'Letter from General Sir Charles Reid to Colonel Travers'.

41 Captain Michael Barney draft Pamphlet The Queen's Truncheon (Nishani Mai) (undated) citing 'The Illustrated London News, 12 April 1862, Page 377'.

42 Macedonia achieved independence from Yugoslavia in September 1991. It became a member of the UN in April 1993 under the name 'The Former Yugoslav Republic of Macedonia', often abbreviated to FYROM. Following a long dispute with Greece, the country was renamed The Republic of North Macedonia in February 2019.

43 John Merriman, *A History of Modern Europe: From The Renaissance to the Present* – Third Edition (W W Norton & Company, 2010), 1210.

44 Milošević was elected President of the Presidency of Serbia on 8 May 1989 and re-elected on 5 December that same year. Following the adoption of a new constitution in Serbia on 28 September 1990, Milošević was elected to the newly established office of President of Serbia in elections held on 9 and 26 December 1990; he was re-elected on 20 December 1992. See: www.pbs.org/newshour/world/europe-july-dec01-indictment for a brief summary of Milošević's political career.

45 John Merriman, *A History of Modern Europe: From The Renaissance to the Present* – Third Edition (W W Norton & Company, 2010), 1212.

46 Peacekeeping in Bosnia, http://www.globalization101.org/peacekeeping-in-bosnia/ accessed on 3 April 2019.

47 Former Yugoslavia – UNPROFOR, https://www.un.org/Depts/DPKO/Missions/unprof_b.htm accessed on 1 April 2019.

48 Former Yugoslavia – UNPROFOR, https://www.un.org/Depts/DPKO/Missions/unprof_b.htm accessed on 8 April 2019.

49 NATO Involvement in Bosnia – The Evolution of NATO's Assistance, https://www.nato.int/cps/en/natohq/topics_52122.htm accessed on 3 April 2019.

50 It's been 20 years since Europe's worst atrocity since the Second World War, https://www.businessinsider.com/20-years-ago-today-europe-saw-its-worst-atrocity-since-wwii-2015-7?r=US&IR=T accessed on 9 April 2019.

51 Peacekeeping in Bosnia, http://www.globalization101.org/peacekeeping-in-bosnia/ accessed on 1 April 2019.

52 Dayton Peace Agreement, https://www.osce.org/bih/126173 accessed on 5 April 2019.

53 Peacekeeping in Bosnia, http://www.globalization101.org/peacekeeping-in-bosnia/ accessed on 1 April 2019.

54 NATO Involvement in Bosnia – The Evolution of NATO's Assistance, https://www.nato.int/cps/en/natohq/topics_52122.htm accessed on 3 April 2019.

55 J C Lawrence, *The Gurkhas: 200 Years of Service to the Crown* (Uniform Press, 2015), 183.

56 The company deployed under the command of Major Simon Archer who handed over to Major James Robinson in theatre.

57 'Op RESOLUTE – A Coy 3RGR deploy with the NATO Peace Implementation Force (IFOR)', The Kukri, No. 49 (Headquarters Brigade of Gurkhas, April 1997), 42–45.

58 NATO Involvement in Bosnia – The Evolution of NATO's Assistance, https://www.nato.int/cps/en/natohq/topics_52122.htm accessed on 3 April 2019.

59 NATO Involvement in Bosnia – The Evolution of NATO's Assistance, https://www.nato.int/cps/en/natohq/topics_52122.htm accessed on 3 April 2019.

60 Which lasted from December 1995 to December 1996. Operation Grapple (which ran from October 1992 to December 1995) was the name given to UK deployments in support of the UN's UNPROFOR mission.

61 Which lasted from December 1996 to June 1998.

62 The company was commanded by the author.

63 Letter from Lieutenant Colonel G P Cass, CO 2RRF, to Lieutenant Colonel Bijaykumar Rawat, CO 1RGR, dated 14 October 1997.

64 The Irish Times, Office of UK, US Embassies Sacked, https://www.irishtimes.com/news/offices-of-uk-us-embassies-sacked-1.167562 accessed on 9 April 2019.

65 'C (Cassino) Company 2PARA – Newsletter', The Kukri, No. 52 (Headquarters Brigade of Gurkhas, April 2000), 57.

66 'C (Cassino) Company 2PARA – Newsletter', The Kukri, No. 52 (Headquarters Brigade of Gurkhas, April 2000), 57.

67 Nicholas Rees, 'The Kosovo Crisis, the International Response and Ireland', Irish Studies in International Affairs, 11 (2000), 57.

68 Nicholas Rees, 'The Kosovo Crisis, the International Response and Ireland', Irish Studies in International Affairs, 11 (2000), 57

69 John Merriman, *A History of Modern Europe: From The Renaissance to the Present* – Third Edition (W W Norton & Company, 2010), 1213.

70 Nicholas Rees, 'The Kosovo Crisis, the International Response and Ireland', Irish Studies in International Affairs, 11 (2000), 63.

71 NATO's role in Kosovo, https://www.nato.int/cps/en/natolive/topics_48818.htm# accessed on 9 April 2019.

72 The Aims of the Air Campaign, https://www.nato.int/kosovo/repo2000/aims.htm accessed on 9 April 2019.

73 Security Council Resolution 1244 (1999) on the situation relating Kosovo, https://peacemaker.un.org/kosovo-resolution1244 accessed on 9 April 2019.

74 An unmanned aerial reconnaissance drone.

75 Captain T R P Hill, 'Recollection of an Intelligence Officer', in Kosovo Lahurey – Kosovo 1999 (The First Battalion The Royal Gurkha Rifles, 1999), 12.

76 '1st Battalion Newsletter', The Kukri, No. 52 (Headquarters Brigade of Gurkhas, April 2000), 25.

77 Captain R J Rea, 'Recce Platoon Goes In', in Kosovo Lahurey – Kosovo 1999 (The First Battalion The Royal Gurkha Rifles, 1999), 22.

78 Having been promoted to Lieutenant Colonel, Fraser Rea went on to command 2RGR from October 2010 until April 2013.

79 The US Task Force was Task Force Falcon.

80 '1st Battalion Newsletter', The Kukri, No. 52 (Headquarters Brigade of Gurkhas, April 2000), 26.

81 In Kosovo Lahurey, a booklet produced by 1RGR after its deployment, the then Commanding Officer, Lieutenant Colonel Sean Crane, stated that the battalion's deployment on Operation Agricola lasted from 5 June to 31 August 1999.

82 'B (Gallipoli) Company Newsletter', The Royal Gurkha Rifles Regimental Newsletter (January–December 1998), 8.

83 Within the Brigade of Gurkhas, the Gurkha Reinforcement Company (GRC) attached to 2PARA was known as C (Cassino) Company 2PARA but many non-Gurkha organisations referred to the company as C (Gurkha) Company 2PARA.

84 The actual deployment dates were 1 August 2001 until 12 October 2001. See: Macedonia (Operation Bessemer, https://www.paradata.org.uk/event/macedonia-operation-bessemer accessed on 18 April 2019.

85 See: Macedonia (Operation Bessemer, https://www.paradata.org.uk/event/macedonia-operation-bessemer accessed on 18 April 2019.

86 This description was provided in an e-mail from the company commander of 2 (Cassino) Company 2PARA, Major Dan O'Donnell, to the author on 26 October 2017 at 1117hours.

87 This description was provided in an e-mail from the company commander of 2 (Cassino) Company 2PARA, Major Dan O'Donnell, to the author on 26 October 2017 at 1117hours.

88 'Second Battalion Newsletter', The Royal Gurkha Rifles Regimental Newsletter (July – December 2001), 13.

89 'Second Battalion Newsletter', The Royal Gurkha Rifles Regimental Newsletter (July – December 2001), 13.

90 The Company transferred from 1RS to 1HLDRS on 28 March 2000. Whilst with 1RS it deployed to Bosnia and Herzegovina from July 1998 to January 1999 as the Divisional Defence Company; six months later it deployed again from July 1999 to October 1999 in the same role, though the name of the role had changed from Divisional Defence Company to Banja Luka Operations Company (BLOC).

91 MGBD Ops Coy Brief as at 12 Aug 03. A copy of the briefing note was given to the author by the Officer Commanding the Company, Major Quentin Naylor.

92 MGBD Ops Coy Brief as at 12 Aug 03. A copy of the briefing note was given to the author by the Officer Commanding the Company, Major Quentin Naylor.

93 Comprised of the Spearhead Lead Element (SLE).

94 SFOR Deployment to Kosovo, https://www.nato.int/sfor/indexinf/articles/040319a/t040319a.htm accessed on 11 April 2019.

95 1RGR was the first battalion to undertake the pan-Balkans commitment.

96 'First Battalion Newsletter', The Royal Gurkha Rifles Regimental Newsletter (January–June 2006), 4.

97 'C (Tavoleto) Company Tour in Kosovo', The Kukri, No. 59 (Headquarters Brigade of Gurkhas, April 2008), 25–26.

98 'C (Tavoleto) Company Tour in Kosovo', The Kukri, No. 59 (Headquarters Brigade of Gurkhas, April 2008), 26.

99 Lieutenant Colonel S D Crane, 'Foreword', in Kosovo Lahurey – Kosovo 1999 (The First Battalion The Royal Gurkha Rifles, 1999), 1.

100 This connection was proudly explained by His Royal Highness The Prince of Wales in a speech to 2RGR during a visit on 2 July 2015 to celebrate the Regiment's 21st birthday. See https://www.princeofwales.gov.uk/speech/speech-hrh-prince-wales-colonel-chief-royal-gurkha-rifles-visit-2nd-battalion-royal-gurkha accessed on 10 March 2019.

101 From the address that the Colonel-in-Chief gave to the battalion on the day. See https://www.princeofwales.gov.uk/speech/speech-hrh-prince-wales-colonel-chief-royal-gurkha-rifles-visit-2nd-battalion-royal-gurkha accessed on 10 March 2019.

102 Toral took over from Herrick as the name for UK operations in Afghanistan on 31 December 2014. This reflected the change that NATO made to its role from being an International Security Assistance Force (ISAF) to providing Resolute Support (RS) to the Afghan national security forces.

103 Azman Ahmed, 'Brunei Darussalam Towards Reform and Sustainable Progress', Southeast Asian Affairs 2005, A.

104 When the monarchy was abolished on 28 May 2008, the Shah dynasty had reigned for nearly 240 years (from 24 September 1768 to 28 May 2008). See: Greg Hickman, 'The Genealogies of the Shah, Rana and Related Families', The Britain-Nepal Society Journal, Vol 40 (2016), 20.

105 For the duration of his three-day reign, King Dipendra was in a coma following what became known as the Nepalese Royal Massacre.

106 East Timor – UNMISET – Background, https://peacekeeping.un.org/mission/past/unmiset/background.html accessed on 19 April 2019.

107 East Timor – UNMISET – Background, https://peacekeeping.un.org/mission/past/unmiset/background.html accessed on 19 April 2019.

108 East Timor – UNMISET – Background, https://peacekeeping.un.org/mission/past/unmiset/background.html accessed on 19 April 2019.

109 'Operation Langar – A Clerical Perspective', The Kukri, No. 52 (Headquarters Brigade of Gurkhas, April 2000), 43.

110 Resolution 1264 – The Situation in East Timor, http://unscr.com/en/resolutions/1264 accessed on 20 April 2019.

111 Resolution 1264 – The Situation in East Timor, http://unscr.com/en/resolutions/1264 accessed on 20 April 2019.

112 'Operation Langar – Peace Enforcement Operations in East Timor', The Kukri, No. 52 (Headquarters Brigade of Gurkhas, April 2000), 40.

113 'Operation Langar – Peace Enforcement Operations in East Timor', The Kukri, No. 52 (Headquarters Brigade of Gurkhas, April 2000), 40.

114 'Operation Langar – Peace Enforcement Operations in East Timor', The Kukri,

115 'Operation Langar – Peace Enforcement Operations in East Timor', The Kukri, No. 52 (Headquarters Brigade of Gurkhas, April 2000), 41.

116 'Operation Langar – Peace Enforcement Operations in East Timor', The Kukri, No. 52 (Headquarters Brigade of Gurkhas, April 2000), 43.

117 Lieutenant Colonel Lillingston-Price was given local rank as a Colonel for the duration of his appointment as COMBRITFOR.

118 The last British troops left Dili on 10 December 1999.

119 Christopher Bullock, Britain's Gurkhas (Third Millennium Publishing, 2009), 242.

120 East Timor, E-Mail from Colonel Jody Davies, who took part in the deployment to East Timor with A Company 2RGR, to the author of 23 April 2019 @0655hrs.

121 East Timor becomes 191st Member of UN Today, https://www.nytimes.com/2002/09/27/world/east-timor-becomes-191st-un-member-today.html accessed on 20 April 2019.

122 Christopher Bullock, Britain's Gurkhas (Third Millennium Publishing, 2009), 242.

123 Regional Selection Overview – Physical Tests, https://www.army.mod.uk/who-we-are/corps-regiments-and-units/brigade-of-gurkhas/gurkha-recruitment/regional-selection/ accessed on 28 April 2019.

124 UNAMSIL – United Nations Mission in Sierra Leone, https://peacekeeping.un.org/mission/past/unamsil/ accessed on 22 April 2019.

125 Sierra Leone – UNAMSIL – Mandate, https://peacekeeping.un.org/mission/past/unamsil/mandate.html accessed on 22 April 2019.

126 Tony Blair, A Journey (Hutchinson, 2010), 246.

127 Tony Blair, A Journey (Hutchinson, 2010), 247.

128 In answer to a question raised during a debate in Parliament on 26 February 2001, the Government confirmed that 58 members of C (Cassino) Company 2PARA had taken part in the operation in Sierra Leone from 5–25 May 2000.

129 Parachute Regiment – Operational History – Sierra Leone 2000, Operation Palliser, http://www.eliteukforces.info/parachute-regiment/parachute-regiment-history/sierra-leone.php accessed on 22 April 2019.

130 Secretary of State for Defence (Geoff Hoon) speaking to the House of

Commons on 23 May 2000. See https://api.parliament.uk/historic-hansard/commons/2000/may/23/sierra-leone.

131 House of Commons – Sierra Leone, https://api.parliament.uk/historic-hansard/commons/2000/may/23/sierra-leone accessed on 22 April 2019.

132 Operation Barras – Sierra Leone, https://www.royal-irish.com/events/uk-special-forces-operation-mounted-rescue-remaining-1-r-irish-hostages-sierra-leone-operatio accessed on 25 April 2019.

133 Interestingly, Brigadier P T C Pearson, who, coincidentally, had taken over as Colonel of the RGR the previous year, was dispatched to Sierra Leone by the Commander-in-Chief (General Sir Mike Jackson) to investigate the circumstances in which the soldiers from the RIRISH had been taken prisoner by the West Side Boys. Brigadier Pearson had 48 hours to carry out a quick investigation in-theatre before reporting back to the Secretary of State for Defence (Geoff Hoon) and the Chief of the General Staff (General Sir Mike Walker). At the time, Brigadier Pearson was the Assistant Chief of Staff (ACOS) Training and Development in Headquarters United Kingdom Land Forces (HQ UKLF).

134 '2RGR Newsletter', The Royal Gurkha Rifles Regimental Newsletter (November 2000–June 2001), 14.

135 Colour Sergeant Chitrabahadur Gurung, Sp Coy 1RGR in Op Silkman Sierra Leone, undated draft.

136 The History of the Sierra Leone Army, http://www.mod.gov.sl/docs/THE-HISTORY-OF-RSLAF-v01.pdf accessed on 27 April 2019.

137 Self-Loading Rifle. A 7.62mm calibre rifle.

138 Colour Sergeant Chitrabahadur Gurung, Sp Coy 1RGR in Op Silkman Sierra Leone, undated draft.

139 'First Battalion Newsletter', The Royal Gurkha Rifles Regimental Newsletter (January 2002–June 2002), 2.

140 'First Battalion Newsletter', The Royal Gurkha Rifles Regimental Newsletter (July 2002–December 2002), 4.

141 'The Special Court for Sierra Leone was set up in 2002 as the result of a request to the United Nations in 2000 by the Government of Sierra Leone for 'a special court' to address serious crimes against civilians and UN peacekeepers committed during the country's decade-long (1991–2002) civil war'. See: http://www.rscsl.org/index.html.

142 'Second Battalion Newsletter', The Royal Gurkha Rifles Regimental Newsletter (January 2003–June 2003), 16.

143 'Second Battalion Newsletter', The Royal Gurkha Rifles Regimental Newsletter (January 2003–June 2003), 16.

144 Lieutenant Colonel Thomas commanded 2RGR from May 2001 to November 2003.

145 Tony Blair, A Journey (Hutchinson, 2010), 246.

146 For the details of this story see: J C Lawrence, The Gurkhas: 200 Years of Service to the Crown (Uniform Press, 2015), 150.

147 Major General F J Loftus-Tottenham, Walkabouts and Laughabouts in the Raj, (2nd Gurkha Rifles, Undated), 40.

148 Folkestone Gurkhas switch to rapid response unit, https://www.bbc.co.uk/news/uk-england-kent-33005635 accessed on 27 May 2019.

149 Text of George Bush's Speech https://www.theguardian.com/world/2001/sep/21/september11.usa13 accessed on 19 December 2018.

150 Prime Minister Tony Blair spoke to the House of Commons on 4 October 2001. The extract from his speech is taken from: House of Commons Foreign Affairs Committee, The UK's Mission in Afghanistan https://publications.parliament.uk/pa/cm200809/cmselect/cmfaff/302/30209.htm accessed on 16 December 2018.

151 Richard D Hooker and Joseph J Collins, Lessons Encountered: Learning from the Long War (National Defence University Press, 2015), 445.

152 C (Gurkha) Company, known as Gurkha Reinforcement Company 3 (GRC3), was comprised of officers and soldiers from 2RGR. It was formed in December 1996 for service with the 2nd Battalion The Parachute Regiment and was disbanded in May 2002.

153 Major General J C Lawrence, The Gurkhas: 200 Years of Service to the Crown (Uniform Press, 2015), 203.

154 The battalion deployed three companies and a headquarters element (a total of 220 men). The deployment lasted from October 2003 until April 2004.

155 Lance Corporal Aimansing Limbu of 7GR was awarded the Queen's Gallantry Medal for his actions in apprehending six illegal immigrants on the Hong Kong/Chinese border on 28 May 1979. Find out what happened at: Major General J C Lawrence, The Gurkhas: 200 Years of Service to the Crown (Uniform Press, 2015), pp180–181.

156 The battalion's deployment lasted from March 2005 until October 2005. The official name of the deployment was Operation Herrick 2.

157 J C Lawrence, The Gurkhas: 200 Years of Service to the Crown (Uniform Press Ltd, 2015), 205.

158 1RGR deployed on Operation Herrick 7 in September 2007 and returned to Brunei at the end of the tour in April 2008.

159 B Company was initially attached to the Household Cavalry Regiment (HCR) in Garmsir, although it subsequently became an independent company with its own area of operations. Some of the other companies also deployed for short periods to provide support to other organisations. For example, C Company deployed to support a Canadian Task Force in Helmand and A Company backfilled The Royal Marines in Sangin. Whilst there, A Company seized the opportunity to conduct a clearance operation which led to the disruption of a major IED facility.

160 'First Battalion Newsletter', The Royal Gurkha Rifles Regimental Newsletter (January to June 2008), 4.

161 'Second Battalion Newsletter', The Royal Gurkha Rifles Regimental Newsletter (June – December 2008), 9.

162 The Company was also referred to as Gurkha Reinforcement Company 1.

163 E-Mail from Lieutenant Colonel Chris Conroy to the author on 19 March 2019 @06.27hrs.

164 GRC 2 was formed in December 2008 with soldiers from 1RGR. It deployed with 1MERCIAN on Operation Herrick 12 and, following the tour, was re-attributed to 1RGR on 31 March 2011 to become D (Kandahar) Company 1RGR, deploying on Operation Herrick 17 with 1RGR in October 2012. Its formal disbandment took place on 28 June 2013 at a medals parade in Sir John Moore Barracks during which operational service medals for Afghanistan were awarded by Brigadier Robert Bruce, the Commander of 4 Mechanised Brigade during Operation Herrick 17.

165 The outgoing unit was The Coldstream Guards.

166 Major Bowman's parent regiment was The Rifles. He was completing a two year attachment to 1RGR as a rifle company commander when he was killed.

167 'First Battalion Newsletter', The Royal Gurkha Rifles Regimental Newsletter (June to December 2010), 7.

168 J C Lawrence, The Gurkhas: 200 Years of Service to the Crown (Uniform Press Ltd, 2015), 215.

169 Citation for Acting Sergeant Dipprasad Pun's Conspicuous Gallantry Cross.

170 Citation for Acting Sergeant Dipprasad Pun's Conspicuous Gallantry Cross.

171 'Operational Awards – Citations', The Kukri, No. 62 (Headquarters Brigade of Gurkhas, March 2012), 17.

172 This was the second GRC3. The first GRC3 was formed in November 1996 for service with the 2nd Battalion The Parachute Regiment and disbanded in May 2002.

173 'Gurkha Reinforcement Company 3 – Newsletter', The Royal Gurkha Rifles Regimental Newsletter (January–June 2012), 27.

174 '1RGR Newsletter', The Royal Gurkha Rifles Regimental Journal 2013, 4.

175 The description of the incident involving Rifleman Tuljung Gurung is taken from: Major General J C Lawrence, The Gurkhas: 200 Years of Service to the Crown (Uniform Press, 2015), 219.

176 Citation for Lance Corporal Tuljung Gurung's Military Cross.

177 Warfare.Today, What is the British Army still doing in Afghanistan? http://www.warfare.today/2017/05/12/operation-toral-the-british-army-in-afghanistan/ accessed on 20 February 2019.

178 Gov.UK, UK ends combat operations in Helmand, https://www.gov.uk/government/news/uk-ends-combat-operations-in-helmand accessed on 20 February 2019.

179 The attack took place in the early evening of 28 November 2018.

180 'Operational Awards – Citations', The Kukri, No. 62 (Headquarters Brigade of Gurkhas, March 2012), 17.

181 E-Mail from Gez Strickland to Craig Lawrence, 'RGR Book', dated 18 March 2019 @1245hrs.

182 British Army, Army General and Administrative Instruction (AGAI), Volume 1, Chapter 5 (June 2017), 5/1-2.

183 British Army, Army General and Administrative Instruction (AGAI), Volume 1, Chapter 5 (June 2017), 5/1-2.

184 Joint Service Publication 419: Joint Services Adventurous Training Scheme (JSAT), (31 October 2011), 2-1.

185 'B (Sobraon) Company 1PWRR Newsletter', The Royal Gurkha Rifles Regimental Newsletter (January to June 1997), 18.

186 'B (Sobraon) Company 1PWRR Newsletter', The Royal Gurkha Rifles Regimental Newsletter (January to June 1997), 18.

187 'B (Sobraon) Company 1PWRR Newsletter', The Royal Gurkha Rifles Regimental Newsletter (January to June 1997), 17.

188 Although Brigadier Bullock states that 1RIRISH crossed the border into Iraq on 21 March 2003, The Royal Irish state that this happened on 22 March 2003 – see: 1 R Irish Battlegroup moves into Iraq, https://www.royal-irish.com/events/1st-battalion-royal-irish-regiment-crosses-border-iraq-part-initial-invasion-force-operation-accessed on 23 May 2019.

189 Christopher Bullock, Britain's Gurkhas (Third Millennium Publishing, 2009), 252.

190 MAMS Operations – Operation Phillis, http://ukmamsoba.org/phillis.html accessed on 23 May 2019.

191 For statistics see: 2015 Earthquake: Facts, FAQs and How to Help, https://www.worldvision.org/disaster-relief-news-stories/2015-nepal-earthquake-facts accessed on 23 May 2019.

192 'A (Gallipoli) Company 1st Battalion The Highlanders (Seaforth, Gordons and Camerons) Newsletter: April – December 2000', The Royal Gurkha Rifles Regimental Newsletter (April to December 2000), 20.

193 'A (Gallipoli) Company 1st Battalion The Highlanders (Seaforth, Gordons and Camerons) Newsletter: April – December 2000', The Royal Gurkha Rifles Regimental Newsletter (April to December 2000), 20.

194 PM David Cameron visited 2RGR during Op PITCHPOLE, https://www.gurkhabde.com/pm-david-cameron-visited-2-rgr-during-op-pitchpole/ accessed on 23 May 2019.

195 Gurkha Museum, Brief – The History of the Kukri (Gurkha Museum, undated), 1.

196 Gurkha Museum, Brief – The History of the Kukri (Gurkha Museum, undated), 8.

197 Gurkha Museum, Brief – The History of the Kukri (Gurkha Museum, undated), 2.

198 Lieutenant General Peter Pearson, who was Colonel of The Royal Gurkha Rifles from 1 July 1999 to 1 July 2009, recalls being in Dharan in the east of Nepal and seeing kukri blades being made from old railway tracks as the steel was particularly hard!

199 Gurkha Museum, Brief – The History of the Kukri (Gurkha Museum, undated), 5.

200 Gurkha Museum, Brief – The History of the Kukri (Gurkha Museum, undated), 5.

201 Field Marshal Earl Wavell, 'Foreword', in F Spencer Chapman DSO, The Jungle is Neutral (Chatto and Windus, 1949), v.

202 F Spencer Chapman DSO, The Jungle is Neutral (Chatto and Windus, 1949).

203 Field Marshal Earl Wavell, 'Foreword', in F Spencer Chapman DSO, The Jungle is Neutral (Chatto and Windus, 1949), vi.

204 UN Sustainable Development Goals, https://www.un.org/sustainabledevelopment/biodiversity/ accessed on 15 April 2019. The UN's over 30% figure is supported by the Earth Policy Institute (see http://www.earth-policy.org/indicators/C56).

205 Christopher Bullock, Britain's Gurkhas (Third Millenium Publishing, 2009), 146.

206 Charles Chenevix Trench, The Indian Army and the King's Enemies 1900–1947 (Thames and Hudson, 1988), 255.

207 Major General J C Lawrence, The Gurkhas: 200 Years of Service to the Crown (Uniform Press, 2015), 155.

208 J P Cross, In Gurkha Company: the British Army Gurkhas, 1948 to the Present (Arms and Armour Press, 1986), 29–30.

209 J P Cross, In Gurkha Company: the British Army Gurkhas, 1948 to the Present (Arms and Armour Press, 1986), 51–52.

210 J P Cross, In Gurkha Company: the British Army Gurkhas, 1948 to the Present (Arms and Armour Press, 1986), 83.

211 Charles Allen, The Savage Wars of Peace (Futura, 1991), 79.

212 Charles Allen, The Savage Wars of Peace (Futura, 1991), 82.

213 British Army Gurkha 'super-tracker' hunting poachers in Gabon to save last remaining elephants, https://www.telegraph.co.uk/news/2017/08/28/british-army-gurkha-super-tracker-hunting-poachers-gabon-save/ accessed on 24 April 2019.

214 Gurkha regiment faces axe as Liam Fox insists on £20bn Trident replacement, https://www.theguardian.com/world/2010/aug/29/british-army-gurkhas-spending accessed on 19 May 2019.

215 Defence Secretary visits British Troops in Afghanistan, https://www.gov.uk/government/news/defence-secretary-visits-british-troops-in-afghanistan accessed on 19 May 2019.

216 Second Day – Defence Estimates, https://www.theyworkforyou.com/debates/?id=1994-10-18a.148.1 accessed on 29 May 2019.

217 Love Your Garden 2016, https://kentfilmoffice.co.uk/2016/07/love-your-garden-2016/ accessed on 19 May 2019.

218 Major Bowman's parent regiment was The Rifles. He was completing a two year attachment to 1RGR as a rifle company commander when he was killed.

219 Corporal Arjun Purja Pun was serving with Gurkha Company Sittang (GCS) based at the Royal Military Academy Sandhurst. He had deployed with 1RGR as an individual reinforcement.

220 Rifleman Remand Kulung was serving with G (Tobruk) Company, a Gurkha Reinforcement Company attached to the 1st Battalion The Mercian Regiment (Cheshire), when he was killed.

221 Rifleman Sachin Limbu was initially wounded in an IED strike on 24 June 2010 and subsequently died of his injuries on 2 January 2012.

222 Lance Corporal Gajbahadur Gurung was serving with D (Delhi) Company, a Gurkha Reinforcement Company (GRC) attached to the 1st Battalion The Yorkshire Regiment, when he was killed.

223 On 17 June 2008, The London Gazette published a Supplement which listed all serving Queen's Gurkha Officers (QGO) and effectively did away with the QGO Commission. For example, it stated that "Captain (QGO) Khusiman Gurung (550146) Royal Gurkha Rifles to be Captain 1 October 2007 with seniority 13 November 2001 (Belated Entry)".

224 Lieutenant Colonel Hayes MBE assumed command of the 2nd Battalion The Royal Gurkha Rifles on 1 July 1994, the day it was formed by re-titling the 7th Duke of Edinburgh's Own Gurkha Rifles (7GR).

225 Lieutenant Colonel Pearson assumed command of 10th Princess Mary's Own Gurkha Rifles (10GR) in May 1993 and remained in command of the Battalion when it re-titled to become the 3rd Battalion The Royal Gurkha Rifles on 1 July 1994.

226 Lieutenant Colonel Theobald took over command of the 3rd Battalion The Royal Gurkha Rifles (3RGR) from Lieutenant Colonel Pearson in December 1995 and remained in command when 3RGR amalgamated with 2RGR to form the 'new' 2RGR in November 1996.

227 Major(QGO) Chandraprasad Limbu became the Gurkha Major of 10th Princess Mary's Own Gurkha Rifles (10GR) in November 1993 and remained as Gurkha Major when the Battalion re-titled to become the 3rd Battalion The Royal Gurkha Rifles (3RGR) on 1 July 1994. He remained in this appointment until 3RGR amalgamated with 2RGR to form the 'new' 2RGR in November 1996. Final Draft as at 27 April 2019

228 It has been difficult to confirm the exact date on which Lieutenant Colonel Clive Fraser handed over the appointment of Regimental Secretary to Lieutenant Colonel Bill Dawson OBE. It is highly likely that it was late 1999, but it might have been in early 2000.

229 'News from Regimental Headquarters', The Royal Gurkha Rifles Regimental Newsletter (July to October 1994), 1.

230 GRC 1 was originally formed in November 1996 for service with the 1st Battalion The Royal Scots, joining its new battalion in December 1996. It then transferred to the 1st Battalion The Highlanders (Seaforth, Gordons and Camerons) on 28 March 2000.

231 This description was researched and drafted by Captain M F Barney RGR.

232 This description was researched and drafted by Captain M F Barney RGR.

233 2GR referred to their Commanding Officer as the Commandant.

234 The section is an extract from: Craig Lawrence, 3A Leadership (unpublished draft).

235 Hugo Slim, 'William Slim 1891–1970' in Andrew Roberts eds Great Commanders of the Modern World: 1866–Present Day (Quercus, 2011), p328.

236 Robert Lyman, Slim, Master of War: Burma and the Birth of Modern Warfare (Robinson, 2004), Location 161.

237 Lyman, Location 171.

238 Lyman, Location 161.

239 Field Marshal Viscount Slim, Defeat into Victory (Pan Books, 2009), Kindle Version, Location 379.

240 Lyman, Location 2143.

241 www.winstonchurchill.org/publications/finest-hour/finest-hour-169 accessed on 5 Jun 2018.

242 Lyman, Location 261.

243 Slim, Location 294.

244 Slim, Location 275.

245 Slim assumed command of Burma Corps on 19 March 1942 and the decision to withdraw British forces back to India was taken on 25 April 1942.

246 Slim, Location 538.

247 Field Marshal Viscount Slim, Defeat into Victory (Pan Books, 2009).

248 This description was researched and drafted by Captain M F Barney RGR.

249 Although Junior Leaders Cadres are usually run every year, which would make the Warren Trophy an annual award, operational commitments sometimes preclude this with the result that two intakes occasionally have to complete their Junior Leaders Cadres in the same year. Similarly, occasionally two intakes of recruits have joined the RGR in the same year with the result that, several years later, both intakes need to complete their respective Junior Leaders Cadre in the same year. This explains why in some years, such as 1998 and 2012, there are two recipients.

250 The name of UK deployments to Afghanistan changed from Operation Herrick to Operation Toral on 1 January 2015 when NATO's International Security Assistance Force (ISAF) mission changed to its Resolute Support (RS) mission.

251 Headquarters Brigade of Gurkhas, Brigade of Gurkhas Update, (Headquarters Brigade of Gurkhas, 29 April 2019), 3.

252 Headquarters Brigade of Gurkhas, Brigade of Gurkhas Update, (Headquarters Brigade of Gurkhas, 29 April 2019), 2.

253 MGBD Ops Coy Brief as at 12 Aug 03. A copy of the briefing note was given to the author by the Officer Commanding the Company, Major Quentin Naylor.

254 'OP HERRICK 15, C Company / D (Delhi) Company (GRC 3) 1st Battalion The Yorkshire Regiment', The Kukri, No. 63 (Headquarters Brigade of Gurkhas, July 2013), 24.

255 'Gurkha Company (Catterick)', The Kukri, No. 67 (Headquarters Brigade of Gurkhas, 2017), 107.

256 Figures taken from the Gurkha Welfare Trust, https://www.gwt.org.uk/wp-content/uploads/2018/02/Welfare-Pension-Jan-2018.pdf accessed on 19 December 2018.

Selected Bibliography

In trying to be as accurate as possible in telling the story of the first 25 years of The Royal Gurkha Rifles, I have drawn on numerous sources. These have ranged from books, journals, newsletters and articles through to e-mails, on-line websites and conversations with those who were there. This selective bibliography lists the books, journals, articles and other 'hard copy' sources that I have used. The numbered notes at the end of the book relate to specific points in the narrative and identify which of the references in the bibliography the fact or point is taken from. 'Soft copy' sources, such as websites and e-mails, are identified in full in the endnotes.

Ahmed, Azman, "Brunei Darussalam Towards Reform and Sustainable Progress", *Southeast Asian Affairs 2005*

Allen, Charles, *The Savage Wars of Peace* (Futura, 1991)

Barney, Captain Michael, *The Queen's Truncheon (Nishani Mai)* (unpublished draft, 2019)

Bellamy, Chris, *The Gurkhas: Special Force* (Hachette, 2011)

Biggs, Maurice, *The Story of Gurkha VCs* (FireStep, 2012)

Blair, Tony, *A Journey* (Hutchinson, 2010)

British Army, *Army General and Administrative Instruction (AGAI)*, Volume 1, Chapter 5 (June 2017)

Bullock, Christopher, *Britain's Gurkhas* (London: Third Millennium Publishing Ltd, 2009)

Caplan, Lionel, *Warrior Gentlemen: Gurkhas in the Western Imagination* (Berghahn Books, 1995)

Chapman DSO, F Spencer, *The Jungle is Neutral* (Chatto and Windus, 1949)

Chapple, Field Marshal Sir John, *The Lineages and Composition of Gurkha Regiments in British Service* (FireStep, 2014)

Collett, N A, *The Butcher of Amritsar: General Reginald Dyer* (A&C Black, 2005)

Corrigan, Gordon, "The Formation of The Royal Gurkha Rifles", *6GR Newsletter*, Volume 74 (1994), 46

Cross, J P, *In Gurkha Company: the British Army Gurkhas, 1948 to the Present* (Arms and Armour Press, 1986)

Duffell, Lieutenant General Sir Peter, *A Gurkha Odyssey* (unpublished draft, 2019)

Gould, Tony, *Imperial Warriors: Britain and the Gurkhas* (Granta Books, 1999)

Gurkha Museum, *Brief – The History of the Kukri* (Gurkha Museum, undated)

Gurkha Museum, *The Gurkha Parachutist* (Gurkha Museum, undated)

Headquarters Brigade of Gurkhas, *Brigade of Gurkhas Update,* (Headquarters Brigade of Gurkhas, 29 April 2019)

Hooker, Richard D and Joseph J Collins, *Lessons Encountered: Learning from the Long War* (National Defence University Press, 2015)

Lawrence, Major General J C, *3A Leadership* (unpublished draft, 2019)

Lawrence, Major General J C, *The Gurkhas: 200 Years of Service to the Crown* (Uniform Press, 2015)

Loftus-Tottenham, Major General F J, *Walkabouts and Laughabouts in the Raj* (2nd Gurkhas, undated)

Lunt, James, *Jai Sixth! 6th Queen Elizabeth's Own Gurkha Rifles 1817–1994* (Pen and Sword, 1994)

Lyman, Robert, *Slim, Master of War: Burma and the Birth of Modern Warfare* (Robinson, 2004)

Masters, John, *The Road Past Mandalay* (1961)

Merriman, John, *A History of Modern Europe: From The Renaissance to the Present – Third Edition* (W W Norton & Company, 2010)

Ministry of Defence, *General Staff Order: Authority for Amalgamation of 2 and 6 GR and Retitling of 7 and 10* GR (D INF 54/1 dated 3 May 1994 – Gurkha Museum Folio Reference 'RGR 007')

Ministry of Defence, *Joint Service Publication 419: Joint Services Adventurous Training Scheme (JSAT)*, (31 October 2011)

Parker, John, *The Gurkhas* (Headline Book Publishing, 2000)

Pemble, John, "Forgetting and Remembering Britain's Gurkha War", *Asian Affairs*, Volume 40, Issue 3 (2009) pp361–376

Prinsep, Henry T, *A Narrative of the Political and Military Transactions of British India under the Administration of the Marquess of Hastings, 1813–1818* (John Murray, 1820)

Read, Anthony and David Fisher, *The Proudest Day: India's Long Road to Independence* (Random House, 1998)

Rees, Nicholas, "The Kosovo Crisis, the International Response and Ireland", *Irish Studies in International Affairs*, 11 (2000)

Shore, F J, "Report on the Dehra Doon 1827–28", *Calcutta Monthly Journal and General Register of Occurrences* (June 1836)

Slim, Field Marshal Viscount Slim, *Defeat into Victory* (Pan Books, 2009).

Slim, Hugo, 'William Slim 1891–1970' in Andrew Roberts eds *Great Commanders of the Modern World: 1866–Present Day* (Quercus, 2011)

The Argus (Melbourne, Victoria), Monday 30 November 1891.

The Brigade of Gurkhas, *The Kukri: The Journal of The Brigade of Gurkhas*, Nos., 47–68 (Headquarters Brigade of Gurkhas, 1995–2018)

The Royal Gurkha Rifles, *Kosovo Lahurey – Kosovo 1999* (The 1st Battalion The Royal Gurkha Rifles, 1999)

The Royal Gurkha Rifles, *The Royal Gurkha Rifles Regimental Newsletters 1994–2019* (Headquarters Brigade of Gurkhas, 1994–2018)

Thorn, Sir William, *A Memoir of Major General Sir Rollo Gillespie* (T Egerton, 1816)

Trench, Charles Chenevix, *The Indian Army and the King's Enemies 1900–1947* (Thames and Hudson, 1988)

Wilson, H H, *The History of British India from 1805–1835, Volume II* (James Madden, 1858)

Index

Page numbers in *italic* font are used for illustrations and refer to the page where the caption text is found.

Gurkha names are sorted by the family name and then by the first name of the individual. Ranks are those as they appear in this book, where more than one rank is shown, the most junior rank is listed first. Post nominals are those the individual was entitled to when they appear in the book.

Acknowledgements

This book would not have been possible without a huge amount of support, given with constant good humour and at no cost, from a whole range of people and organisations. My two predecessors as Colonel of The Royal Gurkha Rifles (RGR) have provided invaluable help; Lieutenant General Sir Peter Duffell patiently explained the background to the formation of the RGR, giving me the 'inside track' on what really happened by allowing me to read draft chapters from his own book on Gurkhas, which is due out in October of this year; Lieutenant General Peter Pearson acted as chief proofreader, spotting mistakes, offering suggestions, taking photographs of kukris and generally keeping me on the straight and narrow. My successor as Colonel of the Regiment, Major General Gez Strickland, wrote the Introduction but also edited the chapter on Afghanistan, offering sensible advice in terms of capturing the essence of the Regiment's many tours in the country, as well as making sure that some of the less well-known deployments received the coverage they deserved. His Royal Highness The Prince of Wales wrote the Foreword. As the RGR's Colonel-in-Chief, his contribution gives the book an authority that it would otherwise lack. Moreover, his comments at the outset of the book set exactly the right tone for what follows. I am grateful to all of them for their support.

I was determined that the book would have at least 500 photographs as I felt that this would be the best way of telling the RGR's story. However, to find so many reasonable images covering all 25 years of the RGR's life was a formidable task. It was made easier through the generosity of a number of people who gave me copies of their image libraries, some running to thousands of pictures. With that in mind, I would like to thank: Ash Alexander-Cooper, Michael Barney, Chris Conroy, Ross Daines, Jody Davies, Peter Houlton-Hart, Jamie Murray, Quentin Naylor, Dan O'Donnell, Dave Pack, Peter Pearson, Mike Peters, Paul Pitchfork, Major Chandrabahadur Pun, Sean Statham, Gez Strickland, Ian Thomas, Andrew Todd and Tom Usher. I am extremely grateful to Amrit Thapa for letting me use his remarkable photographs, particularly the book's cover image, and to Richard Pohle, the Times photographer, for allowing me free access to his professional photographs of public duties and Afghanistan. I am also grateful to Corporal Puspa Gurung, the Editor of Parbate, for his patience in helping me master the image library in Headquarters Brigade of Gurkhas and to Doug Henderson, the Collections Officer at the Gurkha Museum, for his advice on where in the Museum's archives I might find the information I needed. I would also like to thank those people who helped me confirm facts or answer the inevitable questions that arise when you are researching events that happened over such a long period of time: Major Khusiman Gurung helped me with questions relating to the Queen's Medal and shooting more generally; James Robinson provided insights into the Balkans deployments; Jody Davies lent me a wealth of material relating to the RGR's deployments in Kosovo and East Timor, and kindly proofread the East Timor chapter; and Michael Barney very generously let me use his impressively detailed research on honours and awards, battle honours, the Queen's Truncheon and Regimental prizes and competitions.

As with the book I produced for the 200th Anniversary of Gurkha Service to the Crown, there are a few people whose unstinting support has been fundamental to me finishing this book. The first of these is Bruce McKay, the Regimental Secretary. Almost every day for over two years, I have been sending him e-mails asking whether he can confirm some fact or other. To his enormous credit, his enthusiasm in addressing these queries, dipping into the battalions or contacting people direct to get the answer, has never wavered. I need him to know how grateful I am because I know that I have added significantly to his workload over the last few years. The other stalwart supporter whose help has been invaluable is Gavin Edgerley-Harris, the Director of the Gurkha Museum. Gavin has sourced images and information, proofread chapters, suggested approaches and given me complete access to the Museum's resources. I would like him to know that I am extremely grateful for his patient and always cheerful support. I would also like to thank Matt Wilson, the highly talented designer and editor, for working so hard to turn my rough drafts into something that is accessible, visually appealing and interesting. Ryan Gearing, my publisher, deserves particular praise for helping me produce the book. Experienced and knowledgeable, he has been a source of ideas and inspiration from the first meeting three years ago to discuss the feasibility of the project through to the selection of the font size and cover image! My family also deserve my sincere thanks. As I mention in the Preface, this book has taken me over two years to research and write. Throughout, my family, and Laura, my wife, in particular, has been hugely supportive despite the amount of time I have spent working on the book rather than being with them. I would also like to thank my mother, Vicky, for her constant encouragement and my father, Michael, who passed away last year but who was always so supportive of this project.

Lastly, I would like to take this opportunity to thank those members of the RGR, past and present, who have made writing this book such a pleasure. It has been a genuine privilege to try to capture the achievements of the remarkable and inspirational people who, collectively, make up the RGR and I am immensely grateful to them for the opportunity.